Wars and Shadows

Wars and Shadows

MEMOIRS OF
GENERAL SIR DAVID FRASER

ALLEN LANE
an imprint of
PENGUIN BOOKS

ALLEN LANE
THE PENGUIN PRESS

Published by the Penguin Group
Penguin Books Ltd, 80 Strand, London WC2R ORL, England
Penguin Putnam Inc., 375 Hudson Street, New York, New York 10014, USA
Penguin Books Australia Ltd, 250 Camberwell Road, Camberwell, Victoria 3124, Australia
Penguin Books Canada Ltd, 10 Alcorn Avenue, Toronto, Ontario, Canada M4V 3B2
Penguin Books India (P) Ltd, 11, Community Centre, Panchsheel Park, New Delhi – 110 017, India
Penguin Books (NZ) Ltd, Cnr Rosedale and Airborne Roads, Albany, Auckland, New Zealand
Penguin Books (South Africa) (Pty) Ltd, 24 Sturdee Avenue, Rosebank 2196, South Africa

Penguin Books Ltd, Registered Offices: 80 Strand, London WC2R ORL, England

www.penguin.com

First published 2002
2

Set in 10.5/14 pt PostScript Adobe Sabon
Typeset by Rowland Phototypesetting Ltd, Bury St Edmunds, Suffolk
Printed in England by Clays Ltd, St Ives plc

ISBN 0-71399-627-7

Acknowledgements

For their help with the illustrations to this book I am particularly grateful to Anne Bradstock, Iona Carrington, Rachel Dacre, Kate Nicolson and Flora Saltoun, as well as to my wife, Julia, whose work on them was tireless and invaluable. I also wish to express my gratitude to my editor and friend Stuart Proffitt of Penguin, and his team, for encouragement, counsel and support.

Contents

List of Illustrations

Photographic credits, where applicable, are given in parentheses. Unless otherwise stated, photographs are from the collection of the author.

Introduction

My memory of the remote past, of scenes and personalities from my childhood and youth, is very clear, and in this book I have recalled some of the people and places making particular impressions on me when young. In so doing I have attempted to recall not only figures but moods now far distant. This memoir begins soon after the end of the First World War (I was born in 1920) and I have commented on language, times and characters, sometimes with reflections prompted by hindsight or more extended study. I have tried to be faithful to the personal feelings I remember to have experienced, and where time has modified these to say so.

Then comes the Second World War, with impressions both more vivid and more recent – and episodic. My later chapters, inevitably, reflect a more even flow. There was plenty of variety in my life in the years between the end of war and my retirement but the vicissitudes of a professional career are more predictable, and the recollection of them less intense. Each professional interlude has its challenges, its ups and downs, but the pace and movement of a career like mine was latterly less feverish than when under the pressures of youth or war.

Throughout, the figures who people my landscape differ widely: no serious historian is likely to find much matter here. A few were famous in their twentieth-century day, whether in war, on the London stage or in public life. Many, on the other hand, were without distinction in the world's eyes but connected to me by affection, merry, light-hearted, often dying young. Inevitably some, of differing ages, were members of my own family whom I have thought it good gently to recollect, delineate, memorialize.

*

This is an entirely personal reminiscence. It is also benevolent. I am well aware that personal narrative can be given increased interest by a touch of acerbity while favourable impressions can be bland and unconvincing. In my case, however, the fact remains that I have been fortunate in quite a long life and have lived much of it among people it was easy to love.

ONE

I

A Melancholy Radiance

Visual memory can deceive. The proportions of a building confound, and as often disappoint, the remembering mind. Sounds, too, may be transformed by recollection – may be found to have lost (or in some cases to have intensified) the magic their music once conveyed. Smell, however, has remarkably durable evocative power. Certain smells – more suddenly than pictures, more strikingly than noise – can bring to mind entire bundles of associated sensations, whole episodes of life.

The smell of the railway station at Dover was unmistakable and thrilling. There were, dominant odour, the hot, acrid fumes coming from the engine itself – a mixture, I suppose, of fire with oil on the gleaming working parts – carried further by the smoke hanging about the roof, with its exciting redolence of heat and dirt. They conveyed, splendidly, power and invincibility; with them there was a strong whiff of the sea; of sodden rope hawsers, fish, brine. The station was poised on a frontier. Just beyond its confines lay funnelled ships. This was where adventure began. The occasional hoots of ships' sirens were no less urgent in making the heart beat faster than the shrill, alarming whistles of the engines themselves.

This was also where foreign visitors arrived or departed. On that winter afternoon in 1926 I had accompanied my father to meet a visitor of great distinction. I cannot remember what I was wearing – probably some sort of leggings, laboriously buttoned by my Nanny from thigh to ankle, and a short brown coat with velvet collar. I was five years old. My father, however, I can certainly remember, dressed as he usually was by day in the uniform of a major in the Gordon Highlanders – Glengarry bonnet, khaki tunic, Sam Browne belt, breeches of Gordon tartan, black field boots, silver spurs; impeccable and magnificent, a man whose slim figure was unchanged when he died in 1964 from when he was a cadet at Sandhurst in 1909. I don't know if he had taken me to Dover station on that occasion from sudden impulse or whether he had discussed it as a 'plan' with my mother. Certainly I was alone with him and unaware of the outing's purpose. I had, however, been at Dover station before and recognized its significance.

My father left me for a few minutes on the platform, in the temporary care of some other officer, I think. There was cold and a drift of fog. Everywhere there was a hissing of steam, piercing, urgent whistles, hoarse cries; and everywhere that magic smell. The smartly painted coaches of the boat train were halted in front of us. Suddenly my father appeared again and led or lifted me on to the train itself, into the corridor of one of the coaches. A few steps along it and I was drawn into a compartment where my father spoke one or two incomprehensible words to the single occupant.

This was a perfectly enormous old man, to whom I realized I was being introduced. He sat in the far corner, by the window giving on to the platform. He was wrapped in a great black overcoat, with what seemed capes or rugs round the shoulders, like a stage coachman drawn on a Christmas card (I was told, much later, that he had complained bitterly of the climate). On his head was a top hat. I remember a white moustache, and that as he pushed out his hand to be shaken by my small paw he said 'How do?' The voice was throaty and genial. He was on some sort of official visit to England and my father (on the staff of a brigade based at Dover) was present at the station to see a distinguished guest on his way to London. This was Marshal Joffre. Papa Joffre.

Joseph Joffre. Marshal of France. Commander-in-Chief of the French Armies facing the German invasion of 1914 – Commander-in-Chief, indeed, until relieved by General Nivelle at the end of 1916, after the First and Second Battles of Ypres, the Somme, Verdun. Joffre, victor of the Battle of the Marne, which had turned the German tide in the first September of the war. Joffre, who had managed to coax cooperation in that battle of an exhausted British Expeditionary Force from its commander, Field Marshal French, with a direct, personal appeal which still has resonance: '*Monsieur le Maréchal, c'est La France qui vous supplie!*'

To me, born in 1920, the name of Joffre, of course, meant nothing; but 'The War', still only eight years past on that winter afternoon, already meant a great deal. The War formed the dominant background impression of childhood, a vivid, ubiquitous memory which hovered around the nursery and everywhere else. Visitors to that nursery – we lived at that time in a small village called Ringwould, six miles from Dover – were, as often as not, young men, friends of my parents, perhaps in their early thirties. To me they seemed ancient. They were, I was sure, heroes. They had, probably in all cases, both fought in and survived 'The War'.

Thus they had spent four years – I knew that statistic very early – fighting the Germans (nobody mentioned other enemies, like Austrians or Turks). Germans were people of extraordinary ferocity, capable of appalling savagery, as well as every sort of treacherous trick. Germans could never be trusted. Fortunately for us, Germans combined barbarity and deceit with cowardice. German officers, I was told (unlike British), did not lead their men in an attack but menaced them with pistols from behind. German soldiers, ready to shoot or bayonet women and children, quailed in terror before the kilted men of our Highland Regiments (with which, of course, I identified early, even wearing a Gordons' Glengarry bonnet on occasion, placed in my Christmas stocking when I was four). The Germans had panicked totally when first confronted by a tank – a British invention. The Germans, after finally being beaten, had been treated with extraordinary (and, my Nanny declared, most unwise) clemency. They should have been ground into the dust.

The German Kaiser, the arch-fiend, was actually alive, after all the wrong he had done. He was living, unmolested, in Holland – a country which had (somewhat ingloriously) been neutral in the great struggles between good and evil just concluded, so could not be counted on to deal justly with this viper. A little later – perhaps in 1928 – my father had some occasion to visit Holland. When he came to the nursery to say goodbye I said, 'I hope you manage to shoot the Kaiser.'

'Why would I want to do that?'

I can't remember my answer – I don't expect there was one. My impression was clear, however. My father (whom I loved dearly but of whose even mild displeasure I stood in considerable awe) did not approve of wanting to shoot the Kaiser.

The passionate partisanship which coloured so much of childhood in fact derived little from my father. All around me, however, were influences – catchphrases, anecdotes, exaggerations, songs, picture-books – which conveyed the same message. England (not even the most dedicated Scot bothered to say 'Britain') had triumphed over incarnate evil in a struggle which had taken the bravest and the best of the nation. England had won against odds. England had been helped by – and almost only by – the French (not much mention of the Belgians as yet, still less of Italians, Portuguese et al., except with derision: none of those Johnnies-come-lately, the Americans). Our generals, to a man, were models of soldierly courage and military wisdom, solid, paternal, indestructible. Our Army was worthy of them – manned by patriotic volunteers; the Kaiser had referred to it (I heard this misquotation also pretty early) as a 'contemptible little Army', and we'd shown him! Our Navy ruled the waves – my uncle George Fraser, a professional naval officer, had been at Jutland and seldom at home throughout the War; he had, however, survived what were apparently unremitting German efforts to scupper him. My uncle Alistair – my father's eldest brother – had been taken prisoner with 1st Battalion Gordon Highlanders in 1914 and had spent much of the time incarcerated, albeit on several occasions escaping, though always recaptured, but he, too, had survived. Nobody, ever, could beat us. It was ordained.

Behind so much nonsense, corrupting in the narrow unrealism and complacency it encouraged as well as the hatred it unabashedly reflected, the tragedy was real; and behind, too, the strident exuberance of the years of victory there was a deeper and worthier sense, a sort of melancholy dignity which a child was well able to absorb and which is more agreeable to recall, more genuinely characteristic, I think, of our people then. I remember another winter weekday at about the same time, perhaps 1925 or 1926. The morning had been spent in Deal, where Nanny had no doubt been shopping. We were on the pavement of a main street. There were not many cars about in those days – and those few were interspersed with some horse-drawn trades-men's vans, an old red and white 'East Kent' bus, errand boys on bicycles, a number of pedestrians. Suddenly all was still, as if petrified by a magic hand. People stood immobile wherever they happened to be. Every car or bus had stopped and the occupants had alighted and were standing in the roadway. Drivers of vans had pulled up, jumped down and were at their horses' heads. Errand boys, dismounted, were standing silent. A clock was striking. The whole of Deal drew itself up, erect and still. I said, 'Nanny, why—'

'Sh, sh.'

After a little life resumed. Nanny said, 'It was The Silence. The two-minute Silence.'

11th November. Eleventh hour of the Eleventh day of the Eleventh month. The whole country stood quiet. If there were Armistice Day services they took place at that hour, whatever the day of the week, everywhere. It was unforgettable. I thought I could hear the heart of England beating.

I learned that my uncle Simon Fraser, third of the four brothers of whom my father was the youngest, had been killed in 1914, serving in the same battalion, 2nd Gordons, as my father. Nanny's brother, in the Army, had died of another enormous calamity called 'The Flu', which had swept through the troops and population in the aftermath of war in 1918; he was honoured by her, no doubt correctly, as a war casualty. My Aunt Mary, my father's only sister, had lost her naval husband, Jack Codrington, at sea at the end of the war, within a very short time of marriage; while my mother's first husband, Billy Congreve, had been killed on the Somme in July 1916. In the Rifle Brigade, and serving as a Brigade Major on the Staff, Billy Congreve had won a posthumous Victoria Cross – his death came within a few weeks of his wedding, where my father had been his best man. Billy's father – my half-sister's grandfather – was General Congreve, an able and popular Corps commander on the Western Front, who had himself won the Victoria Cross in something called The Boer War, impossibly remote in time (although in fact only about as distant then from me as, say, the outbreak of the current troubles in Northern Ireland from today's new generation.)

Slightly older children sometimes had names different from those of their families. Nanny would enlighten me.

'His daddy was killed in the war.'

It was clearly all very sad, but very heroic. To experience – and preferably to survive – such a conflict must set a person apart, must be supremely desirable, whatever the incidental grieving.

And we were, proud destiny, invincible. I was less sure about the French, despite the impression made by Papa Joffre. As I started to read (avidly from the age of six) I began to learn that the French, like the Germans more recently but to an infinitely lesser degree, had on numerous occasions sided with the devil and fought against England. They had, of course, always lost. There had been Crécy, Agincourt, Blenheim. There had been something called Waterloo, at which the atrocious German, the Hun, the Boche, had actually played some sort of part on the right side. Against the French. Painful adjustments were necessary to reconcile these latter defeated French warriors with the blue-grey-uniformed heroes who had so recently stood shoulder-to-shoulder with ourselves. And what of the Germans?

'They were different in those days,' Nanny said.

The war cast a long shadow and I felt always aware of it. Battle seemed the most sublime of destinies. When (rarely) my father actually spoke of the immediate past it was to utter a stern warning against such ideas. War, he said, was a perfectly dreadful thing. If one's country needed one, one must respond; but the best, by far the best future would be perpetual peace.

I didn't believe a word of it, although I said nothing. I had the feeling, which developed gradually and has never left me, that I was being brushed by England's finest generation. Had I known von Moltke's aphorism that perpetual peace is a dream and not even a beautiful dream I would have heartily assented. It was surely desirable that I and my generation should give evidence of as much fortitude as our forebears. Were there never to be more battlefields? More glory?

My first visit to an actual battlefield – of 'The War' – was particularly inglorious, however. It was in 1932. From 1931 we lived in a house in the Avenue Molière in Brussels, where my father had been appointed military attaché to Belgium and Holland, a span of responsibilities to which Spain and Portugal were later added and which lasted four years.

My battlefield visit – one I have often repeated since – was to the flat, low-lying land of Flanders, near Ypres. Out of that dark plain one or two wooded hills rise steeply; and on one of them, Kemmel, a war memorial was being dedicated. My father, there on duty, had taken me along. A Grenadier now (he had transferred from the Gordons in 1927), his gleaming brown field boots and blue forage cap had replaced the Gordon uniform. I was ten or eleven. And, shamingly, I fainted. I was sometimes overcome by these fits of sudden dizziness and nausea which made me unable to stand.

My father was at a short distance away, I suppose on some sort of official podium, and I had been left among friendly Belgians – there was a large crowd of Belgian and probably French dignitaries present, veterans' associations and so forth. I recall a mass of Belgian flags, military music, trumpets whose notes sounded shrilly different from the familiar cadences of British bands.

And amongst all this, amongst the dark-trousered legs of standard bearers, I collapsed. I remember the strong and welcome smell of eau-de-Cologne on a handkerchief someone applied to my forehead. But I remember, too, the faces of those veterans on Kemmel – kind, serious, generally moustached, eyes full of feeling. I had the impression – and never lost it – that I was among men who had undergone an extraordinary experience together, in which ultimate relief and triumph had followed danger, bereavement and pain, unforgettably commingled. Everywhere there was a sense that a great and recent deliverance had lifted a vast shadow from the land. Such senses come mainly with reflection, but children reflect a great deal. There was something else which I recall from that day in the landscape of Flanders – the atmosphere of simple patriotic emotion which accompanied the relief, the mourning and, I suppose, the pride. It was an emotion different from anything experienced today – in any country, I suspect. Mainly, there was love in it.

Every April in Brussels, King Albert rode down the Rue Royale at the head of a considerable body of troops, led by the *Guides*; the military attachés rode behind him *en suite*. The King had personally commanded his unbeaten army, backs to the sea, on the small wedge of Belgian territory unoccupied by the Germans between 1914 and 1918. The last warrior-king in Europe, he was a national hero and affection swelled towards him from the crowd, monarch and commander. I can see, in the Rue Royale, the Royal Palace and the gardens opposite where English nannies congregated with their Belgian charges to discuss the peculiarities of foreigners in general and their employers in particular – I can see the tall, soldierly figure of King Albert, stern, handsome face, trim moustache, and the line of military attachés riding behind him, my father glorious in scarlet tunic and bearskin, surely admired above all.

That was my first recollection of a battlefield – Ypres. I learned of the battles of First Ypres, where my uncle Simon fell in 1914 and my father was first wounded, having personally buried his brother; of Second Ypres in 1915; and of Third Ypres in 1917, which culminated in the taking of Passchendaele – Third Ypres, wherein my father, a subaltern in 1914, had already become a battle-hardened battalion commander, a lieutenant-colonel of 27. He had spent much of the war in the Ypres Salient.

Names, as he spoke them on subsequent visits to that area, lodged in my mind and their resonance still brings images from 1932 to my eyes. Tynecot, with its thousands upon thousands of soldiers' graves. Gheluvelt. Menin, and the Menin road and the Menin gate out of Ypres, where we looked at more thousand upon thousand names; names of those without known graves – including Uncle Simon. He had a quick makeshift grave at first and my father had said a bit of the funeral service over him while the Pipe-Major of 2nd Gordons played a lament: but few graves from the earlier battles could be identified after the incessant fighting and shelling of later years, the broken drainage systems, the ubiquitous water and mud which turned Flanders into probably the most desolate landscape man's eyes have ever scanned. First Ypres had been a terrible killing field – a brutal encounter battle between much of the old British Regular Army, small but superb, which was said to have died there, and the German right wing, reinforced by new divisions hurriedly raised from young volunteers, and suffering such casualties that the battle, in Germany, was given the name of the *Kindermord*, the slaughter of the children. By 1932, of course, landscape, villages and farms had been greatly restored: neat, new and to our eyes generally ugly. But when I said to my father that Belgian houses and villages compared unfavourably in appearance with those in England he remarked shortly that those in England had not been rebuilt after destruction – destruction by 'The Boche'.

Over forty years later, and myself now living in Brussels, I again visited Ypres, to find the same echoes still in the air. And I visited, too, the beautiful country of Picardy through which runs the river Somme, where my father had also served, where Billy Congreve died. On my first visit it was a particularly lovely day, and there was an extraordinary tranquillity amongst those gentle uplands and shallow valleys. Here, on the Somme, were again names with remarkable power to move – names which, to a generation of men almost extinct, had been burned into memory. The sound of them took me instantly to boyhood, childhood, to recollection of some of those men when they were young, old as they had seemed to me then. Another World War had intervened between those early memories and now; but although I took some small part in that more recent war and had not been born when the first one ended I still find the music set up by those names almost intolerably moving: Beaumont-Hamel. Mametz Wood. Pozières ridge. Thiepval. The Schwaben Redoubt.

The Schwaben Redoubt. The enemy suffered as we suffered, and often more. When the military attachés rode through Brussels behind King Albert in the 1930s, my father's German colleague and friend rode at his side. This was Colonel – soon to be General – Leo, Freiherr Geyr von Scheppenburg. Geyr was a large, handsome, heavily built man, a cavalry officer from Württemberg and a distinguished horseman. He had an agreeable, slightly enigmatic smile. I can see him sitting on his horse in the streets of Brussels; and I can also see him lunching with the other attachés at some inn in Holland during Dutch Army manoeuvres. I, once again and with pleasure, had been taken along – I suppose aged twelve or thirteen. It was a very good lunch. After it the military attachés mounted their horses and rode off to witness what they could of the mock battle. Geyr had just been notified of his impending promotion to major-general's rank and my father took the lead in congratulating him, with some gentle chaff thrown in – he himself was still a major. (I had learned a little balance about Germans since the nursery days.) Having commanded a battalion twice in the war my father had, like most British officers, dropped several ranks and would not gain battalion command again until 1936 – at the age of 46. Geyr was profiting from a sudden and enormous expansion of the German Army, and so I deduce that those manoeuvres were in 1933 or 1934. Adolf Hitler had become Chancellor of Germany in January 1933 and soon thereafter for many German officers career prospects were transformed. Geyr was still young.

My father told me, years later, that he had watched Geyr's face that day at the Dutch manoeuvres, and had deduced a good deal of complacency. It seems that the opposing sides had been unleashed at each other at no great distance and that after six full days had still not made contact! Geyr was one of the early German apostles of armoured mobility and although 1940 was several years away his reports cannot have discouraged those planning the forthcoming German offensive.

I can also see Geyr one evening in our house in the Avenue Molière. It was my fate (but I enjoyed it) to wear, when dining with the grown-ups in the evening, a kilt of dress Fraser tartan, velvet doublet, lace jabot: my first dinner jacket did not come until I had gone to Eton in September 1934. Geyr, massive, dinner-jacketed, looked with grave admiration at my Highland dress. But I chiefly remember from that occasion conversation between him and my father, which soon became conversation about the war. They had been, at least once, exactly opposite each other in the Ypres Salient. I sat, fascinated, and listened.

Ultimately my father wanted to broaden the circle and change the topic. Geyr obviously concurred, and as they joined the ladies he said (I can still hear the intonation), 'I don't want any more of that sort of thing! I'm a bloody layman!'

Fluent in English and no doubt pleased with his mastery of idiom, he perhaps intended 'a civilian at heart', although the sentiment in his mouth remains slightly improbable. 'Bloody' was in those days not uttered in polite society, certainly not in front of ladies. I remember a nervous and surprised titter, and Geyr saying, 'Have I, perhaps, said something that is not said?'

Also dining was a famous Eton housemaster, by then retired, Samuel Gurney Lubbock, known to all as Jimbo Lubbock. He was a frequent visitor to Brussels – King Leopold (who had at that time just succeeded his father on the throne) had been in Lubbock's house at Eton, and was fond of his old tutor. Jimbo Lubbock was a man of most distinguished appearance, with grey hair and an eyeglass on a broad black ribbon. Ageing beautifully, he had the sort of understated elegance inconceivable except in an English gentleman of his generation, on whom too tight-fitting a coat would have resembled a vulgar label on a champagne bottle. He took it upon himself to answer Geyr. 'You've said,' he replied, 'what Americans call a mouthful!'

In July 1934, immediately after the 'Night of the Long Knives', when Hitler, using the SS, disposed of the now-inconvenient leadership of the SA, the 'Brownshirts' (and a good many others as well), Geyr came to my father's Brussels office in a distressed state. He burst into tears. Weeping, he implored my father not to believe that these gangster methods were the real Germany – this was a revolutionary spasm, a disgusting phase which would pass, he said.

Later he served in London, also as military attaché. Then he attained high command and another landscape lies before my eyes – twenty-three-year-old eyes by now. The darkness of the Normandy sky is lit by a continuous, unbroken fretwork of red tracer fire from German anti-aircraft guns all round the rim of the Allied beachhead and marking its extent. This resembled a vast firework display, vivid, unceasing and unexpected. It was late June 1944. The initial waves of the D-Day assault and immediate follow-up formations had established in Normandy a continuous front and now we of the Guards Armoured Division were landing, unmolested, to prepare for the great break-out battles we had been promised. After what had seemed to us an excessively protracted period of training in England we were due to meet the famous panzer forces our friends had encountered in the deserts of North Africa.

My father's last letter before we had left England had touched a chord of memory. 'I see,' he had written, 'that my old friend Geyr is commanding the bulk of the armour against you. Very, very thorough but not very, very bright!' (I don't think this was particularly just.) Presumably the English papers had been given the fact that the German armoured forces concentrated in 'Panzer Group West' were under the command of General Geyr von Scheppenburg. So somewhere out there in the darkness of my first night in Normandy, behind the illuminated rim of the beachhead, controlling those hostile forces of legendary skill and power, was a well-remembered figure from my boyhood.

My last encounter with Geyr was in documents rather than the flesh – he had died some years before. I was engaged in writing a book about Erwin Rommel and I needed to sift carefully the heated arguments in 1944 between Rommel (Army Group Commander) and Geyr about the best deployment of the Panzer divisions for defeat of the coming Allied invasion of north-west Europe. Geyr had wanted concentration and a massive counter-stroke at the right time, a classic manoeuvre, what the Germans call an 'Operation'. Rommel had dimissed the possibility – enemy control of the air, he said, would negate attempts of that kind. Necessarily small-scale but immediate counter-attacks in the coastal areas as soon as possible after enemy landing would offer the best, the only hope. There had been acrimony (my own views support Rommel) and ultimate compromise. When the Normandy battles were obviously going disastrously for Germany, Geyr – at the same time as the overall Commander-in-Chief in the West, von Rundstedt – was relieved of his command on Hitler's orders.

When my father died in 1964 Geyr sent a charming letter of condolence to my mother, recalling especially Brussels days (not forgetting to mention me and my kilt). He wrote of 'a good soldier and a dear and respected colleague'. Such sentiments would have been reciprocated. The figure of Geyr von Scheppenburg is clear and sympathetic in my memory. (He was a gentleman.)

Joffre. Geyr. My own father. The kindly faces of Belgian veterans on Kemmel in 1932, veterans who reckoned that they had emerged victorious from a war to end all wars and were giving thanks – yet were to have only eight years before the next storm broke. Men and women standing silent in the street in an English south-coast town on 11th November. The wide skies and the quietness of the fields above the Somme. The First World War brings to the mind very different and sometimes more enduring images than anything which followed it, despite the fact that I was born two years after its conclusion.

It was a war which probably marked the national psychology more than did any other four years of our history. Our human losses were, of course, enormous, and the legend of vast, unprecedented and to a degree unnecessary casualties passed into the folk memory of the British. And after a while, after the period of my childhood and youth when these losses were still dignified as tragedy, the tragedy was to some extent debased by becoming the stuff of vicious criticism (often facile and unimaginative) and the war itself the object of parody. It became the stupid war, the wasteful war, the pointless war, the brutally incompetent war.

This evolution of perspective was wholly absent from my own early memories; and I suspect these were at least as close to the truth of the matter. Continental nations were not unused to proportionate losses in major conflicts and were, perhaps, more temperamentally aware that such, however melancholy, is the way of war. In the First World War the British Army put into the field the largest force in its history, which fought on the Western Front (and in a small way on other fronts as well) for four years. This fact must be contrasted (when assessing casualties) with the comparatively small British land forces deployed in the Second World War until the last two years. Numbers involved and duration must be taken into the balance as well as intensity of combat and skill of leadership, or lack of it. The memory of an unutterably severe – and ill-conducted – First War, set against an intelligently conducted and much less costly Second, is largely (not wholly) myth and has little applicability except to Britain – and in Britain such reality as the myth contains applies to the Army but certainly not to the Navy or Air Force, for both of which the Second War was an unremitting and costly experience.

As to the conduct of that earlier war, the stereotype is of a futile struggle wherein huge numbers of men were killed in predictably vain and thus criminally stupid attempts to break through an enemy system of entrenchments dominated by machine gun and artillery shell, efforts, in Churchill's words, to 'fight machine-gun bullets with the breasts of gallant men and think that that was waging war'. There was something in the stereotype but those who used it, as the years passed and the temper of opinion became more cynical, often ignored the political and thus the strategic compulsions of the time. The German Army was occupying most of Belgium and a large part of northern France; the British and French could not simply stand on the defensive; and the operational offensive was inescapably difficult when fronts were con-tinuous, fortified and manned by enormous numbers of men.

To make a breach in such fronts and exploit it would inevitably need protracted attritional preparation – or so it was not unreasonably believed. The admirably planned 'hurricane bombardment' with which the Germans preceded their successful break-in battle in March 1918 was, it is true, short; but it is still doubtful if that assault would have succeeded had the British defending forces not been significantly thinned and weakened by an attempt to economize manpower. The British and French, therefore, had depended to a huge extent on sustained fire by the artillery arm; and those who used the stereotype of that war for criticism too often ignored the devastating effect the battles of attrition were having on the Germans themselves. Ludendorff, after all, wrote of the German Army bleeding to death on the hills above the Somme. Generally ignored, too, have been the modest but real tactical successes which were often part of these ultimately tragic offensive battles. Consider the notorious first day of the Somme battle itself; in some Army Corps and Divisional sectors the artillery preparation, the rehearsal, practice and phasing of the attack and – perhaps above all – the determination to avoid excessively ambitious targets for subsequent phases led to a significantly favourable balance of advantage to our own side. This has been obscured by the two most quoted statistics – the casualties (horrendous but most unevenly distributed) and the small amount of ground ultimately won. The latter, however, did not really matter if it were accepted that a battle of attrition was, however horribly, being fought rather than a battle leading to operational movement and manoeuvre. What mattered was to kill Germans. It was, of course, a mistake and a tragedy to suppose that the battle could become a real victory, could usher in a phase of manoeuvre. But the latter would one day come – decisively – in the late summer of 1918.

Such critical analysis, of course, lay far in the future. To my childhood and boyhood the figures were heroic and unblemished, their struggle necessary, the outcome deservedly victorious. And my father – on the Western Front and at Regimental duty for most of the war and frequently wounded – certainly believed in the necessity and in the underlying Allied strategy, although critical of some of the tactics and much of the staff work. He had experienced the victory, too. He never attacked – indeed vigorously defended – the reputation of the British Commander-in-Chief, Douglas Haig; and when, much later, I read his diaries from the war I learned more of the contemporary realities. Such realism is now attacked as heartless.

The brilliant pens of gifted and sensitive participant-poets, the Owens and Sassoons, have made indelible marks – and nobly so. But I don't think they were typical in their reactions. Although the squalid circumstances of life in the trenches and the ever-presence of fear obviously affected that whole generation I doubt whether many believed the war futile or unnecessary. Most men believed that the fate of England depended on their readiness to serve and suffer. They reckoned – and probably continued to reckon throughout their lines – that they were confronting the expansionist ambition of militaristic Germany, and that to confront it was both necessary and right. Cynicism, revisionist sentiment, perhaps more objective political judgement – these would come, at least to a later generation; but I am sure that those men – of all ranks – thought their cause good and their destiny honourable, whatever the pain. And in the end they won.

Myth matters, however, and the particular myth of a campaign on the Western Front producing British casualties without parallel, the unnecessary consequence of brutal, insensitive and incompetent military leadership, coloured popular, and therefore political, imagination in the period between the wars to a degree unwarranted by the facts of the matter. It coloured the imagination of such as Neville Chamberlain, inducing him to eschew until an appallingly late hour whole-hearted military cooperation with France, thus significantly weakening the deterrent power of opposition to Hitler. It coloured the imagination of Winston Churchill, even leading him – also at an appallingly late hour – to hesitate (mercifully, only a momentary hesitation) and to appear to have second thoughts about the necessity to open a major front against the Germans in north-west Europe in 1944. It bred a fear of continental commitment which tended to weaken or negate British influence in the councils of Allies and of other nations. Nor has it disappeared. It was born in Flanders and in Picardy between 1914 and 1918.

The myth will continue as subject of historical and strategic dissection. Its spirit, however, a spirit of embittered disillusion, is wholly at variance with the impressions of my own early years and of the figures who populate them. On the contrary, the pictures I formed and retain are of what seemed a people not only extraordinarily at peace – a peace after suffering – within itself but extraordinarily united. There no doubt was – I have described it – a certain perhaps regrettable triumphalism here and there; but there was seriousness and dignity in the pride, just as there was dignity in the melancholy. Already, of course, economic depression, poverty, industrial unrest and selfish mismanagement were starting to undermine the unity; while feeble leadership, loss of energy and lack of imagination would diminish the power of the pride. For a while however, the British seemed to be saying that the war had decimated but had also transfigured a whole generation. We children grew up in that radiance. All must acknowledge that, despite the horrors of this century, the quality of life and especially the health of most people – certainly most Europeans – has hugely improved since those times I first recall. But although the nostalgia of old age is notoriously myopic I cannot help thinking we were a better people then.

2

Northern Lights

Before the Dover era we had lived in Scotland for two years, my father serving with the Gordons at Fort George on the Moray Firth. Fort George is the northernmost of a chain of garrison posts – Fort Augustus and Fort William being the others – named for Hanoverian princes and William of Orange, with which the Government in London aimed, in the seventeenth and eighteenth centuries, to keep potentially rebellious Highland Clans under control. Unlike the other two, Fort George retains its military identity. It has romantic atmosphere – ramparted, defensible, sea-girt by the waters of the firth, poised on the narrows between the Black Isle and the coast of Nairn.

We lived in a small house in the little town of Nairn, six miles distant, but sometimes I was taken to the Fort itself and can still recall with pleasure the sound of the pipes, ever nearer, as they played back to barracks the 1st Battalion Gordon Highlanders from some exercise or route march, my father often marching at their head. He was at that time (1923/24) combining the functions of Battalion Second-in-Command and Adjutant. Like all his generation he had been promoted rapidly in the war – a lieutenant in 1914, a lieutenant-colonel commanding a battalion in 1917 – and even more rapidly demoted after it; indeed as I have said, it was eighteen years before he again commanded a battalion – 'and not nearly as well', he used to remark. Peace, therefore, brought greatly reduced rank and responsibilities. At Fort George the Commanding Officer, Sir James Burnett of Leys, was an old friend and my parents often visited the Burnett home, Crathes Castle in Kincardine, with its exquisite garden. Sir James, seen from childhood, was a gruff, alarming person; but, as I discovered later, one with extraordinary charm and exceptionally funny when he chose – which he often did.

The sights and sounds of the north of Scotland dominated my life both then and later – sea; a wide, wide sky; distant but not immediately pressing hills; the rather throaty, high-pitched, sing-song cadence of the people's speech; the magic of rivers – particularly the Findhorn, where we often picnicked, where my father appeared, as ever, elegant in his kilt of hunting Fraser tartan with a blue tweed jacket, where my mother seemed extraordinarily beautiful and always laughing, where the trees were in dark, thrilling contrast to the sun-speckled grass of the riverbank, where the water was always frothing and bubbling, where the sky was always blue. Memory is generally benign.

Our house at Nairn was on the road to the sea. From the nursery windows we could see a large house with a flagpole. This belonged to a friend of my parents, a judge, Lord Finlay. I found the idea of a judge (explained to me by Nanny, with no holds barred) rather intimidating, and used to gaze towards the flagpole with a certain uneasiness. An outstanding recollection of Nairn was the beach in summer. We spent much time on it and I know that I often howled with indignant discomfort when made to bathe in the sea there. It felt bitterly cold. It *was* bitterly cold. Nairn was a rather fashionable place for Scottish families to bring their children to the coast for a supposedly healthy summer break and many people rented houses there, the elders having a Northern Season playing golf, shooting with friends when 12th August arrived, dancing. The children – in memory day after day, but I suppose we were sometimes rained off – went to the beach with their nannies. The nannies enjoyed a very social time, with plenty of gossip, having lugged down the tea baskets (sand blowing on to honey sand-wiches; milk in the thermos: primus stoves coaxed into action in corners of windy beach huts). Tea followed the compulsory dip, itself with luck delayed until after completion of a sand castle. I greatly enjoyed sand castles.

The children formed quite a large society. Since we had a house at Nairn the offspring of my parents' friends sometimes stayed with us for a holiday by the sea. I particularly remember Nigel Forbes and Charlie Leith-Hay, both slightly older than me but true friends later. Also older and more 'local', in that their parents or grandparents took or owned houses there, were Ludovic Kennedy and Willie Whitelaw – the former, particularly admired, I knew as 'Lukenny'. I was, however, too young to play the part of a friend or attract their notice – I came to know Willie well in later life and Ludo slightly but I have never spoken about the beach at Nairn. It would still be presumptuous.

From the beach we could look across the firth and over the low ridges of the Black Isle to the hills of Easter Ross and Inverness. Largest of these appeared Ben Wyvis, blue-grey, shouldering the sky. For long the very word 'Scotland' evoked that picture of distant mountains, their shapes more graceful even if not more enormous than the mountains of other lands; of huge skies; and of white, sandy beaches bordering the sea. The sounds were of seabirds; the breaking of surf; the occasional hoot of a motorhorn (produced by squeezing a large, round rubber ball, reached by stretching a hand outside the driver's window – it was some time before I was allowed a go at this); and, sometimes, the thrilling sound of pipes, when a military pipe band was playing in the main street of Nairn.

'Recruiting,' Nanny would say, wisely. Sometimes they were the Gordons. Sometimes the members of the pipe band wore white drill jackets with their kilts, on other occasions the more formal scarlet tunic (drummers, drum-major) and green tunic (pipers). However attired, they looked superb. The distant carry of their playing would reach the nursery and lead to urgent demands on Nanny to get out the ancient, high-wheeled pram and set off on the short march from our house to the place of parade. She generally agreed.

Sometimes we travelled to Aberdeenshire, the home county of my family, and stayed with friends. Travel was by train, and movement to the station was still by horse-drawn cab. If we went via Aberdeen somebody had asked the station-master to watch for us, and he would appear, splendid in top hat and frock coat. I remember, too, delicious food in the Aberdeen station restaurant – including my first poached egg, of which I was wary but immediately liked. Like most children I was disgracefully choosy about food and often scolded for it. (It is a trait which persists through the generations: my own youngest daughter remarked at a very early age, 'Other people's *gravy* always makes me *nervous!*')

Of Aberdeenshire friends the most memorable were the Leith-Hays, of Leith Hall at Kennethmont. Christmas 1924, as well as many other occasions, was spent at Leith Hall, and although I passed much time there when I was older and it is easy to confuse recollections, I shall try to draw on the impressions of childhood before those of adolescence.

The seventeenth-century house was built somewhat in the French manner, round a courtyard open only at the back. There were several small ornamental turrets but the general effect was graceful and unfussy, perhaps because the main elevation had elegant sash windows on the first floor – the floor with the principal rooms. The front door was shielded by a large porch and outer hall, built out on to the handsome sweep of drive as an addition in recent years and personally designed by the laird, Charlie Leith-Hay of Rannes. He had summoned the builders, told them exactly the dimensions of what he wanted and then marked the outline on the gravel with his walking stick. The head builder had said something about drawings, but Charlie had waved such ideas aside, pointed to his own marks on the gravel and told them to begin at once, that morning. There'd been mutters of 'The Laird's fu,'* but they'd obeyed and built the porch and hall. I was told that it was, from a design point of view, perfect. I can well believe it. The object was essentially simple, Charlie knew what he wanted, and architects can waste time and clients' money in elaborating simplicities.

I remember the outer hall as enormously useful – a capacious home for any number of coats, mackintoshes, boots, sticks, skates, toboggans and so forth. From it one went into an inner hall which was at that time used – anyway on major occasions like Christmas – as a dining room, a banqueting hall. The dining room proper, which I didn't see used until the 1930s, was a grand room, hung in red, on the first floor.

Also on that first floor were (with much else) an oval room, Henrietta Leith-Hay's sitting room, where we were sometimes gathered round a piano. Much of childhood and boyhood, especially in Scotland, was spent gathered round a piano, singing, or learning to sing, in something like harmony. Scots songs often but at the Leith-Hay piano I remember chiefly 'Frère Jacques', and cannot hear that 'Dormez-vous? Dormez-vous?' without seeing the Oval room at Leith Hall. Then there was the Music Room, a huge room, very beautiful, running almost the whole depth of the house and with portraits of ancient Leiths and Hays along

* drunk, in Scots.

the wall facing the aforementioned sash windows; and the Whispering Gallery. The nurseries were on a higher floor – it was a tall house.

The Whispering Gallery! Off it opened a number of bedrooms, including mine when I was older. The Gallery ran round three sides of the courtyard. If one placed one's mouth half-way up the inner wall (where I think was a dado) and whispered, the whisper was audible, quite clearly, to someone listening, round two corners, at the far end of the corridor; in effect at the other end of a very long horse-shoe-shaped passage. I don't know the acoustic reason for this but it was remarkable. I imagine it is still effective but I have not visited Leith Hall since the Second World War and its charming inhabitants are long dead. The house itself has become the property of the National Trust for Scotland.

'Its charming inhabitants' – Charlie Leith-Hay, whom we knew as 'Old Charlie' to distinguish him from his son 'Little Charlie', my near contemporary, was surely one of the most entertaining and delightful men who ever lived. The family stemmed from a union between the Leiths of Leith Hall – Charlie was Chief of the ancient Aberdeenshire tribe of Leith – and the Hays of Rannes. Old Charlie had spent part of his youth in Australia where he had, among other things, studied singing. Neither that nor anything else had made his fortune, however, and long afterwards I learned that his reputation as a successful man of business did not stand high. A child sensed nothing except that life at Leith Hall when we went there was wholly agreeable, with an atmosphere of security and affection and with the grown-ups – both Leith-Hays – having all the time in the world to be nice to children, play with them, laugh with them.

Old Charlie was a short man, sturdy, with a bushy white moustache, amused eyes and a high-pitched, rather giggly voice. Some years older than my father – indeed, nearer to my grandfather's generation – he found it irresistible to make gentle fun of people in the kindest possible way. A rather precious lady, visiting for the first time, would gush, 'I find your house entirely fascinating, Mr Leith-Hay.' Charlie would respond with hugely exaggerated words of gratitude.

'Oh, you must write that out! Please, write it out! And sign! Then we can frame it, you see!' To some other grand-looking lady he would perhaps say, 'Oh, we're so glad you've come to see us again! We were sure you would – we remember how much you ate when you were here last, and with such enjoyment, too, so that I said to Henrietta, "She'll be back!"' Then would come that infectious laugh, the lady joining in uncertainly. It sounds absurd. It sounds offensive. Accompanied, as it was, by Charlie's cackle it, somehow, was simply funny. And he generally – perhaps always – reserved his real shafts for the high-flown or the pretentious. We children adored him – it was wonderful, in the face of what was generally a united grown-up front, to find someone so unquestionably grown-up as old Charlie flouting the system and showing not a fig of loyalty to his contemporaries if the fancy took him.

He was capable, of course, of taking a high hand with anyone he found forgetful of his position. I remember him once telling us all, in astonished tones, of how the local police constable (new to Kennethmont) had come to Leith Hall that morning, seen Charlie and asked about parking arrangements for the forthcoming garden party – every summer there was a garden party and boys' cricket match at Leith Hall, in which I played on several occasions, without distinction. Charlie had been outraged, telling the policeman in no uncertain terms that what happened to cars at Leith Hall was his business, not that of the constabulary.

But most of the time Charlie exuded laughter and affection. He was very musical. He paid me one of the nicest compliments I've ever received when I was about seventeen, one which was far more appropriate to himself. 'David,' he said, 'you are one of those people who make age unimportant – one's always an equal.' Not true, but how true of him. And in the early days we loved his appearance in the nursery, we loved his hooting chuckle, his jokes, and his understanding – never obtrusive – of what a four-, or a six- (or a twelve-, or a seventeen-)year-old was really thinking and would really enjoy.

He was not, I think, the most practical of managers. Also when about seventeen I found him once sitting in the Music Room, a card table beside him. On it was a mass of silver coin and Charlie was building piles of specific amounts, I imagine to pay some wages personally. Perhaps this was peculiar – such things would be for factor, housekeeper, even wife – but I think times were difficult. I remember the moment because Charlie seemed uncharacteristically depressed.

'All my life,' he said, vehemently, 'I've hated *money*! I've hated everything about it! I hate touching it! And now, late in life, I have to deal with the beastly stuff!'

He meant it. How easy to mock the attitude of one whose circumstances had been so comparatively privileged that he felt able to stand aloof from the actual pounds, shillings and pence those circumstances provided; easy, but only partially just. It was wholly in Charlie's character to dislike money. He could never have made it. He was probably bad at husbanding it. I don't think he spent it with profligacy but his nature was generous, he had inherited a certain position and certain responsibilities which he would never fail to discharge, and I expect he left the balancing of the books to others, with indifferent success.

His wife, Henrietta, was an O'Neill from Ulster and was perfectly matched – also kind to the point of embarrassment in her unselfish thoughtfulness for others, gentle, very quiet, and to her family utterly devoted. In stature both the Leith-Hays were small (little Charlie was considerably larger) – small, smiling and serene. I never saw old Charlie anywhere other than Leith Hall, surrounded by its woods and with a long, heather-covered hill, Knockandy, protecting its north flank. Far to the south-west, lovely especially in the winter snow, stood the hill peak called the Buck of Cabrach. Near the front of the house, next to the grass expanse where the cricket matches were played, was the lake, frozen hard in winter. At some distance from the back courtyard gate were the walled gardens, as in many Scottish properties set well apart from the house, sloped to catch sun, extensive, beautiful.

Winter snow – hindsight may exaggerate but the snow in Strathbogie (as that district of Aberdeenshire is called) did seem to fall remarkably heavily and lie remarkably deep. I remember being handed out of Leith Hall's first-floor windows via a ramp of banked snow to the white, glistening ground because the doors were blocked by drift. The lake was the scene of ice hockey in winter and I can't recall a winter not dominated by cold. It increased the fun – there were great fires burning in every room that mattered. Gaslight – there was no electricity – seemed efficient and friendly. At meals plates – certainly in the nursery – were kept hot by boiling water held in a special compartment built under each plate's base.

In summer the heather on Knockandy was in bloom and on the small moors behind it a fair number of grouse were driven over the peat-built butts, as I found when I was older. And we swam in the lake and skated on it in the winter. And once – it was during the Nairn days, a midsummer, I think 1924 – we gathered near the back drive, which ran long and straight to a rear gate, gathered under the Dule tree, so-called because there, in ancient times, the Chief would hold court, sentence malefactors, and see them hanged from a high branch: gathered, and were asked if we could hear 'them'?

'Hear what?'

'The pipes.'

Sure enough it was a battalion of the Gordons, marching on summer training and about to camp at Leith Hall. The day was hot. The pipes sounded nearer and nearer until they swung in through the gate, far off at the end of the drive, followed by the battalion in their khaki tunics and Gordon kilts. This was perhaps a territorial battalion, maybe the 6th, raised all over Strathbogie and Banff, a battalion my father had commanded at Arras and Third Ypres in 1917, a battalion which had fought on the Western Front from 1915 onwards – Festubert, Loos, the Somme, Arras, Ypres, Cambrai, the final breaching of the Hindenburg Line. Just before the Armistice, with Scottish manpower near exhausted, they had been amalgamated with the 7th Donside Battalion. Which battalion of Gordons marched to Leith Hall that summer under my enchanted gaze I am unsure; but I hope it was the 6th, although in an old photograph album I found a snapshot of the occasion and my father had written 'March of the 92nd through Aberdeenshire'. The 92nd was the earlier designation of the 2nd (Regular) Battalion.

It was at the beginning of another war, in September 1939, that I was in the small train which ran from Fraserburgh to Aberdeen and had bought the day's *Aberdeen Press and Journal*. 'Young laird of Rannes killed', was a small headline. Little Charlie, recently commissioned after a cadetship at the Royal Military Academy at Woolwich, had been killed in a motorcycle accident. Old Charlie died not long afterwards.

Yet the most outstanding figure of my Scottish childhood and boyhood was undoubtedly my uncle Alistair Saltoun. He was the senior of four brothers, sons of my grandfather, eighteenth Lord Saltoun, eighteenth Fraser of Philorth. My father, born in 1890, was the youngest brother and there was one younger sister, my aunt Mary.

The family home, Philorth, was near Fraserburgh, a town on the Aberdeenshire coast in that north-east district called Buchan, the country north of the river Ythan and east of the river Deveron. The lands of Philorth had once constituted the eastern parts (or some of them) of the ancient Earldom of Ross, one of the great fiefs of northern Scotland, a fief stretching from the east to the west coast. The Earl of Ross in mid-fourteenth century had no male heir and the earldom – a source of considerable economic, political and military power – fell to his two co-heiress daughters. The younger – the Lady Joanna de Ross, as she was styled – married in 1369 Sir Alexander Fraser of Cowie and Durris, Aberdeenshire properties.

Sir Alexander Fraser was grandson of another Sir Alexander Fraser, Chamberlain of Scotland, supporter and brother-in-law of King Robert Bruce, whose sister, the Lady Mary, he married. This earlier Sir Alexander had been killed at the battle of Dupplin in 1332; his three brothers – one of whom, Sir Simon Fraser, was progenitor of the Frasers of Lovat – had been killed at the battle of Halidon Hill in the following year. My great-grandfather, who wrote the family history in three volumes entitled *The Frasers of Philorth*, delved extensively into family charters and demonstrated, at least to his own satisfaction (I think it is accepted by the genealogical authorities), that our progenitor was the eldest brother. Most – not all – Frasers descend from Sir Simon, ancestor of Lovat, and since from that line was founded a numerous Highland Clan (source of power and influence) the Frasers of Lovat, albeit theoretically junior, were of significantly greater importance than our branch in the history of Scotland.

The Sir Alexander Fraser who married Joanna de Ross became, by right of his wife, the first Fraser of Philorth, in 1375.* The principal

---

* The portion of the Earldom assigned to Joanna included, beside the lands of Philorth, lands in Ross-shire and in Galloway. These passed from our ancestors' hands long ago and we were generally known as 'The Aberdeenshire Frasers'. To confuse things further, however, another branch of the Frasers, deriving from neither Lovat nor Philorth, became powerful in Aberdeenshire ('The Frasers of Muchalls'), built the noble house called Castle Fraser, and were given a peerage ('Lord Fraser') by Charles I in 1632.

base of the Frasers of Philorth was a castle, itself originally called Philorth but later named Cairnbulg, built on a low knoll a half-mile from the sea, three miles from where the town of Fraserburgh now stands. It is one of a chain of castles on that coast, built to confront the Norsemen. These 'summer sailors' used to bring their longships to a point where they could beach, and the huge crescent of Fraserburgh Bay is exactly such a point. They would then send the fleet to another point, and march across country to join it, looting, raping, butchering all males and kidnapping all children except the sickly, whom they killed by throwing them from rooftops and catching them on the points of spears. The castles of Philorth, Inverallochy, Kinnaird Head, Pittulie and Pitsligo, in our area, were designed to deter this sort of boisterous Viking behaviour. This, however, was before our time – the Comyns, arch-enemies of our patron, Bruce, had been the powers of Buchan in the era preceding our own and had probably built, or rebuilt, the castle of Philorth.

About a mile to the west of the castle, on more sheltered ground, the tenth Fraser of Philorth* built a new house in 1660, called it Philorth House, and made it henceforth the family's home. It was there that my father and his brothers and sister were brought up. Cairnbulg – the original Philorth – passed into other hands and fell into ruin (in which condition the famous artist of Scottish domestic architecture, James Giles, drew it in 1839); it was restored by an Aberdeenshire shipping magnate, by name Duthie, at the end of the nineteenth century.

Philorth House, an attractive seventeenth-century building of modest size, was greatly enlarged – and not visually improved – by my great-grandfather in mid-nineteenth century. My father loved it dearly, and knew every tree and stone in its vicinity. When he was young the estate stood at about 11,000 acres of largely arable land – and very good land, that part of Buchan being known as the granary of Scotland. The family's lands had contracted, expanded, contracted

---

* Through his mother, Margaret Abernethy, he succeeded his first cousin Alexander Abernethy, Lord Saltoun, and became tenth Lord Saltoun in 1668. The Abernethy Lords Saltoun, having become financially severely embarrassed, had sold the house and lands of Saltoun, in East Lothian, to the Fletcher family and the lands of Rothiemay in Aberdeenshire (where the family had long resided) to another creditor.

again, expanded again as, over the centuries, much had been sold, bought, sold once more. The Frasers' financial vicissitudes had been uneven. Younger sons had in several cases been planted as founders of cadet branches on parts of the original estate, although by the twentieth century their descendants had died out. But the tribe was not inconsiderable. Thomas the Rhymer in the thirteenth century referred to Philorth as one of the 'three great barons in the north', with Findlater and Fyvie. The tenth Fraser of Philorth took a thousand men to support the dispossessed Charles II on his unsuccessful march which ended in defeat at Worcester; and the twelfth, succeeding in 1715, boasted that he could summon a hundred Frasers within the hour. Land, men, supporters, kinfolk, were power. Money, however, tended to be in somewhat short supply. Times changed. My great-grandparents' building ventures and general extravagance undoubtedly bled the estate and my grandfather's own inheritance faced difficulties. Nevertheless, Philorth was a home of amplitude and tradition.

Then, on the night of 24th March 1915, an electrical fault caused a fire which largely destroyed the building. My grandfather, aged 63, had returned to the Army and was about to take command of a home brigade stationed in the south of England, so that the only member of the family at Philorth was my grandmother – my father was back in France after sick leave following a wound at First Ypres, my uncle George, the second brother, was at sea with the Grand Fleet, my uncle Simon had been killed at First Ypres and my uncle Alistair had been taken prisoner with the 1st Battalion of the Gordons during the retreat from Mons in August 1914. My aunt Mary was away from home.

Pictures and furniture were mostly saved but the house was uninhabitable. The loss of Philorth meant that the family had no home in Scotland. My grandparents thenceforth lived in their London house and during the war took occasional houses not far from London. After the war's end my grandfather had to make up his mind what to do about Philorth. And, at a time of severe agricultural depression, he also had to make up his mind what to do about his land. He decided not to rebuild; and in 1925 he resolved to sell the estate, or most of it. He took the view that the problems facing large landowners – especially if saddled with large houses – were intractable. Indeed, he had even been thinking about sale as early as 1907. He had few assets or income beyond his land and lacked the foresight or faith to realize how time might one day transform his fortune.

Those were the Nairn days as far as I was concerned, and of course I was unaware of these traumatic family happenings. Only afterwards did I learn that the first news of the sale of Philorth was read by my father in the morning's *Aberdeen Press and Journal*. My mother told me it was one of the worst days of her life, and I can believe it. My father, of course, was not the heir, so that his loss was emotional rather than economic, but he undoubtedly felt as if a valued limb had been severed and he could hardly bear to speak of Philorth thereafter. Something died; and the pain was sharpened by the sense that his own father had regarded him as an outsider to any family debate on the future of the family home, because not personally concerned. This was in character; my grandfather had firm views on primogeniture and the necessity for younger sons to make their own way. But a tradition of land ownership which had lasted five and a half centuries was being broken, the home my father had loved from childhood was being alienated, and he read it in the newspapers. It hurt.

Meanwhile – after the burning of the house but before the sale of the estate – the sympathy of the brothers had largely been directed to their elder, my uncle Alistair, Master of Saltoun and always referred to by his family as 'Master'. He would return from captivity to find his inheritance shorn of a residence. Then, a few years later, the inheritance itself was sold and when my uncle succeeded his father he could look forward to little property and no home in Scotland, although the third senior in the Baronage of that country. He had himself been very fairly consulted by my grandfather about the sale of Philorth and had recognized – or said later that he had recognized – the compulsive economic necessity. He was, however, completely loyal, and what his inner thoughts were I shall never know.

Because Uncle Alistair was a man quite unlike all others – including all other members of his own family – it is unsurprising that he apparently took the loss of home and land somewhat differently from his brothers and sister, although it was he, not they, who was

directly affected. He once told me that he didn't feel particular deprivation that the lands no longer belonged to him; but he felt that he
and his family belonged to the district and that the connection of the
centuries should not be severed by sale. The feus in Fraserburgh were
still part of the Philorth estate, and Uncle Alistair reckoned that our
association was human and historic, and not simply dependent on
property; in fact he also told me that he found his relationships around
Fraserburgh easier for the fact that he was no longer a considerable
laird.

This sentiment led him to start farming one of the Philorth farms,
which was excepted from sale, immediately after the rest of the estate
went. This was a hard life, and he set about it with typical thoroughness. In the process he launched certain initiatives for the Aberdeenshire farm servants, who had, he reckoned, generally been hard done
by. He thus maintained the contact which he believed was a duty –
and a congenial duty, for he loved Buchan and its people. Later he
qualified as a Chartered Accountant in Edinburgh in order, as he put
it, to learn something about money (land having been turned into
money by the sale of Philorth).

Then, in 1933, my grandfather died and Uncle Alistair decided that
the family must, after all, have a proper base in our own territory. It
was still a bad time to own land. Farmers were impoverished, rents
were low or unpayable, farms were hard to let, returns on investment
in farming were derisory, land was sold for next to nothing. But at
that time the ancient and restored castle of Cairnbulg came on the
market and my uncle bought it. Very little land attached to Cairnbulg
but apart from that inconvenience it was a most happy circumstance.
The sporting rights over much of the Philorth estate – it had been
excellent partridge country – had been retained or were re-rented. In
buying Cairnbulg, where I can most clearly see my uncle Alistair, he
had brought the family home.

Cairnbulg consists of two towers, one round and one – the older
and taller – square, with a connecting centre between the two. During
the period of ruin the towers stood, albeit crumbled, but the centre had
needed total rebuilding when Mr Duthie set to work in the eighteen-
nineties. The towers hold fascinating rooms, and Duthie's restoration
appeared well done. The largest room, taking the whole first floor of

the square tower, we called 'The Keep'. It had been the Great Hall of the castle and was the principal sitting room in my uncle and aunt's day. Above the keep was a billiard room and above that, at the top of the tower, another room used for various games; while below it, at ground level, is a low, barrel-vaulted room known to us as 'the dungeon', about whose original function there were many theories. The top room in the round tower was my cousin's, the Master's, bedroom and had an internal balcony running round it, site for his extensive and lovingly assembled collection of model trains. Most bedrooms, including mine, were in the connecting centre.

I used to stay there regularly, and my uncle and aunt treated me as a son and showed me unreserved kindness and generosity throughout their lives. Their own son, my cousin and from 1933 Master of Saltoun, was a year younger than I and a near contemporary at Eton where – very much unlike me – he was a noted scholar, musician and athlete, who excelled in everything he did. Together we explored that part of Buchan on foot or bicycle. Not conventionally 'scenic', it has a peculiar fascination, with its rolling fields, stone walls, wide skies, an extraordinarily subtle variety of colour luminosity which comes from the land, particularly at evening and particularly under a black, stormy sky. Features or buildings change colour quickly, hour by hour, in that variable light; Cairnbulg itself could gleam white when touched by the sun and looked at from the height of Mormond Hill, several miles away; or could lour very dark against the surrounding woods.

And beside my relations another figure is unmistakable in the landscape around Cairnbulg. Because the shooting was still Uncle Alistair's it meant that at the start of a visit I would take a bicycle and ride to a cottage in the Sinclair woods to see Samuel McKechnie. McKechnie had been head keeper at Philorth for many years, and stayed on, a mighty link with Philorth's past. There I always found a great welcome from him and his wife, for his devotion to all our family was absolute, and of the brothers my father had been undoubtedly his favourite. Then we would sit in his kitchen and talk. And then we would go to the kennels and look at any changes in the dog population. (With dogs he was incomparable.)

McKechnie was a man of wonderful presence and both he and his wife conveyed remarkable nobility, a nobility finding expression in voice and manner (in fact McKechnie was not a Buchan man, he came from Ayrshire): in appearance – he had one of the finest heads I have ever seen, as well as one of the most enchanting smiles; and in character, for his integrity and principles were built on rock and there was no mistaking the fact. Physically he was magnificent, tall, craggy, massive – although a little bent with the passing of the years. He exuded authority. He would have made a magnificent Regimental Sergeant Major – 'Not a man would have fidgeted in the ranks,' my father used to say, 'if McKechnie was on parade.'

He had been broken-hearted at the sale of Philorth. I remember once standing with him by his cottage, looking towards the hill of Mormond – the long, solitary, heather-covered hill which, although only 700 feet high, dominates that corner of Buchan. There were still a few grouse on Mormond, but McKechnie was recalling earlier times, when it was well keepered, heather carefully maintained, standards high. Now all was different. 'Aye,' he said, gazing at its outline, his voice unsteady, 'puir auld hill!' McKechnie felt for nature, for woods, hills, water, as he did for human beings or parts of himself.

From the castle windows of Cairnbulg one could see the sea – often grey but sometimes a remarkable deep, dark blue. The bents – the sand hills formed by the wind, covered by coarse grass and enclosing Fraserburgh Bay – were, superficially, of a pale grey-green colour but could turn to a brilliant gold when touched by particular lights. All of this was the setting for my uncle.

My uncle Alistair was a man of brilliant but erratic mind and independent, original, often peculiar opinions – he was, indeed, regarded both within and without the family as an eccentric. Yet 'eccentrics' can – although I think this diminishes genuine eccentricity – be somewhat self-regarding; they can parody themselves, enjoy their quirky reputations and be detected so doing. There was nothing of that in my uncle. He was completely without self-consciousness. Every gesture, action, speech was genuine and made without thought of effect.

Yet eccentric he was. He minded not in the least what he wore or how he looked – he was in fact an extremely good-looking man, although he would undoubtedly have been astonished to be told it. He was widely read, a good classicist, an interested mathematician (although he always disclaimed competence at mathematics, not because of false modesty but because his standards of academic proficiency were so high) and one who enjoyed the byways rather than the high roads of history. His attitude to every matter derived from first principles and owed little to the opinion of any other person whatsoever. To be with him was generally to acquire information and was certainly to develop certain powers of dialectic if one were in any way to keep one's end up.

His gifts were never canalized into what he would have regarded as expertise. He was diffuse, often obscure, and his mind worked along such unusual lines that it was not always easy to follow. He seemed – and he often mocked and criticized himself for it, but it was astonishingly impressive – to know an immense amount about a bewildering multiplicity of things. A polymath and amateur – but he loved experts and recognized them. He had tried his hand at all sorts of things and often attained a certain level of mastery, if only to see what they were like – it was his way. Involved once with a charity for the blind he learned Braille (I suspect very rapidly) and told me it was an indifferent system and he reckoned he could devise a better. This was characteristic.

He played chess better than most people. He knitted with considerable skill. His style at golf was perfectly extraordinary but the ball often went into the hole after surprisingly few strokes. He brought off remarkable shots when shooting. Above all he liked to laugh – generously, if one told him a good story, loudly, unreservedly, with immense gusto.

With children he was kind, amused, enchanting – enchanting, of course, because he never made the smallest distinction between any human beings, whatever their age, sex, class or function. He would engage a workman in animated conversation and one might find my uncle, forefinger jabbing, reminding a man engaged by my aunt to carry out some necessary repair at Cairnbulg of what Cicero had remarked on a particular point, and asking without affectation or patronage whether he'd got the quotation right. He had a disconcerting way of assuming a companion's circle of acquaintances was as wide

34

and reached back as far as his own. Contemporaries, labourers, debut-
antes, it made not the slightest difference.

'You remember what Jackson said about that?'

'Er – Jackson – ?'

'Yes. He had this theory –' He might be referring to a don who had
marked his time at New College in about 1906 or to a fellow member
of the Athenaeum who'd published an obscure treatise the month
before, and the conversation might be being addressed to a girl of
eighteen in 1970. It never occurred to him to explain or modify and
he didn't mind being faced by silent incomprehension; in fact I don't
think he noticed. 'Charming girl, that,' he'd say.

Nor did Uncle Alistair care greatly for the rules and conventions
which govern much of modern life. I was with him once when he was
driving in the outskirts of Richmond; and talking with animation.
It was a Sunday afternoon and there was little traffic. A particular
crossroads appeared. The traffic lights turned to red. 'Bureaucracy at
its worst,' said Uncle Alistair, as he drove through them without
slowing down.

Above all things, however, he hated injustice, and in the House of
Lords, which he attended regularly and where he was a recognized
expert on Parliamentary procedure, he often attempted to use
Parliament to right a wrong which he fancied had been suffered by
some individual, a wrong which Government, if so minded, could
correct. Sometimes he was unsuccessful. Sometimes, I have little
doubt, he was mistaken. Generally the attempts were unpopular, for
to badger a government department and take up the time of Parliament again and again on a particular issue is seldom appreciated: it
leads to mutters about bees in bonnets, about obsessions, about King
Charles's Head. But sometimes, to my knowledge, he was right; not
only right but carried his point so that, with more or less grace,
Government conceded and an official injustice or cruelty was remedied.
He was a poor speaker, once saying to me with a shout of laughter,
'I'm one of the worst speakers in the House!' His processes of thought
in making a case were sometimes over-complicated, a weakness he
recognized. But a few people, probably unaware of the fact, owed him
much.

He did not in the least believe in moderation. If he liked something he did it for as long as he felt inclined. He enjoyed chocolates: and if a box of them had been given to him he tended to sit in his armchair, the chocolates beside him, and eat until the box was finished. He enjoyed music: and if a particular concert was giving him pleasure he would turn up the volume on the radio (like most of us of a certain age he was rather deaf) until it drowned all else. He could – and generally did – concentrate simultaneously on a number of quite different activities. I once called at Cross Deep, his beautiful house on the Thames at Twickenham. My aunt stopped me before I went into the library, his usual lair.

'Alistair has had rather a bad chill. He insisted on getting up but the doctor's with him. Do go in, he'll love to see you, he's in his dressing gown.'

I went in. The doctor, a man of mature years, was sitting perched opposite Uncle Alistair, who, as my aunt had said, was wrapped in a dressing gown in his usual chair. Conversation was difficult because the radio – Haydn, I think – was at full blast at his right hand. Between him and the doctor was a small table on which was a chessboard. A game was in progress.

'Hullo, David. This is Doctor . . . He's giving me a game of chess, I seldom get one now! He's beating my head off.'

The doctor was looking at his patient like a rabbit eyeing a stoat. Tentatively he moved a piece – I imagine he'd been trapped after some sort of examination but there possibly hadn't even been that and he was doubtless urgently wishing to continue visits to the sick. Uncle Alistair was peering at the board.

'Ah, that's what you're up to, is it –!'

He was wearing a green tennis shade which he had decided was good for his eyes – it would have been a personal decision: I don't believe he ever in life sought or took medical advice on such things. He was knitting busily, a pair of stockings. On a reading stand, placed so that he could turn to it in the (longish) periods when the doctor was ruminating his own next move, was a volume of medieval Latin – Uncle Alistair was particularly fond of medieval Latin. On his knees was the *Times* crossword puzzle, from which he occasionally shot a query at the doctor, or me. I think – but cannot swear to it – that, despite the doctor, a box of chocolates was open between the radio and the reading stand. He started an animated conversation with me on the politics of the day. He won the chess.

For fashionable views he cared absolutely nothing. I was lunching with him at Cross Deep once when the periodic debate about the dangers of smoking had just warmed up. I used to smoke – heavily. I began a meditation.

'I wonder about this smoking business, Uncle Alistair – whether to give it up.'

He looked up, not very interested; I ploughed on.

'I suppose that whether or not the link with lung cancer is established it must be admitted it's a dirty habit.'

He opened a book.

'And expensive.'

My uncle looked up again. 'Do you enjoy it?'

'I suppose I must admit I do enjoy it, yes.'

'Then,' Uncle Alistair said, with finality, 'be a man and die, like the rest of us!'

Uncle Alistair knew his Scotland very well – all sorts and conditions of people, their characteristics, their traditions, their prejudices – in all the considerable variety which Scotland affords. He wore his lineage, like his learning, lightly, and although he knew a good deal about Scottish genealogy and something of Scottish heraldry he laughed about it rather than taking it with the obsessive seriousness which makes some Scots of family appalling bores. He had been Grand Master Freemason of Scotland. Perhaps, as the years went on, his greatest enthusiasm was for the Scottish Lifeboat Service, of which he was long the Convenor. The Lifeboat not only gave him enduring links with Scots all round the coast but, as he put it, with much the most superior sort of person, in moral terms, which our civilization has produced – persons who volunteer to risk life for others, on a principle, again and again and again. Lifeboat disasters he felt deeply; and to the end of his days and at a great age insisted on travelling the length of the land to visit 'my Lifeboat widows'. Their affection was the highest reward he ever desired.

My uncle, although he might have denied it, liked company. He would get restive if alone and would hunt out another of the family. The square tower at Cairnbulg is served by a spiral staircase and a sound I would recognize until the end of time is my uncle's footfall on that stair (he became rather lame), the opening of the door from the staircase into the keep (the door is masked from the main room by an interior stone wall) and then his rapid steps as he erupted into that tall, quiet room with some novel idea.

Uncle Alistair had evolved his own philosophy of life and it only occasionally coincided with the usual prejudices of his generation or his kind, or, for that matter, of his family. I remember once being at Cairnbulg soon after leaving Eton in 1939. The *Eton College Chronicle*, the periodic Eton news sheet edited by boys, arrived through the post, and there was an account of a hunt by the beagles (which I used to follow). The *Chronicle* story told how a hare had been started and had run towards a line of boys, the field. The hare would then normally have turned and swung wide of them, hounds in pursuit. In this case the hare had disconcertingly sprung into the arms of a Lower Boy (probably aged 13 or 14) and had lain perfectly still. The Master of the Beagles – a very important and powerful figure in the Eton hierarchy – had run up and ordered the small boy to put the hare down. He had refused. Ultimately, it appeared, hounds had been called off. It didn't say what happened to the boy.

Pompous with the self-importance of a recently senior schoolboy of eighteen I said that things were coming to a pretty pass at Eton when a Lower Boy dared to defy the Master of the Beagles.

Uncle Alistair said quietly – 'that hare went instinctively to a human being it felt would protect it. None of us knows how or why. But if ever another creature, human or animal, *honours* one with that sort of trust one must fulfil it. The boy did right.'

Uncle Alistair had a remarkable memory. I mentioned to him a rather obscure Victorian novelist, a book by whom I was trying to read, I can't remember why. He said he'd once glanced at one of that author's books, while up at Oxford. I said it was the one I was attempting.

'I never finished it,' said Uncle Alistair. 'I didn't care for it. But he's got rather a good passage about –' and he proceeded to quote, more or less accurately as I later checked, something like a complete page of a book he'd half-read and hadn't enjoyed, sixty years before.

*

Uncle Alistair's time as a prisoner of war had deeply marked him.
He had escaped and been recaptured several times, on one occasion
contriving to fashion a file out of an old bit of scrap he'd found in the
prison yard and filing through the cell bars. He had formed his own
views about escaping, and about enduring imprisonment. There had
been, at one point in the war, some sort of debate on the morality of
breaking parole – their word had been given and broken by a number
of officer prisoners and Uncle Alistair deeply disapproved of the sort
of casuistry which justified this on grounds of general German inhumanity or some such. To him honour was honour, although he never
used highfalutin' language. He disliked his German gaolers intensely
(I have been told by men who were in prison with him that he had the
gift of infuriating them more than any other prisoner), but he disliked
even more his own compatriots – then or later – who, in his view,
made the enemy's defects an excuse for their own. Above all he believed
in the virtue of trying to see an issue – and especially an international
political issue – from the other side of the international fence. Loving
his country, patriotic in a simple, straightforward way, he disliked
what would now be called chauvinism – the sort of narrow justification
of a national viewpoint which is ignorant or uncomprehending of the
sensitivities of other countries.

This led Uncle Alistair to a good deal of unhappiness when war next
threatened, in the 1930s. He disliked almost everything he read of
the Nazis but he felt that people outside Germany had too little
understanding of the pressures suffered by a generation of Germans,
pressures which had exploded into support for so extreme a regime.
He had witnessed the starvation in Germany which had accompanied
the Allied maintenance of blockade after the Armistice in 1918. He
thought the British Government had adopted a succession of mistaken attitudes. They had been hectoring and insensitive – and vengeful
– when they had the power to dictate, postures Uncle Alistair deplored.
They had then been feeble and conciliatory when they should
have been firm, and had finally thrown down what the Germans
would regard as a challenge over Poland, without the means or the
resolve which could make it good. He continued for a long time
to believe that the Second World War could have been avoided or
pre-empted, a belief I could not share and which led to many

impassioned arguments. He hated the war, and by its end it had claimed his only son, for my cousin was reported 'Missing' – and his body was never found – in the battles of the Garigliano in Italy, in the winter of 1943–44.

Avoidable or not, the war, when it came in September 1939, was regarded by Uncle Alistair as a personal challenge to get back into uniform as quickly as he could. He was 53, but managed in no time at all to lever himself into the War Office, dressed as a major in the Gordon Highlanders and working in a department responsible for salvage: for what would now be called recycling of waste.

'Absurd,' my aunt said resignedly. 'Alistair is the most wasteful person in the world, he's always surrounded by a confusion of papers and odds and ends all over the floor!' This was certainly true – he was content to live and work amongst the most astonishing muddle. My aunt, however, had her own eccentricities.

My aunt Dorothy – known universally as Dodo – never threw anything away. Recipes, cuttings from newspapers with helpful sugges-tions on how to preserve this, renovate that or mend the other; 'odds and ends' – accurately alleged by her to be strewn to the winds or over the carpet by my uncle; string, of course: everything was preserved somewhere, although only to her was it known, or even guessable, where. She, too, was utterly lovable, with a quiet and very common-sensical understanding – intuition even – of what a young person was feeling; of what, if anything, was worrying.

She was small and birdlike, and carried herself as erectly as a guardsman. She dressed throughout her life (she died in 1985) much as she had at the beginning of the century but – like my uncle – with a total lack of self-consciousness. And although her principles were intransigent, and her affinity with the late twentieth century apparently non-existent, in a curious way she was ageless. I think the truth is that she had a very shrewd, unspoken awareness of how superficial and impermanent were many of the signs of the times which might have been imagined to shock her. They went past her, so to speak (although she missed little), and the fundamentals of life or within people remained, less obvious but alone worth attention.

My aunt Dodo disliked change. She never installed labour-saving devices in a kitchen or anywhere else. She only liked things being done as she had known them done when young, an increasingly impossible attitude. Sometimes they were done to a certain pitch but left in a certain limbo thereafter – it was usual to arrive, year after year, at Cross Deep or Cairnbulg and find a number of large brown paper parcels, addressed to my aunt in her own neat, beautiful hand, ranged in the hall. On the next visit they were still there, and the next, and the next. Clearly there was method in it, but what? What was in them? I never knew. And it was *completely* impossible to ask.

Her kindness, at all stages of life, was immense. She had a great flair for knowing exactly what a schoolboy, for instance, would find enjoyable. In matters of food and drink she was delightfully over-indulgent. She enjoyed amassing (and tabulating, with references and cross-references) details of history and family history which she had discovered. Although herself a Welby from Lincolnshire, she came to love Buchan; and the people there came to love her, for it was impossible to be with her and not appreciate her integrity and her modesty and her unselfishness. To me she was never-failing in generosity and hospitality. Indeed my uncle and aunt were surrogate parents to me, for when I was a boy my father and mother were sometimes abroad, and I was made to feel Cairnbulg was a home. When the war came, too, we had no home in England, my father was with the Army and my mother was engaged in war work from a succession of London flats. A single telegram could announce my arrival at Cairnbulg on some unexpected leave, clothes and impedimenta could be left there, a huge welcome was assured.

My uncle Alistair lived to be 93. By then I was a full general and myself within a few months of retirement from the Army after nearly forty years of service. When he was dying at Cross Deep in 1979 I visited him from time to time. His constitution was immensely strong, his heart like a young man's, and he confounded doctors (as ever) by refusing to fade away. He regained consciousness periodically and on one occasion, I think the last, I managed to get across who was with him, so that he said, 'David!' Then, very slowly, carefully but audibly he said, with curious formality, 'David, we've been very proud of you, as a family. Proud of your achievements.'

I couldn't speak. Then he said, 'But *far* more important than any of that has been the very real pleasure of knowing you, all these years.'

I wish somehow, at some time, I had conveyed back to him that same, simple message.

3

Figures in the Foreground

I was also fortunate in both grandparents and parents; and of the former three out of four show vividly in the landscape of childhood.

My maternal grandfather, Cyril Maude, was a very successful actor-manager of the late-Victorian and Edwardian era. Short and stocky, with an infectious chuckle and charm to which few were immune, he loved above all things to dispense hospitality. He enjoyed life in London and his clubs – the Garrick and the Beefsteak – for he was immensely convivial: but I can see him mainly in, or in the gardens of, his charming house, Redlap, near Dartmouth in South Devon – greeting his friends, making them laughingly welcome as if each was the only creature in the world necessary to complete his happiness. Redlap was white, thatched, a house high on the red Devon cliffs, from which it peered comfortably towards the sea across lovely gardens through which a small stream trickled from pond to pond and in which it always seemed to be a West Country summer, warm, sleepy, languorous.

Grandpa Maude was a superb raconteur and a mimic of dangerously accurate genius. Always immaculate, rosy-complexioned and silver-haired, I see him in summer, generally wearing a blue, blazer-type jacket and Panama hat; and in the evening in a black or dark blue velvet smoking jacket, pleated shirt with diamond studs, stiff collar. Day or night a monocle was stuck in his right eye – not simply for decoration: he was extremely short-sighted – or hung on a narrow black ribbon from the neck.

The Maudes were an Anglo-Irish family but their head, Lord Hawarden – Grandpa's cousin – sold all the Irish property in 1904 and thereafter the family lived in Kent. Grandpa Maude, however, had led an unusual life for those days. Born in 1862, he had a conventional upbringing, being sent to Charterhouse (which, although writing in his memoirs that it was a happy period, he told me he loathed: he loathed anything to do with school). He spent much holiday time at Toddington in Gloucestershire, his mother's family (Hanbury-Tracy) home. Toddington, a huge house designed by Sir Charles Barry, was constructed on similar lines to the Houses of Parliament and my grandfather loved it and his Hanbury-Tracy relations.

Grandpa's parents lived in London, so that Toddington was his home in the country. His maternal uncles were extremely kind to him – uncles, because the eldest, the third Lord Sudeley, head of the Hanbury-Tracy family, died unmarried and was succeeded by Uncle Charlie Sudeley when Grandpa was fifteen. The third Lord Sudeley had something of a menagerie and I have a photograph, touched up in colour, showing Grandpa, in what appears to be Zouave uniform, aged about four, standing by a governess cart in which is seated (I think) his mother. On the box has been placed a smaller child, perhaps one of his younger brothers, wearing clothes similar to those we associate with the child-Emperor of China. Harnessed to the governess cart is a zebra, and standing by its head a coachman, with top boots, green livery, tall hat and gold band – probably this was Shepherd (affectionately described by Grandpa in later life), who taught him to ride in Toddington's indoor riding school and introduced him to hunting with the North Cotswold hounds.

He learned more from his Hanbury-Tracy uncles than country pursuits and how to ride. On one occasion, when very small, he was accompanying his uncle Charlie on a walk when they passed a ragged and dirty tramp, who gave Uncle Charlie a respectful salutation.

'And this is my nephew, Cyril Maude. Cyril, shake his hand,' for a grimy hand was being extended. But Grandpa had never seen a creature so hirsute, strange and apparently menacing as the old tramp. He was frightened. He put his hands behind his back. They walked on a little, and then Uncle Charlie stopped and confronted him.

'Cyril, you will soon go home to Toddington, have a good supper, sleep in a warm bed. That man may sleep in a ditch and probably doesn't know whether he'll have any supper at all. *But God loves him as much as you, and probably more.* And now YOU WILL WALK BACK AND SHAKE HIS HAND.' Which he did. And did not forget. But Toddington suffered from Uncle Charlie's ill-fortune in various investments* and has long passed from Hanbury-Tracy possession, together with 6,600 acres of Gloucestershire and over 17,000 acres in Wales.

Yet despite my grandfather's customary and happy upbringing he had very different ambitions and these, at the time, were regarded as peculiar and irregular. He wanted to go on the stage. He had always wanted to go on the stage – indeed when six years old he told his father so (but when he saw my great-grandfather's awful countenance he quickly changed tack and said he thought he'd be Bishop of London instead). From boyhood he shone in the amateur theatricals which played a large part in Victorian country house life. At Charterhouse, too, were friends with similar ambitions – Aubrey Smith, who later captained Sussex at cricket as well as becoming a star of stage and screen: Johnston Forbes-Robertson, a theatrical knight-to-be. Grandpa's greatest friend there was probably the later Dean Foxley-Norris of Westminster, who went into the Church rather than the theatre but would have certainly been a resounding success in either. Grandpa finally made up his mind, and never changed it, when he was nineteen.

The family had enormous misgivings. He was delicate, often ill. He was always regarded as touchingly frail (though he died at the age of eighty-nine). He was sent on long journeys, supposed possibly therapeutic both of health and theatrical ambitions. He was sent to Australia and was back in a few months. Then he was sent to Canada as a pupil on a farm, where the healthy outdoor life might, it was thought, be decisively curative. After a very short while, aged twenty-one, he escaped to New York, determined, somehow, to find opportunities to act. He had very little money. If he wished to stay alive he needed work. It was 1883.

Grandpa got a contract with an ancient German tragedian to tour various parts of a still fairly primitive American West and Middle West at fifteen dollars a week. Before the tour he somehow managed to exist in New York boarding houses, which cost him some six pounds

---

* Very fully recounted in 'The Sudeleys, Lords of Toddington', Manorial Society of Great Britain, 1987.

weekly. He never wavered in his aim. And when the tour started he found he could raise laughs in even the roughest communities – and exulted in the fact.

The company toured – Colorado, Arkansas, Montana, Washington State, California, San Francisco. Grandpa was playing for, he calculated, the equivalent of £3 a week – Shakespeare, *East Lynne*, *Woman of the People* and many, many more. Then back to New York, to more cheap lodging houses (but lodging houses where other actors and actresses also stayed, so all the time he was meeting, gossiping, learning). Occasional work – as often as not still owed salary when a company disbanded, broke. But he was gaining experience and he was doing what he knew he could and should do.

Finally he returned to England, to London, and to more search for work. He was proud, penniless and determined. His family, understandably, were firmly resolved never to subsidize what were thought to be utterly irresponsible ambitions by any sort of financial help. Sometimes he dined with grand relations, very aware of the poor condition of his evening coat and suspecting that the footmen in silk stockings and plush breeches were better fed than him. Provincial tours in broken-down companies. He kept going. Grandpa intended to make the grade in the theatre and make it by his own efforts alone.

And back in London he was starting to make a name. Comedies, burlesques, melodrama, musicals, classical theatre – he played the lot. And then one better part led to another better part, and ultimately a good part in a successful play in the West End of London and highly complimentary notices. By the nineties he was playing with Charles Wyndham and George Alexander. In 1893, by now an experienced actor, he played Cayley Drummle in Pinero's *The Second Mrs Tanqueray* (the best male part, as he rightly said). Only the fact that my grandmother was busy producing my own mother prevented her from playing Paula Tanqueray, the part made famous by Mrs Patrick Campbell: Grandpa told me that the whole cast were jittery on the first night – they thought they might be booed, so daring did the theme and the language seem.

For by now Grandpa had married. Without much security in life or prospects he had married in 1888 my grandmother, Winifred Emery, already a well-known actress; one who, although young, had 'arrived'.

She was the only one of my four grandparents who does not stand out in my memory because (although I remember once being in a room with her and being aware of a rather overpowering presence) she died when I was three years old. In 1896 Grandpa acquired the management lease of the Haymarket Theatre, in partnership with Frederick Harrison, holding it for nine years and achieving thereby a permanent and leading position in the London theatre. He was thirty-three and was going against all the best advice, including particularly that of Henry Irving, whom he revered. 'Don't take a theatre!' Irving wrote. 'You'll lose money!' He did and he didn't.

I miss not having known my grandmother. Winifred Emery was, I suspect, an enchantress – a difficult person but an enchantress. Unlike my grandfather she had the theatre in every drop of her blood. Her great-grandfather had been on the stage in the reign of George II; her grandfather, John Emery, painted by Zoffany, had been among the great of his time – as well as being a musician, a patron of prizefighting, and having seventeen pictures accepted by the Royal Academy. Her father, Sam Emery, had made a huge name in creating certain Dickens parts – Peggotty, Quilp – when the novels were first produced in play form. He had then deserted his family and gone to Australia, leaving them near-destitute. My grandmother, on the stage from the age of sixteen (but always chaperoned by her mother to and from the theatre), had supported the family. Emery blood was theatre blood, but by many accounts pretty unreliable.

Grandmother Winifred, however, was far from unreliable. I only know her from (excellent) photographs and the accounts of others. She was beautiful, outspoken to the point of embarrassment, high-principled and somewhat puritanical in outlook. She was, I think, determined that no vestige of the rackety side of the profession – perhaps exemplified by the Emerys, of whom, nevertheless, she was extremely proud – should touch her life or her family. Professional to the finger-tips, she was a perfectionist, caring only for the integrity of a performance and the credibility of a play. 'Society' bored her and she disliked the intermingling of social and theatrical persons and occasions. Visited in her dressing room by friends, she only wanted their reactions to the play, their 'feedback' to a performance. Grandpa, on the other hand, wanted from visitors to the dressing room gossip about family, about friends, about fishing. For him the play was over and despite his love of the stage it was time to think of more agreeable and entertaining things. For my grandmother there were no more agreeable and entertaining things.

My grandmother had understudied Ellen Terry, had toured with Henry Irving, had come to the Court Theatre in Sloane Square when still a girl and had progressed rapidly. By the time she agreed to marry my grandfather (who was two years younger than her) she had a considerable name. When they went to the Haymarket, after eight years of marriage and with two children, they went as a famous husband and wife team. Their combination as Sir Peter and Lady Teazle in Sheridan's *School for Scandal* was long talked about by anyone who saw it. But I think that the partnership grew increasingly difficult, although the Haymarket years were splendidly successful. Grandpa liked doing comedies, even farces, and excelled in them – he could be funny, charming, relaxed (or as relaxed as expert theatrical performance permits). Grandmother, I suspect, could play anything, but thought they should 'stretch' the company with more serious attempts.

Everyone spoke of Grandmother's voice, probably her most effective attribute. Grandpa – who, whatever his affections, was entirely objective when judging anyone or anything to do with the theatre – wrote of Winifred –

She got her effect subtly. The mellow contralto was unusual. It came upon one as a surprise, that full, round, low-pitched voice . . . her first, soft, velvetlike note fell on one's ear with a sudden delight, and a delight that held one unwearied to the end. One of her peculiarities was that she did not raise her voice. There was no touch of the so-called restrained force in her acting. She was intense enough where the opportunity for intensity offered but in her intensity there was no taint or blemish or rant. The full effect was produced by mental rather than physical effort.

My mother adored her. Aubrey Beardsley drew her, rather effectively, for an edition of the *Yellow Book* – and Oscar Wilde often came to gaze at her while Beardsley was at work on the drawing. My grandmother tolerated this, although she disliked Wilde (as did Grandpa – very emphatically).

Grandpa, a widower from 1924, remarried – Beatrice Trew, herself a widow, a kind, delightful and efficient step-grandmother, a most knowledgeable maker of gardens, who ran an admirable household. Baden-Powell – 'BP' – a Charterhouse friend greatly and rightly revered by Grandpa, was best man. Grandpa had left the stage – by his own account with absolutely no regrets, having successfully played his part – soon after the First World War, apart from occasional returns for some particular occasion; he also took a surprising number of early (silent) film parts. When I first remember him, at Redlap, he was simply enjoying to the full the leisure and prosperity which success had earned. The New York lodging houses were as far behind him as was the dubious disapproval of his family in early days. Now everyone was proud of him. A stream of visitors came to Redlap, and visitors of every kind, for Grandpa's career and connections had spanned several worlds. He seemed to welcome everybody – relations, Maudes, Hanbury-Tracys, Tottenhams, Petos: old friends from the world of the stage, Allan Aynesworth (always called Tony), Henry Ainley, the Trees, the Vanbrughs, George Alexander's widow, wearing remarkable clothes of great extravagance: Devon neighbours – I remember a very old and very local Miss Bidder, who claimed not only to believe in fairies but often to have seen them. Dressed in deep black, she was thought to be a hundred years old, and I can hear her at tea, describing the fairies very effectively. 'They are,' she said, 'like a cluster of very small electric bulbs, moving all the time. One can't, of course, see them by day.' Of course not.

Everyone seemed to like Grandpa, and he everyone. He saw life not so much as a drama but as a sequence of agreeable theatrical happenings in which he had, quite rightly, been given a suitable role. An old man (who did not not know him personally) once said to me, 'There was never anyone on the stage like your grandfather for making an audience *happy*. His personality was so charming that whenever he came on everyone felt better.' It may not have been the highest piece of theatrical commendation. One cannot imagine it said of a Kean, an Irving, an Olivier. But it says something credible about Grandpa Maude.

Grandpa was sentimental – that might be called the 'down side'. He relished – on or off stage – scenes of unalloyed pathos. Enjoying children, he liked concealing from them in places like flower vases little notes addressed to them by name and allegedly placed there by a fairy (Barrie was a great friend). This sort of whimsicality, unlikely to be tolerated today, was all right until we reached a certain age, when embarrassment overtook pleasure. My half-sister, Gloria Congreve (having reached that certain age slightly ahead of schedule), once said to Grandpa, 'We know *you* put them there, really!' He was not best pleased. And I suspect that his own judgement of plays was inferior to my grandmother's – he liked sentiment, he liked saccharin, he disliked the challenge of brutality or, perhaps, truth; *The Second Mrs Tanqueray* must have been tough for him. His success, I think, had been rooted in a delightful stage personality combined with a hard-working mastery of technique and indefatigably high standards.

But although I see my grandfather most often in his own setting, benign, hospitable, affectionate and amusing, I remember another side and am glad of it. There was at Redlap a large room, originally a barn, projecting from the back of the house. We called it 'The Barntop'. Because Redlap was built on a steep slope one went up two flights of stairs to reach the Barntop, and yet found that at its far end was a door opening at the same level on to the back drive, the sort of curiosity which always appeals to a child. The Barntop was used for parties, games and so forth – it was a very long room, dark, agreeable, vaguely mysterious and exciting.

And in the Barntop the Dartmouth Players, the local amateur dramatic society, used to rehearse, having persuaded Grandpa to do a bit of direction or, anyway, coaching. I remember a session after dinner one evening. The play was *The Late Christopher Bean* – one of Emlyn Williams' earliest successes. I sat in the background enthralled.

I was watching a totally different grandfather. There was no shred of sentimentality, of kindly charm, of the Cyril Maude said to put everyone at ease and make them feel loved. Not a bit of it! Grandpa was a martinet. I can see him now, in his smoking jacket, sitting on a low stool, script on his knee, the cast in a circle around him, speaking or reading. His comments, when they came, were harsh, sharp, insistent, devastating. 'No, no! How *could* she say it like that? She's upset! Now listen to me!' His voice would drop, convey the required emotion in a sentence. Then – 'Back two pages, all of you.' And so on. Discipline was total. Grandpa was on the job. Thus it must once have been.

My paternal grandfather's upbringing and early years had also been somewhat unusual, although in a very different way from Grandpa Maude. Born in 1851, Grandpa Saltoun had been brought up at Philorth with one brother, my great-uncle David, whom I never knew, and a large number of sisters. His mother was notable for good looks and a violent temper, which he inherited. She was extravagant, with large ideas – larger than her husband's income. Within the family she became an unpopular figure of legend, referred to as 'Milady'. Reminiscences have her throwing china objects or anything else handy in the drawing room at members of the family who offended, particularly her daughters, who were frequently belaboured by her, whoever was present. Life at Philorth was stormy.

I imagine Grandpa was sometimes taken to London when young; his mother undoubtedly preferred it and his father played an appropriate part in Parliament. On the whole, however, he grew up in the north, at Philorth and at Ness Castle, a property near Inverness brought to the family by Grandpa's great-grandmother, another Fraser. He was encouraged to be hardy, enduring and uncomplaining. He brought up his own family on similar lines.

Grandpa and his brother were very good-looking boys. He was also extremely strong. The brothers were once – in their teens, or perhaps even less – placed in the care of a holiday tutor while their parents were in London. The tutor found it impossible to exact obedience and wrote to my great-grandfather asking if he had His Lordship's permission to impose discipline with the cane. Great-grandfather replied that he gladly gave permission – but wrote by the same post to my grandfather saying what he'd done but adding that if his sons actually allowed themselves to be beaten he'd think the worse of them. This unpardonable behaviour, disloyal to an employee attempting to do his duty, led – inevitably – to the tutor attempting to flog, whereupon the boys chased him out of the house and up a tree, loudly explaining what they'd do to him when he came down.

At the age of eight Grandpa was sent to Eton. Accounts of mid-Victorian Eton are gruesome and the idea of a child of eight being there is disturbing. The official record shows my grandfather there from 1861, when he was nine or ten, so there may be some question mark over it but, eight or ten, it was a rough start. He was first committed to a special form created for him and two others at the bottom of the school. This form was called 'Nonsense' and I think Grandpa stayed in it for several years. The only work done was composition of Latin verses, which didn't have to mean anything comprehensible but which had to scan, and to be composed of actual Latin words. False quantities, therefore, were beaten out of him at a very early age. (My grandfather's great-uncle, the 'Waterloo' Lord Saltoun – the 16th Lord, who commanded the light companies of the Guards at Hougoumont – had a rather more distinguished career at Eton, if only because he was reputedly the first boy to jump from Windsor Bridge into the river far below.) One of the three in 'Nonsense' was later to become Earl of Southesk, then Carnegie. Carnegie was two years younger than my grandfather but became a lifelong friend and crony; and if Grandpa was still in the form when Carnegie reached it, it argues for quite a long stint before he reached Third Form, the ordinary bottom rung on the Etonian ladder. 'Anyway,' Grandpa used to say comfortably, when recalling schooldays, 'Carnegie was sacked and went to Harrow!'

My great-grandfather's views on how to bring up boys were not, therefore, such as would commend themselves today. When the family dined at Philorth Grandpa, from a very early age, sat at the dining room table throughout what was generally, I expect, a pretty long session. He didn't eat dinner (indigestible for one so young) but simply and silently sat, learning how to behave and decorating the table with his youth. At the end of dinner he was allowed fruit. Then the butler placed in front of him whatever was left in the decanter of claret and the decanter of port; he had to finish both. Penalty for not completing the task, a severe thrashing.

Grandpa left Eton at the age of fifteen and was at some time thereafter sent to Heidelberg University. Duelling in German universities was customary, governed by strict etiquette. A student was elected and admitted to a particular club or circle, after rigorous initiatory procedures, and was then expected to fight a duel within the club. The duel itself was fought by alternating cuts with short sabres, no movement of feet permitted, cuts aimed only at the opponent's face. Bodies, and parts of the face, were protected by padding. Cheeks and forehead were exposed, so that the keenly desired scars could be collected and borne through life. The duel stopped when blood ran to a stipulated amount. It was a highly stylized rite of passage.

Grandpa said he didn't wish to fight because he'd nothing against the (first) chosen antagonist. Told he must, or lose honour, he squared up and used his first cut to strike his opponent a blow on the top of the head with the flat of the sabre, with enormous force. My father told me that the other student died. Grandpa was expelled from Heidelberg after this remarkably brief academic career. He was, I think, sixteen or perhaps seventeen. By the time he was just eighteen, in 1869, he had been commissioned in the Grenadier Guards. Old photographs show him as an exceptionally handsome and elegant young man.

My grandfather served as a Grenadier for sixteen years, with great enthusiasm and enjoyment, only retiring when his own father died. He resigned his commission because he found the problems of running Philorth (and restoring the estate and its finances to some sort of order after the extravagances of his parents) impossible to combine with a military career – even with the fairly undemanding military duties within the Brigade of Guards of those days. He had applied for, and been refused, a year's leave of absence to put his personal affairs in order. So he left – very sadly. His interest in the Army never waned.

I remember Grandpa Saltoun almost exclusively in London, where he lived most of the time from the destruction of Philorth until his death in 1933 – first at No. 1 Bryanston Square, then in Gloucester Place. I can't remember the house in Bryanston Square – I expect I was taken there as a child but I have no picture of it. It is a handsome, double-fronted building and must have been a very large London dwelling, even for those days, since it included the long house now running along George Street, adjoining it. Until after the First World War it had to act as home to all my grandparents' children, as well as accommodate pictures and furniture from Philorth, but it is unsurprising that after his children were all married Grandpa moved to a more modest house at No. 110 (later renumbered No. 25, as now) Gloucester Place, and it is there that I will always see both my grandparents. I used to stay there, more often than not, at the beginning and end of each school holidays, before or after the journey to wherever it was.

Arrival at Gloucester Place never varied. A press on the front door bell, school trunk having been deposited by the taxi driver. Heavy door then swung back by Tomlin, the butler, with a curious turning-away movement which caused his coat tails themselves to swing, as if in a breeze. Tomlin always wore an intimidating frown, as if to say that grandsons were a nuisance, made work, and probably didn't know how to behave. There was a footman – generally quite a young boy, terrified of Tomlin's frown and menacing mutters, especially in the dining room, where they both hovered throughout meals. Luggage disappeared with the boy footman and Tomlin, frown never relaxed, invariably said in his grim controlled voice, 'Her Ladyship is in the drawing room,' and left one to make one's own way up. When slightly older I was sometimes preceded by him, to make the announcement. He then, of course, appeared, dead on time, before each meal: 'Luncheon is served, My Lady,' or to relay the transport situation: 'The car is at the door, My Lady' (no parking problem in Gloucester Place in those days).

Tomlin was so well-drilled, such a disciplinarian, so alarming (yet so utterly loyal) that it was hard to discern a more human side. But it most certainly existed. Once he had to accompany me by train to my preparatory school, St Aubyn's at Rottingdean, I can't remember why. I had never before seen him without his tail coat. He became a delightful companion. He talked, freely and interestingly, about the war – he had served in the Army, on the Western Front. Next time I saw him, however, the frown was back, the bushy eyebrows knitted with menace: 'Her Ladyship is in the drawing room!'

In the Second World War, both my grandparents being dead, Tomlin moved to my uncle Alistair's house, Cross Deep at Twickenham, and was a brave and notably distinguished air raid warden during the Blitz attacks on London. By then in the Army, I visited it often, as I have recounted, and on one occasion there was Tomlin (no tail coat). To my absolute astonishment his face broke into as warm a smile as I remember. He wrung my hand and spoke words of real pleasure – I had never before seen Tomlin look pleased. He was a splendid and devoted man, and my family was extremely lucky. I recognize that now, but at the time Tomlin generated in the young nervousness and a sense of inadequacy.

Back at Gloucester Place, I would bound up the stairs to the drawing room, a comfortably sized room, cluttered in the Victorian manner, with tall windows overlooking the street and family portraits on the walls. In the drawing room was my grandmother, and adjoining it was Grandpa's study. He would emerge from it to talk to both of us for a little, then retreat again to the dark panels and lined bookshelves of his own lair.

Grandpa, when I knew him, had a ruddy complexion, a white moustache and not much hair. He was rather stout, wore a stiff, high collar, a broad tie, spats (I think) and an eyeglass (but less obtrusive than Grandpa Maude's; and perhaps less necessary). He was increasingly deaf but was still notably elegant, as befitted one who had been a formidable Grenadier adjutant. He had the reputation of an equally formidable parent, a great believer in corporal punishment and a man with an explosive temper – his mother's temper, not improved by frequent attacks of very painful gout. He was ironically known by his contemporaries as 'The Dove'. All his children feared him, although it is clear from my father's letters during the 1914–18 War that he also respected him greatly, and I think affection grew with age.

But to a grandson he was charming. He was obviously warm-hearted – a child is instantly aware of that. He made me feel welcome and important. He took trouble with any enquiry or request for advice, however trivial or infantile. He showed interest in the doings of boyhood. He once visited me (to my astonishment – it was unannounced) at my preparatory school and the Headmaster, a pretty formidable figure on his own account, was very obviously and deeply impressed in a way which did me nothing but good; indeed, Grandpa *was* impressive. He always tipped me £1. In 1933, in the last weeks of his life when he was certainly dying, I went to Gloucester Place and was sent in to see him 'just for a minute'. Grandpa had grown a white beard. I was warned not to be surprised if he didn't know me: he hadn't been well. But he not only knew me but said, 'Last time you were here, David, I wasn't well and *neglected my duty*!' And out of his wallet came two pounds.

Grandpa's recollections were extensive. When he had joined the 3rd Battalion of the Grenadiers the Quartermaster had actually fought at

Waterloo – Quartermasters in those days were permitted to serve until an advanced age after commissioning and this one had, I think, been a drummer boy on that memorable June Sunday in 1815, so Grandpa had learned about Waterloo from a participant. When he talked – never boringly – a boy felt, without articulating it, that a certain kind of historical experience was in the air. He had played an active part in the House of Lords, had been a Tory Whip, and in the Parliament Bill battles of the pre-1914 period had organized the 'Ditchers' – those who rejected compromise on Lords reform and thought it best to die in the last ditch against the Liberal Government. Grandpa had been unimpressed by the Conservative Party's craven surrender (as he saw it) and by the King's undertaking to create enough Liberal Peers to pass the Bill – 'Let him. Best fight now. Got to come some time. Lose later.' He persuaded a good number of peers in the same direction, which does not surprise me. He would have scared the daylights out of most of the politicians I have met since.

I doubt if this line of my grandfather's will be thought high political wisdom by posterity but it was in character. Grandpa had not found the course of political history in the early years of the twentieth century much to his liking. He had little regard for intellectual fashion, believed in the primacy of the landed interest and lamented its difficulties, disliked Liberals of every sort, thought it his duty to look after people God had called to a less elevated station, and believed in the right and the obligation of himself and his kind to give a lead in the governance of England. He had the rosy self-confidence of one never disposed to doubt that his position in life was part of a reasonable and beneficent divine plan.

I only saw Grandpa's legendary temper explode once. I was taken shopping by him – or, rather, I accompanied him on a round of visits to shops, driven by Tyrell, the chauffeur. Grandpa, stiff-brimmed Homburg hat and gold-headed cane added to the ensemble, communi-cated with Tyrell through a speaking tube – the front of the car was separated from us by a glass partition. The speaking tube was rather fascinating but sometimes Tyrell didn't seem exactly to get the message because I remember some pretty sharp corrective orders.

We must have gone to the City. At the site of Temple Bar Grandpa indicated the Griffin and pointed to No. 1 Fleet Street.

'Child's Bank. That's your bank.'

I hardly knew what a bank was but it sounded impressive, and Child's my bank has remained. It had belonged to Lord Jersey (Child-Villiers), who was a close friend of Grandpa's.

We called at a cigar merchant – I think it was Robert Lewis in St James's Street – and I heard for the first time the expression 'Damme', so far only met in historical novels. Grandpa had ordered cigars and had kindly asked after the cigar merchant's gout. The answer was clearly depressing. 'Damme, that's bad,' Grandpa said. Then we went to an optician.

And it was there that it happened. I think Grandpa had been told that some spectacles would be ready for collection, and they weren't. I remember the appalling suddenness of the explosion. I hadn't been ready for it. The optician hadn't been ready for it – I don't think anybody else was in the shop. Grandpa *roared* like a wild beast. He picked up his gold-headed cane and struck the glass counter (I know it was glass because I remember astonishment that it hadn't shattered). He lashed the optician with his tongue. Then we drove off, Grandpa apparently in perfectly good humour.

Grandpa, as I have said, believed strongly in primogeniture, in the importance of an heir being recognized as such by his siblings. This didn't stop him, Uncle Alistair told me, being particularly harsh and demanding to the eldest, but it led him (for instance) to send my father to Charterhouse rather than Eton like his father and brothers. It may have been inspired by economy – though I rather doubt it in those days. I think it was to rub in the fact that younger sons were on a lower step of the staircase. Uncle Alistair, characteristically, told me in later life that he thought it one of his father's worst mistakes.

Similarly, when my father was nearing the end of his time at Charterhouse Grandpa asked him his ideas on a career. The Army was mentioned and Grandpa said, 'Regiment?'

'I thought I'd try for the Grenadiers.'

'Why?'

'Well – it was your Regiment. And others of the family. And –'

'The Brigade,' said Grandpa with finality, 'is for elder sons.' This was palpably untrue (indeed his brother, Uncle David, had joined the Scots Guards at the same time as Grandpa's entry into the Grenadiers).

It was, presumably, another example of the put-down of a younger son who might get grand ideas. And, of course, the Brigade of Guards was comparatively expensive for an officer at that time and Grandpa felt short of cash.

In describing my grandfather it may be hard to avoid caricature. He was generous but illiberal, of a high sense of duty but reactionary in probably all his opinions, kindly but hot-tempered and immoderate. All that said, he was no fool. His judgements were generally acknowledged as shrewd. In serious dealings with people he was fair, scrupulous and highly regarded. He was a certain sort of human being, whose like can now only be conjured from the pages of fiction, but I don't think our country was badly led by such people, in a certain sort of way.

My paternal grandmother was Irish. She was born Mary Grattan-Bellew. The family's homes were Mount Bellew in Galway and Tinnehinch in Wicklow. They stemmed from the marriage of a Catholic Bellew of Mount Bellew (Granny's father) with a Grattan of Tinnehinch, granddaughter of Henry Grattan, the celebrated Protestant Irish statesman. Henry Grattan worked hard for equality and amity between the two religions but he had, of course, made his great career – devoted to the independence of the Parliament and Government of Ireland from London – well before Catholic emancipation.

Grattan, however, believed in the British connection. He disapproved of the Irish revolutionaries of his day, the Wolfe Tones, the Robert Emmetts, because he thought they were putting back the cause of reform. He deplored their willingness to seek help from England's French enemy. He was a patriot by his own lights, broad-minded, perceptive and witty, a brilliant orator and debater. His face, from some portraits, is not dissimilar to my grandmother's, with a rather quizzical expression and laughing mouth. I like the story of a guest dining with him at Tinnehinch, who, as he prepared to mount his horse and ride away, pointed to a large tree.

'The roots of that tree might give you trouble, Mr Grattan. It's very near the house.'

'Yes, I know. I'm going to move the house.'

By Granny's day both her parents were Catholic and she herself was extremely devout. Grandpa Saltoun, an Episcopalian (as the Frasers of Philorth had generally been), had simply agreed that in the matter of religion she should go her own way, sons of the marriage following their father and any daughter their mother.

On entering the drawing room at Gloucester Place I always moved straight to Granny's chair, to the left of the fireplace. She would get up, arms wide outstretched to greet me.

'Darling!'

She called everybody darling, almost without exception. Then she sat down again and usually took up the *Times* crossword puzzle (I remember very early editions, including some of the clues). I sat by the arm of the chair and contributed what I could. Doing the puzzle was interspersed with anecdote, called to mind, perhaps, by a clue or its solution. She was a lively raconteuse with a good sense of timing – in this resembling Grandpa Maude – and with a very musical voice and laugh. Jokes which particularly amused her were often what might be called 'black humour' – a virtuous pillar of society receiving a disastrous come-uppance, a missionary ending in the cannibals' pot – but they were well told. Granny enjoyed reminiscing and – a trait bequeathed to Uncle Alistair – made the unspoken assumption that one not only understood what she was talking about, but whom.

Although demonstratively affectionate, Granny never showed the slightest interest in our, or anybody else's, recent activities. This was, in fact, a relief. There were none of the 'Had a good holidays?' or 'How did the term go?' usual from adults, who must have been wholly indifferent to the answer. This seeming unconcern infuriated my mother, but at any age I found it comfortable. Granny liked talking about things, ideas, subjects. She liked talking about scientific theories and definitions. She would launch at one, without preamble, a thought from whatever was uppermost in her mind, a book she'd been reading, a discovery reported in some scientific journal – 'Come along, darling. I've just read something rather fascinating.'

Granny had been an enthusiastic amateur photographer, developing and printing her own pictures. She had fitted up a room at Philorth – and later at Gloucester Place, and presumably before that at Bryanston Square – as a laboratory, and conducted scientific experiments, widening her own knowledge to her own satisfaction. She was very manually dexterous, and had a workbench, lathe and so forth – accomplishments by no means customary in the Victorian and Edwardian society she also adorned, for Granny, as can been seen in early photographs, had been very pretty and clearly very attractive; a studio portrait of her in peeress's robes for, I think, the coronation of Edward VII is stunning. Granny was also – I only learned this after her death – a distinguished astronomer, recognized as such by the Astronomical Society. She had an excellent memory and was a quick learner; deciding to learn Spanish she did so extremely fast and wrote a play in the language, which was actually produced in Madrid. I believe that she learned Chinese – probably because someone told her it was difficult for Europeans to tackle. Granny also tried her hand at writing fiction and produced a book, a fantasy, published by Duckworth in 1930, called *After*. It is largely set in Hell and is rather disturbing.

Granny enjoyed conversation and appreciated the company of a few chosen cronies but she was not, in the ordinary sense of the word, very sociable. She enjoyed intrigue, however – enjoyed getting her way with subtlety, approaching an objective obliquely, often with a disclaimer and a degree of evasion. She smoked – Turkish cigarettes, held in a long cigarette-holder – and she had certainly done so well before most women of her kind. I don't think Granny ever actually offered me a cigarette on pre- or post-school visits, but it would have been unsurprising.

Sometimes, when alone, Granny felt like a bit of company and Tyrell was summoned with the car, to drive her to Selfridges, where she would go to some department like 'Gloves', get herself rather grandly established by a counter and start exchanging enquiries, smiles and talk with one of the sales girls. Soon there would be laughter and other girls would come along and be drawn by Granny with a word or two, a flattering enquiry, an Irish smile – and all, I'm sure, called 'Darling' – into the circle of gossip and pretended purchase. I don't expect she bought anything. Selfridges no doubt lost some business from the distraction of their employees and Granny would be driven home by Tyrell, in excellent spirits. She could twist anybody, of any sex, race, age or class, round her little finger.

Sometimes Granny felt strongly about an issue, so that it dominated conversation. One such was the Spanish Civil War, which started in 1936. This caused a good deal of heat and partisanship in other countries and places – including Eton, where I then was and where strong factions were formed. Granny, unsurprisingly, was a convinced and vigorous Francoist and gave me many pamphlets, with blood-curdling details of what had been done by the Reds. Later reading, thought and investigation have indicated to me that much of this was true: but it was, of course, one-sided, although probably less one-sided than the equivalent propaganda produced by the other side. My father, a well-informed man of generous sympathies who knew Spain, gently advised me to take Granny's output 'with a pinch of salt'. But when Granny was a partisan she did it thoroughly.

I don't think my grandmother was an easy mother-in-law. On most Sundays those of the family in London – and at intervals in my childhood and boyhood we lived in London – would lunch at Gloucester Place, with Grandpa at the head of the table rather like an unexploded bomb waiting to go off and with my parents' eyes nervously on me. The dining room, on the ground floor, was dark. A large table was adorned with silver candlesticks and silver statuettes, both Grenadiers and Gordon Highlanders (Grandpa, although a Grenadier, had been given Honorary rank in a militia battalion of the Gordons after leaving the active Army). A long sideboard was ranged along one flank, and a shorter one occupied the end of the room, opposite the window. Tomlin prowled around hissing commands at his acolyte. The food was invariably delicious. There was also what seemed an extraordinary amount of it – the 'starter', as we'd now call it, being followed by roast or cutlets, and that in turn succeeded by Tomlin's approach to one's left ear and a gratifying whisper, 'Ham, Sir?' And a huge cut of York ham was served, accompanied by a slice of day-new bread, warm and blissfully indigestible. My mother was always rather puritanical about food (and even more about drink) and thought that I, and everybody else, was done too well for our stomachs' good at Gloucester Place. My grandparents, however, were used to doing what suited them.

My mother's place at table was often next to Grandpa. She got on well with him but yelling at his deaf side was hard work, and inevitably the rest of the table would suddenly listen in.

'Father,' she yelled on one occasion, seeking to entertain, 'a cousin of mine [it was one of the elderly male Maudes] has just got engaged to be married for the *first time*! He's eighty! They're marrying next Thursday!'

'What was that, Pam? Speak up, my dear.'

'A cousin, Father! He's eighty – '

'Well?'

' – getting married. On Thursday. For the first time!'

The whole table was silent, and Grandpa simply said, 'Damn fool! He'll be dead in a week!' My father, recounting this later, used to end triumphantly by saying, 'And he was!' It was all somehow rather characteristic of both the Maudes and the Frasers.

Granny sat somewhere at the other end of the table and I often sat next to her. In front of her, at the appropriate moment, was placed a coffee percolator and spirit lamp. She used to give a brief lecture on the particular physical laws which made the heat drive the water up into the ground coffee and then allow it to percolate down again, ultimately turning into this splendid, very black, beverage. Then – 'Pam, I expect David would like just a *little* coffee, mixed with a lot of cream and coffee sugar.' Coffee was on my mother's black list and cream was 'terribly rich', but she was generally some distance off and her anxious interventions seldom if ever had effect.

On wine, too, my grandmother was remorseless – she loved wine and knew a good deal about it. I was, when eleven or twelve, thought to suffer from a vulnerable stomach and to be rather anaemic.

'I think David's a little pale, Pam darling.'

'He's been put on a tonic, Mother.'

'You should give him wine, regularly. A glass or two of Burgundy is the best thing.'

'Oh no, Mother, I *don't* think that would be a good idea – '

'I think it would. Very strengthening. Or port. Now, we're drinking a very light port. Tomlin, give Master David a half glass of port.'

'Very good, My Lady.'

'Mother, I think it may upset him – '

'Well,' Granny used to say equably, 'we'll just have to see, won't we?' The port glasses were huge, and as I, with nervous delight, lifted mine Granny would turn to me with something not entirely unlike a wink.

I hardly saw Granny Saltoun after the Second World War began.

She died at Gloucester Place in October, 1940, having endured the 1940 blitz on London with a good deal of sang-froid, as I heard. She was unenthusiastic about the war, and I also deduced this from her letters to me at Eton or during my short time at Oxford after the war itself began. She thought the war likely to lead to the advance of the Soviet Union and the United States – not her two most favoured nations – and to disaster for most other countries. I doubt if the run of events would have changed her mind had she lived to see them. But with all her partisanship, circumlocutions, eccentricities and naughtinesses I remember my grandmother as one of the most enchanting people I have ever known.

Grandparents were one thing, but dominating the foreground of the successive landscapes of childhood were, of course, my parents. So far my father and mother have been touched in by me almost as auxiliaries to the main themes of the picture – my father greeting Marshal Joffre; my mother humouring my grandfather or in uneasy remonstrance with my grandmother's indulgences; but they were, of course, ubiquitous, and illumine almost every recollection. And how does one describe parents? Some people have done so with malicious wit – I think of Osbert Sitwell. Others have indulged in hagiography, tending a sacred family flame. Most of us, I think, wish for neither extreme, but parents are difficult to view externally, as people. Grandparents, uncles, cousins are sufficiently remote to appreciate or disapprove without any particular sense of obligation or betrayal. Parents are different.

I am lucky in that I loved and admired both parents and, on reflection, know that I was justified. My father often appeared strict and formidable and I was in awe of him – something which greatly upset him when he learned it later, for having feared his own father he was determined that the pattern should not be repeated. What I feared, of course, was that I should disappoint his expectations, let him down. I needn't have bothered because whenever I struck disaster or failure in later years no man could have been quicker to sympathize and support.

My father was well-read, quick-witted and physically very agile. He was exceptionally good with his hands, a handy man. He was expert at most games and field sports, with an excellent eye, good balance and natural grace. I had little of this – but just enough to lament that I hadn't more. I longed to be as good a shot, a cricketer, a golfer, a horseman as my father: I knew I wasn't and wouldn't be, and – completely erroneously – I supposed my comparative inadequacy pained him. It didn't in the least, but I was slow to realize that. He had a quick temper and a sharp tongue.

I was, however, rather more on terms with him in academic matters. I was no great scholar but as the years went on I read and wrote and thought and argued, and in all that side of life I could meet my father on a more equal basis. This brought us increasingly together. What really bound us, however, was my developing appreciation of his deep affection, his utter loyalty. He would, right until death, have put his hand in the fire for us and never have hesitated. He was a man with extraordinarily little selfishness, but in his devotion to his family self came nowhere. I sensed this always and ultimately I knew it completely.

My father had very high standards – of performance in whatever one was attempting, of manners and appearance, and of conduct. If he took something up he studied, learned, practised with great thoroughness. It was not possible to imagine him doing anything in a slipshod style. He was generally courteous and considerate; but, although personally unostentatious, he had great common sense and a very quick sense of how to get his own way, how to protect his interests. He was not a man to upstage or push around, and I cannot easily visualize my father in a queue unless pretty near its head; he was impatient. These high standards and dislike of the mediocre often made him a demanding parent, and his impatience exacerbated things.

He was, however, extremely kind, quick to drop everything and help another. Bad manners revolted him; and I cannot say that he was a tolerant man, though later in life he often openly condemned himself (and me, from time to time) for intolerance. He frequently, from my childhood onwards, urged me to see more than one side of a question; but I doubt whether the readiness to do so was his own longest suit when he was young. When older, however, he was touchingly frank and humble about his own shortcomings, as he saw them.

My father got great enjoyment out of life, although the exacting standards he set himself seemed, at least superficially, to reduce that enjoyment. He was, for instance, an expert golfer with a handicap of 4 most of his life; yet one bad shot seemed able to send him into an abyss of angry despair and self-accusation. A fish getting away which should have ended on the bank stabbed him with the reproach of actual sin – though it was an infrequent occurrence. He drew – by no means badly – and painted in watercolour, and I think this gave him particular peace because he knew he would never be very good, so that the attempt rather than the achievement was accepted as sufficient for happiness; yet a botched sky threw him into melancholy. His sense of visual beauty was strong, and he loved pictures – and, when he could afford it, collected in a modest way, with considerable shrewdness.

Above all, my father was pertinacious. He never wearied if he set his mind to something. If he entered a shop – in this utterly unlike myself – he refused to leave without examining every article on offer, of the sort he was seeking. A determined bargain-hunter, his face on such occasions assumed an expression of incredulous contempt – dismissive of the goods being displayed and incredulous that anyone should have the impertinence to ask so high a price. He shopped as a Frenchwoman shops. No doubt it was this persistence which made my father so successful a fisherman. It may be that in this catalogue I have conveyed a certain grimness – nothing could be less accurate. Like my mother, my father loved laughter, and as a family we laughed a great deal. But seriousness often broke in.

My father was a man of exceptional neatness and good looks. To the end of his days his appearance gave one pleasure. His face lightened with happiness when he greeted me, especially if we had not seen each other for a while. He was – the phrase is calculated, not conventional – the best of fathers; and of all my departed friends I miss him the most.

My mother had exceptional charm, in this resembling both her parents. She had a wonderful sense of humour. She had never felt tempted to follow my grandparents on to the stage but she had a strong theatrical bent. I used to get somewhat fed up at the frequency with which people said, 'Your mother is the most charming/most delightful/ loveliest/most amusing person I've ever known', but it was generally sincere, and, clearly, a matter of congratulation. I sometimes sensed (and resented) that the warmth of the compliment implied a tacit criticism of my father, an unspoken comment that his quality was less attractive than hers. But that my mother was greatly admired was a fact of life and we grew up in its shadow. At times, naturally, it made me jealous and protective. I didn't always welcome the adulation which seemed to surround her.

She, however, exuded affection so that we had no sort of complaint on that score. She was in many ways the exact opposite of my father. She was impractical where he was immensely practical. I once said to her, explaining some requirement, 'It's just a matter of common sense,' and my mother, without the slightest affectation, said, 'I have *no* common sense'; she was perfectly right, and it was distinguished of her to recognize the fact. She was inept at most physical pursuits, attempting golf and tennis but succeeding not at all, and very unsafe at the wheel of a car.

My mother was musical – she played the piano competently, sang agreeably, and had a sensitive and appreciative ear (this was in strong contrast to my father, who could never sing in tune or distinguish one melody from another). She responded to all forms of visual beauty – in this her tastes coincided with my father's; and, like him, she loved books, and relished the music of language. I could always make my mother laugh, and she me. As with my father, she never compromised over principles. Light-hearted and affectionate, her sense of right and wrong was nevertheless immutable, and behind her charm was a certain amount of puritanism (in this like her mother), as she herself readily admitted.

My mother had adored her own childhood, and has skilfully evoked it in a book of recollections.* Like her father she had a certain sentimentality about childhood; but, like her mother, she balanced this with a good deal of impatience when sentiment degenerated into sloppiness. She had a no-nonsense side which was often in evidence – sometimes at surprising moments – and which was good for us.

My mother liked getting her own way, and as she was widely admired she had come to regard this as the pretty natural order of things. She wasn't exactly spoiled, but people humoured her whims, enjoyed giving her pleasure, liked being generous to her. My mother

* *World's Away* – John Baker, London, 1964.

accepted this with a certain unconscious complacency, and – in later years – a certain resentment if it was not forthcoming. But this was offset by her humour and her readiness to laugh at her own foibles.

I was extraordinarily lucky in both parents.

4

Foreigners and Others

I rate it a benefit that much of my childhood was spent in foreign lands, and a good many of the figures I remember from it are foreigners.

The first of these were American. My aunt Margery Maude had married Joseph Burden in the United States at the end of the First World War and there were cousins of like ages to my half-sister, Gloria Congreve, my young brother Alistair (born in 1926) and me. The Burdens spent frequent summers in England – they lived in New York, with a holiday home on Nantucket – and we met at Redlap, or on occasion took a holiday house together.

My eldest cousin Joe – called Jo-Jo – was two years older than me. He was a charming and gifted boy, good-looking, dark, rather serious, extremely thoughtful. He later went to Groton and then to Christ Church, Oxford. In the Second World War – just down from Oxford when it began – he immediately joined the British Army, thereby forfeiting his American citizenship, since the United States was neutral until the Japanese attacked them and the Germans declared war on them in December 1941. Joe had visited Germany during University vacations and he had decided that the Nazis represented something fundamentally evil. It was morally imperative to fight them. When Britain – his temporarily adopted country through University, and by blood through his mother – went to war in 1939 Joe was not prepared to stand aside. He was eventually commissioned in the Scots Guards, served in the same Division as myself and was killed in Normandy in 1944.

Joe first led me to the essential discovery that foreigners are different, have different tastes and views, and look at England through different spectacles; not necessarily with hostility, but with open minds and – sometimes – no little scepticism. And of all foreigners Americans are in many ways the most foreign, a fact effectively disguised by a similar language, a culture in much of the United States (but certainly not all) derived from that of eighteenth-century England, and a history which was constitutionally linked to our own until the Americans broke the link in circumstances which still provoke argument.

Joe was very firm in his American patriotism, but he also had a (very good) quizzical and enquiring mind. As we grew up I was prone to positive, prejudiced and passionate opinions and wasn't backward in expressing them. Joe deflated me – often, of course, infuriatingly because he was both older and cleverer than I. He had a gentle laugh which accompanied the deflation, and I sometimes grew heated. He had the most absolutely decent standards of anybody I have known – honest, honourable and generous; but, in his own way, inflexible. Voices are almost more evocative than faces and I can hear my cousin's voice, his sceptical laugh, his decisive statement of a principle at least as clearly as I can see his dark, narrow, high-cheekboned face. Of course our more serious conversations – and arguments – came later; in boyhood and adolescence and in the war when, fortunately, I saw him often. But, from the first, I recognized that Joe was an important person, and that he was, as an American, absolutely different. There were angles of vision completely unlike my own.

In 1928, after the Dover years, my father had transferred from the Gordons to the Grenadiers, his father's Regiment – and not only his father's but that of the sixteenth Lord Saltoun, 'Waterloo' Saltoun, my father's great-great-uncle, who had become a general but had died without legitimate offspring and been succeeded at Philorth by his nephew, my great-grandfather. Although, as I have said, the idea of a commission in the Guards had originally been thought inappropriate for the youngest of the family, in transferring to the First or Grenadier Regiment of Foot Guards my father was following family tradition, as have both I and my eldest son. My father's transfer meant that we moved first to Aldershot and then to London. He joined the 3rd Battalion of the Regiment as a company commander.

He was thirty-eight. He had commanded a battalion on the Western Front at the age of twenty-six. Had he remained a Gordon Highlander he would probably never have again attained battalion command, so sluggish was promotion between the wars in Regiments of the line. This was not very stimulating for a man who had led a battalion through some of the greatest battles of the war, collecting a Military Cross and three DSOs in the process. In the Grenadiers there was a chance of battalion command, although he had inevitably joined with forfeited Regimental seniority, and command would come late, if at all. There were other reasons for the transfer – as a Gordon Highlander he would have moved to India and although he had hugely enjoyed service there as a young man on first joining the Army in 1910 he had no desire to return with a wife and young children. There were other factors. Even more than most of his generation he had lost his particular Regimental friends in the war. The Gordons had changed, there were new faces: and he had changed too.

In the 3rd Grenadiers my father's first Commanding Officer was Andrew Thorne, 'Bulgy' Thorne. He had a great name as a trainer, as one dedicated to his profession in a way which in those days was comparatively rare, and as being a fanatic for physical fitness. Like my father (but slightly older) he had commanded a battalion on the Western Front with considerable distinction. He was at this time 43, which was then young for a Battalion Commander. Later in life I got to know him (his wife, a Douglas-Pennant, was a distant cousin of my mother's; my mother's great-grandmother, Lady Sudeley, had been a Pennant, while the Pennants, too, had Maude blood). Bulgy Thorne was not only a fine soldier but was one of those rare people who could talk to one when young as an equal, showing interest and concern in what one was thinking (however inept) or feeling (however immature). In modern terms, he could 'communicate' – wonderfully. He – like many excellent soldiers of his generation – subsequently had a disappointing career in the Second World War, commanding a Territorial Division in 1940 but then – albeit reaching the rank of General – not seeing active service again, condemned to various commands in the defence of the United Kingdom, which became frustrating when the threat of invasion had passed. It was, with a few exceptions, a slightly younger generation which led the Armies and Corps of 1943 and 1944, when the British Army was again employed against the enemy on a significant scale: and, wisely or not, they were regarded as representing fresher ideas, more youthful vigour, military modernism and a wave of success. There was probably something in this, but not as much as was popularly supposed. I can see Bulgy Thorne now, short, trim, vigorous, modest in his speech and manner, a soldier respected by all. With a slightly different fall of the dice he could have done different and more resounding things, but at least one boy remembered him with great affection.

Transfer to the Grenadiers meant Regimental service in Aldershot and London. My father bought a house in Brechin Place, South Kensington. Unfashionably far down the Old Brompton Road, it was – so my mother later confided to me – the only one of my parents' homes which she really loathed.

I see it as dark – every room seemed dark, whatever the hour, whatever the season. I had never lived in London before and it was very different from our house at Ringwould, near Dover. There we had lived next to a farm with its sounds and smells, there my father had kept his chargers with a neighbour, a soldier-groom tending them: he had usually ridden the six miles to work at Dover Castle over the turf above the cliffs there. There the summers seemed spent haymaking and riding home on the banked haywains behind the huge and splendid horses. There I rode out on a pony with my father, on frequent occasions sternly corrected as to seat and hands but nevertheless feeling most superior. Brechin Place was even more different from the beach at Nairn. Furthermore I did not welcome my father's Regimental transfer – the Gordons had signified Scotland, and although I had spent most of my short life in England I felt very much a Scot.

There were compensations, however, to living in London. I had never been to a theatre and was taken to *Peter Pan* – and was suitably enchanted, and intrigued (of course) by the flying. Gerald du Maurier played the doubled Mr Darling and Captain Hook and I am glad to be able to say I saw him, although it may not have been in one of his greatest roles. Jean Forbes-Robertson, daughter of Grandpa Maude's old Carthusian friend, Sir Johnston, was Peter.

There was a large communal garden at Brechin Place. Often, in the garden, there were Russians. A family of Russian émigrés lived in one of the houses and we had a good deal of international bickering and violence, chiefly stemming from arguments about who had won the war. I was prepared to be generous about this, conscious of the victor's good fortune and inherent superiority. I was amazed to find that the Russians – touchy on this, and most other points – saw the matter in a completely different light. The Russians, they told me, had confronted the bulk of the German Army – and defeated it – while the British and French were sitting in trenches and not daring to get out of them. 'Not daring . . .' I still remember the sensation of almost choking with rage.

Nor did it stop there. I apparently knew nothing about the military profession itself. There was mention, once, of officers' swords. On this I knew my stuff. 'In the war,' I said, 'officers, after a bit, didn't wear their swords. Anyway, not infantry officers. There was no point – not after it became trench warfare.'

'Of course officers *always* wear swords!' One of the Russians, very confident, a leader, was called Cypie, Cyprian. He was a great putter-down, thin-faced, crafty-eyed. I can see him now. I said that my father was, now as well as in the war, an officer. I knew what I was talking about. Cypie said that if he hadn't worn his sword, throughout, he couldn't have been a proper officer. There was trouble.

But the Russians were sociable and the girls were sweet. When we weren't quarrelling they were enchanting. Cliques were formed, sides taken. Tears were not infrequent. Above all, however, I became aware of an atmosphere, a level of thinking and feeling, completely different from my own, often perplexing, but also deeply attractive.

I also, inevitably, became aware of the Russian Revolution. All these children and their parents were refugees from it. My mother told me enough to show me something of the sort of horror they had escaped, and the complete overturn of any decent order of things which Russia now apparently represented. All this was recent – we moved into Brechin Place in 1929 and these frightful happenings were only eleven years behind my Russian acquaintances. Most of the children, of course, were under eleven, but in family memory for them it was as if today one were to recall an era when Margaret Thatcher had already been many years Prime Minister – recent, in other words. The Revolution dominated the consciousness of most of Europe (however people viewed it) in a manner whose only precedent was the cataclysm in France from 1792 onwards.

*

And soon there were Belgians. After a few years' Regimental service with the Grenadiers as a rather elderly company commander, my father was sent to take up his military attaché post in Brussels. My young brother – five years old at that time – meant that our nanny was still with us; and the public gardens in Brussels – whether on the Bois, at the end of the Avenue Louise, or fronting the Rue Ducale, near the Royal Palace – were, as I have said, the meeting points for Belgian children of the reasonably 'Haut Monde' and their (invariably English) nannies.

I was a bit old for this, having gone to my preparatory school, St Aubyn's, Rottingdean, in January 1930, but I had suffered a rather protracted illness immediately after our move and I had a longish time off school. I therefore found myself in the gardens as often as not, and although most of the children were of nursery age there were some older ones thought appropriate companions for me. And from them – as well, of course, as from listening in to the gossip of the nannies from time to time – I acquired a picture of a strange world, and of a people whose immediate experience again differed wholly from our own.

Brussels had been occupied, throughout the war, by the Germans. Some of the English nannies (acquiring thereby heroine status) had lived there, more or less unmolested, throughout. There were stories of the tricks played on German soldiers, of the mockery to which the Germans had been subjected, of the occasional brutality – but mostly the heavy-handed stupidity – shown by the occupiers. It all sounded exciting, periodically heart-stopping, undoubtedly inspirational and, above all, fun. It was also very recent. Nothing like it, of course, could conceivably happen again – I had been born to a less heroic age – but it was good to listen to stories of these epic happenings. Unlike the Russian boys I'd met, the Belgians seemed thoroughly and properly appreciative of what England had done for them. The atmosphere – in all generations, I think – was immensely friendly. It may have helped that King Leopold (Crown Prince when we arrived, but succeeding on King Albert's accidental death while we were in Brussels) had been at Eton, whither I was one day bound.

The Belgians were full of noise, quarrel and affection. They were lively. They enjoyed intrigue. They lived at a more colourful level than ourselves, or so it seemed. The children were always forming alliances, enlisting support, declaring war. My brother Alistair was in his element and became a very popular figure in his generation – years later, when I returned to Brussels in the Second World War, I met people who immediately spoke of him when they heard my name.

A disadvantage in the Brussels days, a figure recalled without warmth (I am aware of the ingratitude in this), was Mademoiselle Leloir. My mother – most laudably – was determined that I should use those times to learn adequate French, something which an English education almost totally neglected, despite the school fees. She therefore engaged, during the holidays, Mademoiselle Leloir to come to 315 Avenue Molière, almost every afternoon.

Mademoiselle Leloir was a stern task-mistress; we did not really get on. I can see her now, fussily dressed, hat with a sort of plume, busy, bustling, critical, unquiet. I have no doubt that her ministrations were extremely good for me. Every lapse of grammar, every distortion of accent was savagely reproved. I had to learn a great deal of Racine and Corneille by heart. Nevertheless I was unimpressed. It seemed to me that in a language with so regular a grammar as French the use of rhyme in verse became too easy, lost its punch, resembled cheating. I said this to Mlle Leloir, who was outraged. She said that the word-endings in English were also limited and facilitated rhyme: the difference was that they were hideous and irregular instead of sonorous and beautiful. She said that the sacred and ancient Latin hymns of the Church employed rhyme, although Latin was a most regular, consistent and grammatical tongue. She said much more.

The only way I could cut a lesson short was to tempt her to the ping-pong table. She enjoyed the game, and played it noisily. She was a bad loser. I think, nevertheless, that I owe her a good deal. I have always thereafter been comfortable with the French language. And – Mademoiselle Leloir notwithstanding – I have always had considerable affection for Belgium and the Belgians, and have visited often and lived there again in later life.

In the summer holidays we took a house in Le Zoute, by the sea, and I learned (with excellent tuition) to play tennis better and greatly enjoyed it. Tennis, bathing, and bicycling round the mercifully flat roads of Flanders under the huge Low Country skies – these were our summers, or part of them. On the beach, where a lot of each day was spent, a craze seized the children one summer (our first). They made paper flowers, set up shops, and then bought them from each other with buckets of shells. Accumulation was the name of the game.

The unimaginative children simply exhausted themselves collecting shells in buckets, to buy the flowers. Others busied themselves making them. My brother Alistair watched it all intently. After a while he made his plan. I cannot remember all its details – it consisted in creating monopolies in certain flowers and then charging immensely high prices. When we had amassed huge amounts of shells by this means we bought the flowers again from the (impoverished) purchasers; and ran child after child out of business. I remember that after a day or two of trading we had swept the beach, and we felt triumphant. Then we made an important discovery. To get trade going again we had to lend shells to children in order that they could buy. In fact we learned a lot – I have never got the better of a Belgian since. It was all Alistair's doing.

And how safe were the cities of those days! London, Brussels or wherever, I was encouraged to go everywhere by myself, to walk, to travel on trams (Brussels) or bus and underground (London), to shop (without much to spend), to learn my way around. I also travelled alone, armed simply with my ticket and a small ration of cash, from London to Brussels at end of term – taxis, railway (3rd class, 2nd abroad), cabin on boat (1st class), dinner ordered with great enjoyment in the boat's restaurant, school trunk registered at Victoria (via Ostend) or Liverpool Street (via Harwich–Antwerp) and recovered at the Customs shed in the Brussels Gare du Nord, where my parents met me. It was inconceivable that anything could go wrong. Nobody was anxious. None of the sort of horrors were prevalent which are now brought to us daily by newspapers. I got to know Brussels well. The knowledge stood me in particularly good stead one September evening some thirteen years after our first arrival there.

On that later September evening I was in the Place Brouckère, in the old city, not far from the Bourse and the Gare du Nord. The night sky was lit by a huge bonfire, fuelled by the furniture and possessions of alleged collaborators with the Germans. The whole population of Brussels were in the streets, cheering us. For the Germans had left that afternoon, 3rd September 1944; and the British Second Army, led by the Guards Armoured Division, were entering. It was liberation.

It was also total confusion. Traffic columns were inextricably mixed, and whenever they halted excited Bruxellois would swarm over every tank, scout car, vehicle, pressing bottles of wine on all, pressing kisses on all, shrieking, exultant, free. The noise was indescribable. I had spent the day attached to the Household Cavalry, who had been scouting forward, leading the advance – an advance which covered a hundred miles, from south of the French frontier. Nobody knew where we were, and nobody knew where we were meant to be going. No communications were working. All was chaos. Somehow – I have completely forgotten how – somebody yelled to me, 'The Royal Palace. We're harbouring there. It's called Laeken, or something.'

Laeken! The Royal Family's residence, rather than the official, and central, Palace at the end of the Rue Ducale. Of course I remembered in general terms on which side of Brussels Laeken lay – it is in the suburbs, well clear of the city centre, in its own park. A perfectly appropriate place to harbour. The same authority (I think) yelled, 'But God knows where we are!'

But I did. Place Brouckère! Very distinctive. Old street maps of Brussels, boyhood walks, tram journeys of long ago came back to me. Indeed I knew where I was. I also knew the direction in which lay Laeken. I set out, edging a scout car, leading an armoured column, through the delirious mass; and ultimately, hours later, we got there to find the Queen Mother of the Belgians standing by the side of the drive insisting on shaking hands in the darkness with, as far as I could see, every member of every crew of every tank.

Laeken: the name brought back, on that September evening in 1944, a whole swarm of memories which mingled with the astonishing present. My mother told me that the return of King Albert's body from Laeken to central Brussels in 1932, to lie in state in the great cathedral of St Gudule, was the most impressive ceremonial occasion she'd ever witnessed. The landscape of Brussels is one of contrast – a 'new' town, begun in the eighteenth century, looks down on the medieval city with its superb Grand Place, capital of the Emperor Charles V, and the cathedral juts out over that mediaeval city like a great ship about to be launched from a slipway. When it was known that the king was dead – he had been killed climbing in the Ardennes – and that his body had been recovered and brought to the palace of Laeken every light in every house and building was put out. Brussels was in complete darkness. Nobody dreamed of breaking this instruction. Then – starting far away, from Laeken – came marching an immense column of soldiers, I imagine most of the troops of the considerable Brussels garrison. Every soldier carried a flaming torch. In the centre of the column was the gun carriage carrying the body of the king. They marched, in total silence, the considerable distance. Everybody watching from the heights of the new town, from windows, from rooftops, could see – the only points of light in the darkness – that immense column wending its way through the night to St Gudule, escorting their king to his long rest. Spontaneous ceremony can be more impressive than the carefully rehearsed kind.

My father and mother lived in Brussels for four years. They had a legion of Belgian friends. It was home. It was also, and unforgettably, scene of family tragedy, for my brother, Alistair, was killed there in an accident at a children's party. He had been playing hide and seek at the house of great Dutch friends of my parents, the Van Boetzelaers, had climbed out on to a glass roof which had given way, and had fallen the whole height of the well staircase of that tall house. I was away at boarding school, and was summoned by the Headmaster one day early in the summer term of 1932 with a mutter of 'your parents'. My mother and father had just arrived to break the news to me. They knew how I loved him; of all the tragedies in my mother's life – and she had plenty – she once told me that the hardest recollection was having to give me that news. I knew that life would never be the same again, and in some ways it never was.

Many, many years later, in 1975, Brussels again became home – I was sent as Military Representative to the Military Committee of the North Atlantic Treaty Organization. We lived in Boitsfort, in a house which looked across a lake at the Forêt de Soignes, that superb stretch of beech woods, planted in honour of the Empress Maria Theresa, which acts as a generous lung to Brussels and reaches as far as Waterloo. I walked daily in the Forêt, just as we had almost daily gone there or to the Bois de la Cambre (the fringe of the Forêt within Brussels proper) in those long-ago Avenue Molière days. There was a large lake in the Bois de la Cambre and as children we could pay a few francs and hire a rowing boat. One holiday two beautiful Swedish girls of about eighteen somehow came into my life, and I used to row one or the other on the lake. I was, I suppose, twelve. The affair never progressed. I think they may have regarded me as rather young for them.

But in that last return, in the 1970s, memories of the long-ago persistently came back. The pages of *High Life*, Belgian society's book of reference, were still dominated by names familiar to me from the friends of my parents, whose children and grandchildren still gossiped, intermarried, did periodic good works – and periodic scandalous things – in a most traditional way. Britain found itself at war in 1914, very largely because of a sense of outrage at the violation of Belgium. The sense of outrage was wholly justified.

The Dutch were altogether different. My mother's cousin, Hubert Montgomery, was the British Minister to the Netherlands. In those days our missions to most countries were Legations, headed by Ministers, rather than Embassies led by Ambassadors. I was told, rightly or wrongly, that in nations which had been allied with us in the war we had upgraded Legations to Embassies. Certainly there was a British Embassy in Brussels but a British Legation in the Hague. The Legation was the name given both to the Minister's residence and the place where his staff did their work – the chancery. At the Hague, and in those days of small staffs probably in most other capitals too, the chancery was, in fact, in the same building – in an adjoining annexe overlooking a courtyard. We were extraordinarily fortunate in Cousin Hubert's appointment. My father, covering as military attaché both Belgium and Holland, generally did part of his Dutch business during the school holidays, and so kind and hospitable were the Montgomerys, Cousin Hubert and his wife, Cousin Grace, that we stayed at the Legation during such ostensibly business visits.

The Legation (now, alas, alienated from the British Crown) was a large and beautiful house in the Westeinde. Presiding over it was the hugely efficient butler, Brinkmann, and cohorts of assistants. I particularly remember the plate of sandwiches with which he greeted us after some evening outing, ensuring there would be no night starvation. The house was lively and laughter-filled. We first went there during my own transitional period between preparatory and public schools, so that in that earlier time I listened, nervous and fascinated, to my cousin David Montgomery's awesome expositions of life at Eton (he was some three years my senior and when I got there helped me greatly). But I particularly remember my cousin Hubert.

He appeared a man of great patience. He was small, trim, moustached, and seemed quite a lot older than my father. His brother, Archie Montgomery-Massingberd, was Chief of the Imperial General Staff, a man with whom contemporary history has on the whole dealt harshly – Liddell-Hart in his memoirs showing particular venom about what he recorded as Montgomery-Massingberd's obstruction of progressive ideas. I don't know whether the brothers resembled each other – from what I have read I somehow doubt it. But the quality I found remarkable in Cousin Hubert was the way he tolerated a positive hubbub all around him when (presumably) working on important matters of diplomacy. His study, where he did all his work, opened off the hall, and had a door opening on one of two connecting drawing rooms. In the room next to the study was the radio-gramophone. It was an era – and we were of an age – when dance music, songs, the latest hits, were irresistible: 'Smoke Gets in Your Eyes', 'Stormy Weather', 'Night and Day'. That gramophone had a record playing on it from breakfast time onwards. I only once remember Cousin Hubert complaining – I was alone in the drawing room, had just put on a jazz record *fortissimo*, after breakfast, and Cousin Hubert appeared from his study to ask, in the gentlest imaginable manner, whether I'd mind turning the volume down a bit.

I can particularly see the Hague in winter, the frozen lakes and the introduction to skating. The Legation chauffeur – his name was Lein – was very expert, and everybody had to learn, Lein doing some coaching as well as driving us to and fro. On the ice I met Dutch children, effortless and amiably contemptuous of my efforts – they were born to skates. The Dutch used to skate hundreds of kilometres along the canals.

Golf played a major part in life at the Hague – my cousin David being not only older but naturally good at the game. People were kind and played with me, but I was less skilled than most, and so it has remained – my father could never really understand why I found so difficult the essentially simple task of hitting a small stationary ball in the required direction. And life at the Legation was enormously social – with very little exclusion of younger generations. There was a huge ballroom and I remember a ball – all ages allowed, very formal dances mingled with a few more modern. There were Quadrilles, 'Lancers' and so forth; it seemed antiquated and charming, even to a twelve- or thirteen-year-old.

Sometimes, if we were in the Hague during the Easter holidays, Lein would drive us out to see the tulip fields on the Haarlem road. It says something about traffic conditions that this expedition often took place between teatime at the Legation and the hour (7.30) when it was obligatory to change for dinner. During that two-hour interval we could drive from the centre of the Hague, view the bulbs and return. Today the journey would probably demand a day in a queue.

Christmas parties at the Hague were for all ages, and every Legation or Embassy seemed to give one. I was generally the youngest present, and felt a little conspicuous in my Highland dress. After supper there would be games of one sort or other, then the drive home with Lein through the cold night, flushed and excited. On one occasion I did very badly. I can't remember who was the host but dinner was at a number of round tables. National contingents were broken up, and, since nobody knew who 'M. David Fraser, Legation de Grande Bretagne' was, I found myself at a table without a relative in sight. It was here that I first tasted oysters and loved them; and there was champagne, and plenty of it.

Conversation was animated, but my father and mother told me in later years that they had been disturbed at the particularly loud laughter coming from one table, punctuated by silences in which my treble could be heard holding forth. I was, in fact, well away; I felt a friend to all the world. I was giving them a series of imitations and anecdotes. Later I felt unsteady but glorious. We played some sort of riotous game, and eventually David Montgomery had to drag me off the sixteen-year-old daughter of the Polish Ambassador, whom I had assaulted with energetic and unbecoming affection.

The British Legation was supposed to be haunted, a fact I didn't know at the time. One winter evening the older grown-ups had gone to some reception, some 'Jour'. It was about six o'clock, the time between tea and dressing for dinner when card games and so forth were played. Somebody suggested table turning.

We, the younger element, pushed a large, heavy, round pedestal table into the ballroom, which was otherwise empty of furniture. We then put out all the lights – there wasn't total darkness but the next best thing – and stood round the table with our hands upon it, our outer fingers touching. There was a good deal of giggling as somebody said, 'Is there anyone there? One knock for yes, two knocks for no.'

David Montgomery said in his drawling voice, 'Two knocks will be a bit suspicious, won't it?' There was (slightly nervous) laughter, and some whispering.

'You're pushing it!'

'I'm not! It's far too heavy!' And the table was indeed extremely heavy, so that it had needed united and muscular effort rather than finger-tip touch to shift it.

'Is there anyone there? One knock for yes.'

After a few minutes of this, and some (rather reassured) whispers about it all being nonsense, we were suddenly electrified by a *deafening* bang, as if the table had been raised and dropped from a height. Total silence.

'Is there anyone there?'

Another immense reverberation. Someone tried to give instructions about spelling the name of whoever or whatever it was but by then we had lost control. The table started to rotate. It rotated – with ourselves walking round with it, just managing to maintain finger contact – faster and faster, and at the same time it started to move around the ballroom. In the dim darkness we scampered round it. Eventually it stopped – some way from its original point.

'Who is there?'

The table suddenly started to tilt on its pedestal. Heavy as it was, it tilted until the under-rim was nearly touching the ballroom floor. The participants on that side contorted their bodies to keep their hands in contact with the table and with each other. At last the table tilted back to true, creaked and was still. Somebody said, 'I've had enough of this,' and broke the circle. We put the lights on. We said little, then or later. We all knew that none of us could have caused that effect by cheating.

Inevitably, because the life was diplomatic, the people we saw – and their children – were of many nationalities, and the Dutch, natives of the place, seemed almost outnumbered. But plenty of Dutch figures people that landscape of the Hague, and I chiefly remember reflecting how enormously like ourselves they were – far more than were Belgians, certainly than were Russians, even than were Americans. The Dutch appeared not only to look more like us, but to thiink more like us (I suspect this was something of a misapprehension). Above all they tended to talk perfect English, and to a Briton there is no more decisive proof of civilization and sense.

And then there were Germans. I do not remember Germany until I was sixteen, but my memory of it is especially vivid. Germany in those days (1937) was on everybody's lips.

We were again living in London. After Brussels my father had returned to Regimental duty in London in 1935 and we had bought No. 6 Cheyne Gardens, just off the Embankment. It is a tall house – six floors if one counts the basement – and has now been knocked into flats by sideways extension into the adjoining houses. I only learned from Victoria Glendinning's superb biography of Anthony Trollope that his widow had moved to that house after Trollope's death – I am sure my mother was not aware of that, and I regret it, for she would have relished the knowledge.

The times were uneasy. Hitler had become Chancellor of Germany while we were in Brussels. Thereafter there had been the revolutionary period, the time of violence, the 'Night of the Long Knives'. Everybody knew that Germany was rearming, but there was a general feeling that this was only natural, and not necessarily menacing. Widely accepted was the view that the Germans had been treated with the sort of harshness which would inevitably provoke a reaction, and one aspect of this reaction would obviously be the need to get some sort of parity with other nations in the sphere of military power; to walk tall again. Few people supposed that, if seriously confronted by France and Britain, Germany would start another war. Like everyone else, she'd surely learned her lesson. 'Confronted by France and Britain' – almost nobody else counted. There were small nations in Europe – we had been living in two of them – which would obviously look to France and

Britain to keep international order. There was America – ostentatiously neutral, in our view a laggard in the war, and not seriously to be counted upon in any direction. And there was Russia, generally regarded (in our sort of world) as dominated by so evil and incompetent a regime that contact, let alone alliance, with her was near unthinkable. To keep the peace was for Britain and France.

After the revolutionary period matters in Germany seemed rather quieter. There were periodic stories of the bullying nastiness of the Nazi regime, in some of its aspects. Jews were discriminated against, were made to register as such, were limited in their employment opportunities, were sometimes knocked about, with the authorities doing too little to protect them. This was wrong, of course – the sort of way Germans (and, it was easily said, not only Germans but many foreigners) found it acceptable to behave. But, it was also said, the Germans had some cause for their resentment – the great inflation, the economic distress after the war which we could not imagine and which, rightly or wrongly, they tended to blame on the Jews, Jews who had flooded into Germany from the east in many cases, alien, predatory. Nazi conduct was bad, but perhaps it was not altogether surprising. And it certainly didn't spell danger. Thus people talked. Hitler occasionally made speeches about neighbouring countries – Austria, Czechoslovakia, Poland – which could be interpreted as holding a degree of menace; but, soon afterwards, he spoke words of friendship to them, concluded pacts, talked of the absolute necessity of peace. The situation seldom seemed exciting for long. Because, of course – it would be humbug to conceal this – to a boy the prospect of war, not the continuance of peace, was what excited.

The only German I had met was Geyr, described already. My father shook his head a good deal at the news reported from Germany, but he had been so marked by the sheer horror of the war that he refused to believe anybody could be stupid enough to start another. Hitler, I think he reckoned, was a nasty, vulgar and unprincipled little dema-gogue, with contemptible prejudices and the gift of the gab; but pro-vided it was made clear that there was a line in international affairs which he would not be allowed to cross, sanity would prevail in Germany, responsible hands would bridle the volatile chancellor, and peace would last. Anything else was unthinkable. For my father – in this wholly consistent, even where less than prophetically perceptive – the absolute necessity was for Britain and France to form and cement an alliance, and for that alliance to speak with a united voice. He also regarded it as important to support Czechoslovakia, since it had a not-inconsiderable army and armament industry.

In the summer of 1937 my father decided we would take a holiday in Austria and Germany. We crossed by car ferry to Ostend and spent the first night in the Ardennes at Ligneuville, very near the German border. I knew the Ardennes well, since we often picnicked there in the Brussels days, and it was curious to connect them to the possible imminence of war. There had not been much war talk recently; it had died down, and the international scene appeared once more peaceable, and consequently dull. My mother, however, said, 'One doesn't know, ever, how people in these parts [Ardennes] would react –' I was rather startled.

'To a war, you mean?'

'To the Germans. There are a lot about, they've got plenty of friends.'

It seemed rather fanciful, although the proprietor of the inn where we were staying was German. Next day, with an agreeable sense (for me) of penetrating a mystery, we crossed the frontier into Hitler's Germany.

We drove through the Palatinate, Württemberg, Bavaria, and then spent some time in Austria, first in Salzkammergut then in the Tirol. In Germany we visited – either en route to Austria or on the return journey – Cologne, Coblenz, Frankfurt, Heidelburg, Rothenburg-ob-der-Tauber (and other exquisite medieval towns on the so-called 'Romantische Strasse', Dinkelsbuhl, Nordlingen), Munich. Everywhere we saw the sights – as a sightseer my mother was indefatigable. My father and I climbed and walked for miles in the Austrian Alps. And, more memorable than the mountains, the museums, the castles, the churches, we collected impressions of National Socialist Germany. Germany in 1937 is still clear to my eyes.

My first impression was of relative scarcity and hardship. I, naturally, knew little of the economic circumstances with which the German Government was faced (or, to a large extent, had itself brought about, with a huge expansionary programme of State spending on infrastructure and armaments). I knew – every newspaper and every German said it – that Hitler had 'solved' the unemployment crisis which most European countries, including Britain, were suffering with a good deal of internal poverty and unrest. We didn't know how he'd done it: the first Autobahns (which we drove down), splendid novelty, Darmstadt–Frankfurt, and then Munich–Salzburg, presumably gave part of the answer. But one upshot was scarcity. On particular days of the week no restaurant was allowed to serve meat. On other days there were different prohibitions. I had never experienced this sort of rigour.

But it didn't seem unpopular: for the next impression was of what seemed near-universal contentment. I have never experienced an atmosphere of greater cheerfulness and friendliness. One saw a column of 'Hitler Jugend' riding bicycles, led by their leader, his bicycle sporting a tiny Nazi pennant. All waved, cheered. One saw the crowds drinking in the street outside the taverns of Rothenburg, where a Party occasion coincided with our visit, where the whole exquisite medieval main street was hung with the blood-red Nazi banners, the black Swastika in its white circle on each. The crowds were boisterous but joyous – and friendly. Good humour and high morale were in the air. Later – in Austria – we talked to numbers of delightful young people, met in the *Gasthof* at which we stayed. Effusively friendly young men, pretty girls. To my astonishment they all explained that the sooner Austria joined the German Reich the better – Austria, with the old Empire carved up by the victors of the war at Versailles, made no sense, no economic sense, whatsoever. Austria needed size, company, a proper place in the world. She needed Adolf Hitler. And the sooner the better.

But I also see very different scenes and figures.

My father was an excellent linguist. He was, of course, reasonably well-informed – he was commanding a Grenadier battalion in London at that time, but he had only been some two years returned from Brussels and the diplomatic world; he saw a wide circle of friends. Wherever we went in Germany he talked to people in his fluent German and people – particularly older people – talked easily to him, although the ease was circumspect, and the conversation was conducted with careful glances to and fro, gestures which even I (having little German) could not mistake. I see a middle-aged man putting petrol into our car at a filling station – pale blue overalls, blue cap, heavy moustache. Unmistakably, an old soldier. My father chatted. Sure enough, he had been in Flanders in the war and I heard long-familiar names: 'Ieper: Gheluvelt: Menin.'

When we drove on my father was quiet, simply saying that he'd seemed a nice chap and that they'd not been far from each other in the war on several occasions. 'All he wants,' my father said, 'is that there shall never be another.' This was the theme of anybody one spoke to in Germany. There might be problems, but they were soluble. The young people might be a bit excitable but the Führer, it was frequently said, had brought strength, security and the guarantee of peace.

'Does he [the filling station attendant] think there will be another war?'

'He just sighs and shakes his head. And says, softly – you saw him – "These people! These people!"' I think one of the joyous Hitler Jugend columns of bicyclists was passing us at the time. In terms of reaction to the regime what we would now call the generation gap was very marked.

I can see a restaurant in Cologne – I think it was on our return journey, through the Rhineland. Rather bleak, bare floor, bare tables. Few people – the evening meal. An old, shambling waiter, complaining of arthritis and again exchanging reminiscences of the Ypres Salient and suchlike with my father – and this time enjoying showing off his own English.

'Ach – that Ieper! It was the vurst place, the vurst place!'

My father heartily agreed. Then the old waiter seemed to see something and suddenly shuffled off. Into the restaurant, tall, immaculate, handsome, marched two young officers of the SA. In spite of Hitler's purge of their hierarchy the Brown-shirted 'Storm Troopers' were much in evidence (and in Munich the black uniformed SS had been everywhere). The two halted at our table, heels clicked, charming smiles, the Party salute.

'Heil Hitler!'

Then a tin rattled and a short, courteous speech was made. They were collecting for widows and orphans (or something). It was a good cause.

My father put in a coin. Then followed a most friendly harangue.

From England? Yes. Then we were most welcome. Welcome to the new Germany. A small medal was slapped down on the table for us. A small gift from the new Germany. 'Heil Hitler!' Exit.

After their departure I see the old waiter limp back to our table and pretend to be surprised at seeing the medal lying there.

'Vat that?'

We showed him – unnecessarily.

'You give 'em money?'

'Something,' said my father.

'Vey not get *my* money!'

He slouched off. And I remember arrival at the walls of Rothenburg – the beautiful rose-red walls which entirely surround that enchanting town. Beside the gate was a wooden board nailed at head height to the wall. On it was painted the caricature head of a Jew – Shylock locks, exaggerated nose, malevolent eyes. Obscene. Beneath, in Gothic script, was a verse. My father translated. I cannot remember anything but the gist – 'I am a Jew. I cheat Christian merchants. I violate Christian maidens –' etc., etc. Because it was so prominent and so permanently fixed there could be no question but that this was officially sanctioned. It was certainly not simply the spontaneous emotion of the citizenry which Nazi propaganda so often proclaimed. And in every shop window in Rothenburg we saw '*Juden unerwunscht*' or variations on the same theme. Nevertheless there could be no doubt that National Socialism was a mass, popular movement – a fact often denied by subsequent generations for entirely understandable reasons. And much struck us as good, reluctant though we were to admit it.

A final scene. In the great Odeonsplatz in Munich was a columned memorial to the Party dead of some occasion in the German revolution. The Munich streets were thronged with the black-uniformed SS, silver lace and buttons, white rubber truncheons swinging at the hip. At the memorial, two helmeted, rifle-carrying SS ceremonial sentries. A continuous stream of citizens climbed the steps of the memorial. Then each stood silent for a moment, when level with the sentries, and shot up an arm.

'Heil Hitler!'

We asked my father what the memorial was about. He said he thought he'd have a look. 'We'll stay here,' said my mother, and we watched from a distance while my father climbed the steps, paused opposite the sentries, at whom he directed the critical, fault-finding and formidable stare I knew rather well, and then advanced into the centre of the memorial to subject to a prolonged inspection, noticeably lacking in reverence, whatever was therein displayed. No Heil Hitler. No acknowledgement of any kind. When he rejoined us I merely remember – 'Oh, it's one or two of those fellows who died in . . .' A few glances were directed at us. No lowering of my father's voice. His expression of dislike, when he felt it, was always unmistakable. I felt curiously reassured.

The figures of Germans in my boyhood are therefore of uneven intensity and most uneven sympathy. On the one hand were the deplorable, bullying texts of anti-semitism in the windows, on the tower gate of Rothenburg, conveying a curiously medieval atmosphere, like a mad, bad fairy story. On the other the infectious music, the simple, happy faces and voices of people, especially young people, who looked, spoke and acted as if they had suddenly walked from darkness into the sun – an atmosphere which was inevitably impressive. Whatever came later it was clear that, at least for the young, Hitler *was* Germany. Of hostility or menace towards ourselves there was nothing.

5

A Long Summer Afternoon

The 1930s, as far as I was concerned, were the days of boarding school, and more than foreign places it is the memory of school which dominates the decade. At the beginning of 1930, and soon after arriving at Brechin Place, I was first sent to boarding school. St Aubyn's, Rottingdean, was built on a slope of the South Downs, so that the main playing field had a considerable downward tilt towards the sea. The buildings, austerities, peculiarities and food of such establishments have been frequently described, and St Aubyn's has had the attention of several authors, notably – and with asperity – Wilfred Thesiger. I think that as preparatory schools went in those days it was a good one. The headmaster was utterly dedicated to the school and had considerable character and generosity – his name was Lang – and some boys retained in later years the sort of affection for St Aubyn's which is generally only accorded to more mature establishments. Some, of course, loathed it both at the time and in retrospect.

I belonged to neither extreme. Games overshadowed everything, and I wasn't a star at them, but I enjoyed cricket – in a moderate sort of way; the cult of games in English boys' schools has been the subject of much writing and I can add no particular insights. The cult was sometimes, I think, excessive and unbalanced; but there are worse obsessions. St Aubyn's was not distinguished academically, and when I reached Eton I discovered, rather unnervingly, how backward I was compared to contemporaries from such places as Ludgrove, Heatherdown and Sunningdale. At St Aubyn's I had, to some extent, shone. I don't think that Lang's deliberate under-emphasis on learning was necessarily a bad thing – he himself was a distinguished mathematician as well as an athlete – but I doubt if he always struck the balance in the best place. The balance, I suspect, is better kept nowadays.

The worst thing about any school, of course, was the other boys. Boys – and no doubt girls – in the mass are not improved in character thereby. It is a weakness of the boarding school system that the emphasis placed on the corporate spirit can generate its travesty, the herd instinct. To teach children to subordinate personal desires to a common good may be sound: to enforce this by sanctions against those who 'let the side down' too easily develops into a witch hunt against the unusual, the underperforming, the unlucky or the weak. Few children disclose misery: they have pride and reticence. Self-respect is one of the strongest emotions and the young will go to great lengths to conceal suffering.

I made a few good friends at St Aubyn's and was relatively happy but by the age of thirteen I was ready to move on. Unlike modern times it was comparatively rare for parents or anybody else to visit boarding schools and take a boy out – perhaps particularly so in my case because of our domicile abroad after my first year. Sometimes when my father and mother did come – and they were with me for several weeks after Alistair's death, constantly taking me out and comforting me – we went over to Plumpton to see my godfather, Edward Hudson.

Edward Hudson, founder, proprietor and editor of *Country Life*, had a throaty and rather pedantic voice and a bald head of roughly egg-shape. He seemed to know everything about birds, plants, trees and the countryside and would shoot out questions (unanswerable) in a disconcerting way. I think children bored him. He had been devoted to my mother's first husband, Billy Congreve, and had planned to leave him the restored Lindisfarne. A great friend and collaborator of Edwin Lutyens and of Gertrude Jekyll, these three had formed something of a triumvirate over a certain sort of house and garden taste.

Uncle Edward, as I knew him, had a huge fund of knowledgeable appreciation of everything beautiful, whether domestic or in open spaces. That even a boy could sense. He was restoring an old house with stepped lakes, at Plumpton; and in London his superb house, 15 Queen Anne's Gate (running round a corner, with the Queen's statue outside the drawing room window), was a treasure house of rooms in which it was entirely satisfying – even preferable – to be left alone. A birdcage in the drawing room, constructed (I think) like a large ornate Chinese pagoda, was irresistible. Uncle Edward was kind, shy, obviously clever and curiously formidable, although not in the least seeking that effect.

In 1934 I took the Common Entrance Examination for Eton, satisfactorily achieving the top attainable form for a new boy – Remove. I thought this pretty good, and so did St Aubyn's. When I got there, however, in September, I soon discovered how poorly I had been instructed compared to other Remove new boys. They all knew Greek, whereas at St Aubyn's only two of us had taken Greek, and that as a sort of rather unstructured extra, so my Greek was indifferent. The shock was accentuated by a mistake in the Eton School Office. When I arrived I was surprised to discover that on school lists I was down as 'Hon. A. S. Fraser', and at the first 'Absence' (roll-call, when each boy answered his name, lifted his top hat and called out 'Here' to a Master's call of his name from the list) I was also disconcerted to be called out as 'Mr Fraser'; 'Mr', although I didn't at first know it, is the Etonian form of 'Honourable'. What had happened was this. My cousin, the Master (one year younger than me), had taken his first scholarship exam at the same time, but had elected to wait another year before coming up to College – the home of King's Scholars. He was an excellent scholar, in a different class from myself, and was ultimately top 'King's Scholar' of his year and Captain of the School. They thought I was he. Later – again very unlike me – he won every sort of athletic as well as academic distinction, Captain of the Boats as well as top scholar and pre-eminent musician.

Fortunately I had taken the Common Entrance Exam and received the results before he took his scholarship, so there was no awful doubt raised about my having attained Remove at all. If successful scholars didn't choose to take up their scholarships they could come up to Oppidan houses and into Remove; and in his case, of course, it would have been into the cleverest division of Remove, for his papers had been outstanding. I was, therefore, placed in classical forms well above my abilities. The error was discovered within a week and I was moved down to a lower Remove division – rather humiliating but certainly merciful. It mattered little, for with Eton a new and magical chapter of life had begun.

As so often, I was lucky, although I think my parents' good sense had designed the luck to some extent. Uncertain what a public school would be like I was, before going, nervous. My mother pointed out that huge numbers of people had done what I was about to do and had survived and enjoyed it, but the unknown is always daunting. We fear death not for its incidental suffering and its finality but because our friends have not lifted for us the curtain which protects its secrets. In the case of Eton, however, plenty of older hands had been ready to lift the curtain a little – often somewhat alarmingly, and relishing the alarm, as boys do. But a few days before the start of the Eton year, September 1934, I was taken to dinner with a Congreve great-aunt of my half-sister Gloria, and after dinner was deliberately left alone with her husband, my host. A wizened, delicate little man, years older than my father, he was an old Etonian of fanatical loyalty and devotion.

He talked to me. He talked with such enthusiasm and happiness that I began to see life through different spectacles. He talked of Eton as a glorious inheritance (his words), of the extraordinary good fortune of anyone enabled to share it. He spoke, unaffectedly, of its beauty, its traditions. He mentioned its (to me mysterious) language, customs, peculiarities with immense reminiscent affection. He congratulated me on being about to experience all this. He could think of no brighter destiny. Afterwards I learned that he was regarded in the family as something of a joke, a bore, because of his single-minded love of Eton, a boy who had refused to grow up. So be it. He did a great deal for me, and I slept happily that night.

Then the formidable preparations had to be made. There was much visiting of tailors and problems of how much money I would need. Eventually, in grey flannel suit (wrong), blue shirt and white detachable collar (wrong) and Old St Aubyn's tie (utterly wrong), I bowled in a car over Barnes Pool Bridge and was introduced to my Housemaster, known henceforth as My Tutor: Mr J. D. Upcott, at Keate House in Keate's Lane.

My first impression of Eton was of size. I imagined 'school' as being a coherent collection of buildings. This seemed a sort of town. I said to my mother, as we approached the junction of Keate's Lane, 'Which is Eton?' She said it was all Eton. Later that first afternoon we new boys were taken on a brief tour by Upcott, during which we began to get to know him.

For Etonians the character of the Housemaster was all-important. There were good and bad Houses, dull or stimulating Houses, unsuccessful and star Houses, miserable and happy Houses. It all depended on the man at the top. If he was weak, boys arrogated too much to themselves and – exactly as in any society – freedom from ultimate higher control could be hell for those at the bottom. If he was boring, dullness tended to prevail. If he was obtuse – one could continue indefinitely. Most Eton Housemasters in my time had character and, I think, a good deal of wisdom. Bad Houses were rare. I think it was a benefit of the era that most men of the Housemasters' age had served as officers in the Great War. They knew something about command.

Jack Upcott certainly did. A Wykehamist, he had served on the Western Front in the Devonshire Regiment. He ran the House like a good battalion or company commander – trusting his subordinates (the 'Library' of senior boys and in particular the Captain of the House), loyal to them, and backing them up, apparently not interfering, never spying on his boys: but, without advertising it, quietly knowing what was going on. Every evening 'after prayers', when we were confined to our rooms before Lights Out, he visited every boy for a minute or so; I doubt he ever missed this ritual. If he had guests for dinner he took them round with him. He expected not silence but some sort of conversation, some initiative: '*Say something, boy!*' He strode about the House noisily, with éclat, advertising his presence, disdaining any attempt to catch people in misbehaviour. He had a considerable sense of humour. He never asked questions or obtruded his own reading of a situation; yet that reading was profound. He knew his boys well, and sometimes they hardly guessed it.

Upcott was a man of the world, openly derisory of some of the pettier habits of schoolmasters and frankly mocking of some of his colleagues. He taught us to laugh at a lot of life, and especially at ourselves. He taught us to laugh at misfortune or punishment – if one was beaten (with a cane, by the Captain of the House, for some often trivial misdemeanour) Upcott would, on his evening visit, say, 'Oh, I know! You've been beaten, haven't you!' and roar with laughter. Unfeeling? I don't think so. He calculated such things very shrewdly and he was a kind man; but he never encouraged a boy to take set-backs tragically or make much of physical pain.

Upcott affected a mild eccentricity and flamboyance of manner, but with a touch of self-mockery always working behind the eyes. A dedicated fly-fisherman, he had a house in Devon; his expert subject was the English seamen of the Elizabethan age, a choice wholly in character. He was also a skilled maker of models of the ships of the period, accurately rigged. He was an erudite and devout Christian of High Church convictions; his wife was a shy and gentle Frenchwoman, who took little part in the management of the House but who knew more about us, I suspect, than we guessed.

As a boy grew older he received, more and more, Upcott's friendship, always extended on equal and uncondescending terms. He relished the English language, easily communicated enthusiasm, and liked an argument, which he would conduct fairly but vigorously, using a good deal of personal abuse, which he expected to be reciprocated. He would say, after some verbal exchange of shots with me on his evening tour of the House to say goodnight, 'What's the use of arguing with you, you're a reactionary and obstinate little Scotsman,' and I would retort, 'And you're a narrow-minded Devonian pedagogue, sir,' and he would stride off, slamming the door, and loving it. He understood exactly how to run an Eton House, and in my five years at Eton I never remember, even with retrospective judgement, that he made a serious mistake. He was a little bored by some boys, but always kind to them. His somewhat pyrotechnic manner used to dumbfound and silence a few. But most were stimulated and admiring: and the House had an atmosphere of fairness, friendliness, laughter and trust.

From the start I loved Eton. I liked the sense that it was, to an extraordinary degree, a free and adult society. One sank or swam. From the first day one had one's own room, to decorate as one wished, a little private kingdom where one did much of one's work, had one's tea in a 'Mess' with a friend, could be alone.

It is said that the age of going to such a school is too tender for exposure to the raw competitions of life. I cannot see why. One of the prime curses of the English private educational system, as it has evolved, is the artificial immaturity it imposes. Some schools appear –

or certainly used to appear – to go on the premise that the longer boyhood is prolonged the better. Some parents appear to condone the treatment; in particular by a typical – although not universal – aversion to 'cramming' and to demanding intensive effort at an early age. If a boy has real intellectual quality the earlier and harder his mind works the better. Eton, in this, resembled the world. If one wanted to get on one had to work, and if one failed that was one's own misfortune. There were plenty of stimulants, encouragements, and an excellent tutorial system of 'Private Business', discussions of a subject by a small handful of boys with a Tutor; but more work was left to us to do in our own time than in most schools. The curriculum was comparatively uncrowded. We were remarkably free. It is no exaggeration to say that Eton, unlike most schools, treated boys as the world treats adults – that is, frequently with indifference, expecting obedience to often irrational laws, and rewarding the intelligent, the gifted, the handsome, the entertaining and the strong with generosity and applause. Also like the world – at least the civilized world – it was indulgent to eccentrics and expected the minumum conformity necessary for communal existence, health, and the assurance of a comfortable life for those in power.

I loved Eton for its beauty, too, in all seasons. The walk through School Yard, the Cloisters, Weston's Yard and then along the river was always enchanting, and I hope always will be. The mellow colour of Eton's brick set a standard against which Etonians generally measure Tudor and Jacobean brickwork thereafter. The sense of bustle in the winter evenings, as the dusk fell and the boys' Houses hummed with light and life among the smells of frying sausages and browning toast, and 'Lock-up' approached; the long summer afternoons and evenings, in which cricket was played or watched, bumping races were conducted on the river amidst huge enthusiasm, new books were discovered, new friends made; all these things and a hundred others soon brought home to me that I had been rightly informed. Eton was, indeed, a glorious inheritance. The sense of continuity and history was irresistible.

Eton believed in liberty, in the old, brutal sense of leaving people to get on in their own way. This was, of course, frightening at first, particularly in the first days. There was a sense of being entirely lost, without identity, unrecognized by the mass of boys and masters sweeping past with the confidence of familiarity; of finding that one had to discover where to go, what lesson was to be learned, what books to bring; of finding that the books needed buying, and were sometimes unobtainable, but that Eton was indifferent to such individual problems. There was a sense of a strange language, and of the sudden impact of unfamiliar customs and awe-inspiring sophistication. There was also, however, a sense of opportunity: to follow any hobby or interest, to play any game in good company, to read what one liked and discover more and more and more. Eton was more like the world than any other school: it had more tolerance, perhaps suffered more evil, perhaps enabled more good. I have said that it was built on the belief in liberty. It was also something of a relic of an aristocratic and pre-Victorian past. It did not seek to turn out 'gentlemen'. In fact I don't think it seeks, or in my day sought, to turn out any particular article. We were not greatly pressed upon or stifled by the team spirit, the need to conform. Inevitably – since Eton is a school, although quite unlike any other and in Etonian eyes entirely superior to all – a certain amount of corporate feeling existed: and we got unreasonably elated about the success of our particular House, although this was tempered by a rational mistrust of enthusiasm, and a scepticism which owed more to Lord Chesterfield than to Dr Arnold. Individual prowess was admired, and individual sports – boxing, fives, fencing, racquets – held almost equal prestige with those in which a spurious unselfishness was accounted the highest of virtues.

For these various reasons, among a thousand others, Eton was a school where most boys could be happy: it was also a school to which a good many boys gave their love. I was one.

Eton was, above all, about friendship, about people, and about the characters who composed our world and awoke in us, in varying degrees, admiration, curiosity or mirth.

When I arrived the Provost of Eton was M. R. 'Monty' James, a previous Provost of King's College, Cambridge and the author of some of the best ghost stories in the language. I was familiar with these and had often re-told them, after lights out, to fellow occupants of my St Aubyn's dormitories. The Provost – the resident Chairman of the Fellows, or Governors – was the highest individual authority at Eton, but seemed to have little contact with the running of the school. He was, however, one of the three individuals (the others were the Vice Provost and the Headmaster) who were saluted by passing boys with the removal of hat or cap, as opposed to the 'capping' – the raising of finger to hat-brim, executed with maximum slovenliness – which was obligatory for other masters ('beaks', as they were invariably known). Monty James died in my second year, in June 1936, and the funeral took place at Eton one afternoon. It is the only funeral I remember which was accompanied with what, in earlier times, would have been customary ritual. We all had to remain in our Houses while the procession weaved its way through Eton from, I suppose, Provost's Lodge to College Chapel and from Chapel to Cemetery. We had to remain not only in our Houses but in our rooms, alone, with the blinds drawn! I can imagine a reaction of 'How absurd! How much better for boys to be out taking exercise, or working for that matter! Confined to room, blinds drawn in the middle of the afternoon!' Such reaction would be disproportionate. What does it matter whether or not I played another game of fives, looked at another book in the library or ate yet another ice-cream in Rowlands? It is of absolutely no consequence; while it is something to remember Monty James's funeral. Its always best to give the young memories, especially unique memories; and not to consult their transient wishes in the process.

Monty James was succeeded by Lord Hugh Cecil, a distinguished Churchman and Tory Parliamentarian of an earlier age – he had led some of the rowdiest wing of the Tory Party at the turn of the century. He had never married and I believe that Provost's Lodge was his first individual home beyond rooms in London – he had always had the same room at Hatfield which had been his as a boy, in that great Jacobean palace from which the Cecils contemplate the adjacent industrial town and the Hertfordshire countryside, princely, affable and detached.

Known as 'Linky', he had a squeaky, precise voice which was much imitated. He immediately began to institute changes in the College Chapel services. The general thrust of these was to restore the Eucharist to its central position as the main service on Sundays (we went to chapel twice on Sundays, or three times if one attended Early Service, Holy Communion before breakfast: and once on weekdays, after breakfast). Hugh Cecil didn't think much of the Sunday morning service (Matins, more or less) and abolished it. He was then prevailed upon (I think) to cut the replacement, the extended Choral Communion, in half; so that one could go out after the sermon but before Communion, which made it to some extent resemble what had gone before but to a significant and welcome degree shorter. Pretty well everybody availed himself of this privilege; the Cecil innovations never really 'took'. As a matter of fact I think Linky was right, but the manner of his attempt ran against the immense conservatism of boys.

He was intransigent in all things, however. One Conduct (at Eton the Chaplains are known as 'Conducts') by mistake uttered a blessing after the sermon and before we trooped out. We heard him verbally chastised by the Provost in the ante-chapel: 'Mr So-and-So, because the less religious members of the congregation choose to leave half way through the service that is no reason why they should be blessed!' When Linky was installed as Provost he was welcomed, according to ancient custom, by the Captain of the School (the senior scholar) and the Captain of the Oppidans (the senior non-scholar) on the steps running from School Yard up to College Chapel. Each of the two boys reads a Latin address and the new Provost, in replying, removes his headdress (a velvet cap) and replaces it. The whole school is in attendance at the foot of the steps. Linky put his velvet cap back on the wrong way round, which delighted us.

Linky used to entertain senior boys to breakfasts and dinners; and at dinner wine flowed. I never rated one of these parties but good stories always emerged from them, and although the stories have in many cases gained wider currency it was something to have heard them, even at second hand, from Linky's own mouth. His father had been the long-serving Victorian Prime Minister, Lord Salisbury, surely one of the most distinctive political figures of his day. Linky, memorably, described to an audience of boys how he remembered, as a tiny child, peering through the upper banisters of the great staircase at Hatfield and recognizing a visitor, just arrived, as none other than his father's arch-enemy, Mr Gladstone.

The infant Linky piped through the banisters, 'Go away! You wicked man!' Mr Gladstone looked up, masterful, impressive. 'Why am I wicked?'

'Because my father says you are.'

'Then why has Lord Salisbury invited me to stay at Hatfield?'

Hugh Cecil simply replied, 'Because he's going to kill you!'

Linky had been a formidable and witty controversialist, well-known for his propensity to espouse, if he thought it necessary, the most unpopular causes (certainly in conversation and sometimes in Parliament also). He pursued every point from first principles. He was merciless with illogicality. He was no respecter of persons, including his own. In the Great War, at the age of forty-five and completely unmechanical (he regarded bicycling as both difficult and alarming), he had learned to fly, with the Royal Flying Corps, and joined Trenchard's staff. He was the subject of innumerable anecdotes, the inspiration (if not always accurately reported) of some inimitable quotations. I think the majority of Eton masters found him perplexing and often exasperating. We found him a great source of enjoyment, and it enhanced our sense of Eton's uniqueness that so eccentric a human being, with so utterly independent a mind, should reign over our little kingdom.

The Headmaster's name was Claude Elliott. He had, I suspect, a great deal to endure at Linky's hands. He had succeeded Cyril Alington shortly before my own arrival – a contrast of chalk and cheese. Alington had been stimulating, handsome, theatrical in voice and manner, an incomparable preacher who, when he returned to preach to us, as he frequently did (he was by now Dean of Durham), had every boy in College Chapel silent, moved and tense on the edge of his pew. Elliott did not, I think, have that or any other very memorable effect on anybody. The Headmaster of Eton's job is not to know individual boys – there are far too many and if he attempts to he will muddy the waters; it is to know the masters, and in particular the Housemasters. It is with them that the school's reputation will lie. It is also, I imagine, to run the scholastic and business side of the school with competence: to be a respectable academic, an organizer, a manager. I daresay it is also important that a Headmaster has a sharp eye and ear for Public Relations: the school's image is bound to be one of his primary concerns.

I suspect that in all this Elliott was efficient, in a low-key, uninspiring way. I never met him while at Eton (not, as I have emphasized, a matter of criticism of a Headmaster) but once or twice afterwards our paths crossed and he was invariably agreeable. He had little direct impact on our lives and he was not, like Linky, a 'character'; but he never tried to be, and I have no doubt that his decisions were sensible, and that his somewhat self-effacing personality was not unhelpful to the school, in contrast to the dramatic atmosphere which had surrounded Alington and the roaring eccentricity which appeared to dominate Provost's Lodge. Later, Elliott became Provost himself.

The King, George VI, and the Queen, having only recently succeeded to their thrones, visited Eton – I think in Ascot week, 1937. The school was assembled on the main cricket field, Agar's Plough, where the 1st XI played, and Their Majesties arrived in an open landau with a sovereign's escort of Household Cavalry. They then walked round the large circle we formed – close inspection of the great seemed much rarer and more memorable in those pre-television days.

Queen Elizabeth was walking with the Provost. I tried to eavesdrop as they passed me, talking.

'Did you have a good Fourth of June?'

'It was exactly as ever, Ma'am, I'm glad to say,' I heard Linky reply, 'I cannot recall the weather.' A characteristic exchange.

Friends abounded, and as my own tastes and interests developed new friends were made. Inevitably my closest Eton friends, certainly for most of life there, were in my own House. Almost all those who were dearest to me at Upcott's have died long before me. Of the five who were elected to our Library – the 'House Prefects' – with me at the beginning of my last year three were killed in the war, which began in September 1939, as were a particularly large number of my friends in other Houses. Like the friends I was later to make and lose in my Regiment I often – quite a usual experience, I believe – feel them extraordinarily close to me as life extends, hearing their voices, above all their irrepressible laughter. Youth, after all, is very much a matter of laughter; of a good many tears as well as some ecstasy, but above all of laughter.

English education – even up to the time when I was a boy – has been severely criticized for its classical bias, its emphasis on the humanities, even its idealism. The great Victorian promoters of the modern public school have been vilified for their absorption in building character, for their concentration on Christian principle and civilized taste, rather than on science and practical skills appropriate to the creation of wealth. Certainly the cap fits. If one took an adverse report, a 'Rip' (an inadequate paper in form was torn or 'ripped' at the top, and one then had to get it signed by one's Housemaster, to ensure reprimand or punishment), from a science master to Upcott he simply observed, 'Oh, science!' and signed it with a yawn and without a second glance. 'Practical skills' he regarded as not in the least what education was all about. 'You are here,' he would say, 'to exercise and be made to exercise that thing called a mind. Just like a muscle.' And he regarded the classics as particularly good training for that muscle. When the time came for me to specialize and we had to state preferences he roared with laughter at me when I said I would like to read History. He himself was a historian.

'Don't be absurd, David! You'll read history all your life. You enjoy it! You're here not to indulge your tastes but to stretch your mind.'

So I read Classics.

The attitude I have attributed to my Tutor has been held to be responsible, in large part, for our decline as a nation, and our lack of industrial competitiveness – and military preparedness – in the first half of the twentieth century. I understand the argument, and the point of view is held by several observers and historians whom I respect: but I don't agree. Our principal failures in that century – I am particularly thinking of the period between the two World Wars – derived from refusing to face facts as they demonstrably were and in substituting hope for objective realism. Wishful thinking is essentially human, and it can, obviously, afflict high-minded idealists very especially – since the idealism can lead to such an aversion from the disagreeable as to distort the vision. But I don't think men trained primarily in the humanities are particularly prone to this: and I doubt whether scientists and engineers are immune. I accept the reality of the symptom but question the diagnosis of the cause.

I confess to impatience with products of the English school system of my time who portray the whole experience, often in lurid terms, as unimaginably tough, brutal and backward. This may have been true in the early or middle nineteenth century (although even then evidence is by no means all one way) but, in my day and certainly after, such caricatures are ludicrous. Memory plays tricks, of course, and the desire to exaggerate and dramatize past experience is natural; but I suspect some portrayals have derived both from self-pity and from a desire to deprecate privilege. An Eton – or any privately financed – education is described, and often denounced, as 'privilege', and it is probably true that some products of it have felt the need to offset this by explaining how ghastly it all was, and how truly unlucky the privilege. Understandable – but wrong. Of course we were privileged – and lucky. We grew up among cultivated men in beautiful surroundings and in an atmosphere where such brutality as existed (and it was very little) was totally overshadowed by the enjoyment, the ease and the atmosphere of friendship and civilization. Of course life was unpampered and often comfortless; but that applied everywhere, and is not a subject of tragedy.

Public events sometimes memorably intruded. Etonians probably often took their opinions from the atmosphere at home, although a few reacted in an ostentatiously contrary direction. These were years of mass unemployment. A large body of 'hunger marchers' from the North of England tramped through Eton on their way to Windsor to present a petition to the King. The Red Flag and the hammer and sickle were prominent. But only later in life did I realize fully the bitterness those years caused, and the confused political attitudes they produced. Sir Oswald Mosley's Blackshirts used to come down, selling the Fascist newspaper outside the school stores, where they were often assaulted by irritated boys. The Spanish Civil War, which broke out in 1936, aroused a good deal of feeling in one way or another. My own views, influenced a good deal by Granny Saltoun, were ferociously Francoist, and although (as my father patiently emphasized) there were two sides to the question my later acquaintance with Spain and Spaniards – and the course of European events after 1945 – strengthened this sympathy rather than the reverse. Few could deny that there was cruelty shown to the defeated Republicans at the end of a war in which such horrible things had been done by both sides, but much written in this country about Franco and his regime has been prejudiced and absurd. He no doubt made mistakes but at the start he saved Spain. When I later discovered that Kim Philby, the British traitor, had been involved in an NKVD plot to assassinate the Spanish Caudillo it provided a further indication of his merits. My uncle Alistair likened Franco to the Emperor Augustus in his ability to rule strongly and ultimately smooth earlier animosities. Meanwhile the war went on – reported in the British press on the whole in anti-Nationalist terms – and we took some interest in the military side, where, unusually, I found my team winning.

But domestic affairs had the most impact at that time and a more compelling picture is of Upcott's drawing room one winter evening in 1936. It was already after 'Prayers', the nine o'clock ritual in the House dining room. We were summoned from our rooms, and assembled in dressing gowns, to My Tutor's drawing room on the 'Private Side'. His wireless was playing loudly.

'You will now hear the King's final words to his people.'

Edward VIII had probably had a poor press in most Etonians' homes, certainly of the more conventional kind. We had all heard horror stories of his behaviour – of how he had cancelled some charitable visit, purely in order to meet Mrs Simpson; of how he had worn extraordinary clothes on some stuffy occasion, outraging the proprieties; of how 'Americanized' he was, with his peculiar twang, his hat or cap worn at a rakish angle. The better-informed boys muttered darkly. The old King, George V, had been a father-figure, remote, revered. At his funeral boys of the Eton Officer Training Corps had lined part of the route through Windsor Castle from the Long Walk across the Lower and Middle Wards to St George's Chapel, wearing the peculiar maroon-khaki uniform of the Eton Corps, resting on their arms reversed. The rest of us – I was still too young to join the Corps – had been allowed up to the Castle to squeeze in behind them and watch the procession. I can see the massed dignitaries stepping past in close order, identified by the knowledgeable: the Prince of Piedmont in long and splendid white cape and gold helmet: the representative of Finland, the magnificent Marshal Mannerheim, in the furred cap and pelisse of a cavalryman from another age; the King's Company of the Grenadiers slow marching on either side of the gun-carriage drawn by sailors on which the King's coffin lay. We had seen all that. That was Kingship. And now we had a youngish man who wore odd clothes of the kind we had all been taught to regard as caddish, and who talked like an American.

Then the stories about Mrs Simpson had at last reached the press and suddenly the crisis broke. Abdication – it all happened, as far as the public were concerned, with extraordinary speed – was so bizarre as to be almost incomprehensible. A whole order of life was being overturned. There was a good deal of resentment. The Waits were already out singing carols and hoping for pennies in Windsor and Eton, and we heard –

> 'Hark the Herald Angels sing,
> Mrs Simpson's pinched our King.'

In Upcott's drawing room we listened. Most of us had heard the King's voice before, probably on newsreels at the cinema. I had seen him once – inspecting a battalion of Grenadiers at Chelsea Barracks after their return from Egypt. He served with the Grenadiers in the First World War, made many friends and maintained a particularly strong affection for (and knowledge of) the Regiment. Now he was talking to the whole Empire. We were, on the whole, appalled. He said he couldn't go on 'without the woman I love' – surely, we felt, instinctively, a gutless, undignified attitude for a king. Our reactions were hurt, unsympathetic, contemptuous. A few boys whose parents knew him spoke up for the King but they got little support. When it was reported that others who were on his side included Winston Churchill (pretty generally execrated as unreliable, particularly by my Saltoun grandparents) and Lord Beaverbrook, for whom absolutely no words of disparagement were adequate, the cause of Edward VIII did not improve.

My memory moves on from that drawing room on a December evening in 1936 in Keate's Lane. Twenty years later, in 1956, I was Regimental Adjutant of the Grenadier Guards (at that time a Regiment of three battalions – there had been four in the First World War and six in the Second). A great Tercentenary celebration was in preparation – the Regiment was founded in 1656 by Charles II in exile, in Flanders. One of the Tercentenary events was to be a huge exhibition of pictures and memorabilia, for which the Queen had made available the State Rooms in St James's Palace. In Wellington Barracks, at Regimental Headquarters, the telephone rang on my desk one morning.

'Duke of Windsor here. Can I speak to the Lieutenant-Colonel?'

Taken a good deal aback I explained that this officer would not be in his office until the afternoon. What could I do to help His Royal Highness?

The Duke explained that he'd heard about our exhibition. He had some things we might think it appropriate to borrow. He was visiting London. Could he come and talk about it? We agreed a time that very afternoon and at three o'clock, accompanied by Lord Dudley, he arrived.

Before this the Lieutenant-Colonel, Tom Butler, had ruminated on what we should do to entertain the Duke. 'We must present Fred Turner to him,' he said. Fred Turner, retired Lieutenant-Colonel Quartermaster, a past Regimental Sergeant Major and Quartermaster of immense character and distinction, had an office in the same building as ourselves in his capacity as General Secretary of the Grenadier Comrades' Association. Like the Duke of Windsor he had served in the First World War.

When the Duke arrived he immediately showed enormous interest in – and infectious enthusiasm for – all our plans and arrangements. He told us what he planned to lend – his collection of Grenadier prints and artefacts was considerable. He looked around, inspected various glass cases, which took up a lot of the floor space at Regimental Headquarters, pointed things out to Lord Dudley, commented – restless, energetic, amused. At one glass case he stopped. It held a full-dress tunic and on it was a plaque – 'Tunic worn by His Majesty King George VI as Colonel-in-Chief of the Grenadier Guards.'

'Look at this, Eric,' the Duke called out to Lord Dudley. 'Look at this! They've got my tunic!'

I saw Tom Butler's mouth start to open and prayed he wouldn't try to put the record straight. I needn't have worried, as the Duke simply chuckled and said, 'My tunic! My tunic!' and, turning away, 'Then I passed it on to my brother!'

After quite a bit of this, with conversation never flagging, Tom Butler brought in Fred Turner to present. I will always see the Duke of Windsor's face during this conversation, bright, eager, features mobile.

'What Battalion did you join, Turner?'

'Second Battalion, Sir, in early 1917. Just after they came out of the Somme battle.'

'Ah, well, I was never in the Second Battalion but I used to visit them often, of course, look up my friends and so forth.' (He had been made to stay on the GHQ staff, to his intense annoyance.) 'Which Company did you join?'

'No. 3 Company, Sir.'

'Right. — was Company Sergeant Major and — was Pay Sergeant. Then there was that nice Pioneer Sergeant, what was his name?'

Fred Turner was floundering a little. 'Would it have been —, Sir?'

'No, no, he was Pay Sergeant of No. 2. Great character, Nottingham man, huge number of children!' And so on. Afterwards Fred told me that he'd been able to check and that the Duke of Windsor hadn't made a mistake. He hadn't known he was going to meet Fred Turner; he was confronted, unprepared, with a man he'd never met; he talked of a Battalion of Grenadiers – not one in which he'd served – visited occasionally forty years before, talked with lively recollection, names not forgotten, of the members of the Sergeants' Mess of that Battalion; and had shown every sign of being able to keep it up as long as we wanted. Fred Turner was completely overcome. When I took leave of the Duke at the steps down from Regimental Headquarters to the parade ground of Wellington Barracks he simply took my hand and said, 'Thank you. I enjoyed my visit greatly,' as he spoke my name and looked very directly into my eyes.

There have been many disagreeable stories of the Duke of Windsor as a monarch, as a public man. There has been plenty of adverse criticism and it will continue. He has been alleged to have fallen for Nazi overtures, to have hoped for an end to the war in which he might play a constructive part; to have been disloyal. There may have been something in some of this, although much is transparently ignorant as well as malicious. Neverthelss it is easy to forget the yearning for peace in the 1930s and the readiness to hope that people of all countries – and especially countries which had confronted each other and suffered in a frightful war less than twenty years before – could find more understanding of, and patience with, opposing viewpoints. When, as Duke of Windsor, Edward toured Germany in 1937 this was certainly the emotion which chiefly moved him. Of course he was indiscreet, but he cared. Descriptions of him as a traitor (as were produced in a malicious and ill-informed British television programme in 1995) were, and remain, ludicrous rubbish.

It is easy to forget the misery of the unemployment at that time and of how as King he visited South Wales – a visit later disparaged – and was met by a huge concourse of unemployed miners. Old soldiers, to a man. I can still hear a later radio programme about it, in the 1950s, and one of those present remembering, 'I stepped forward, saluted, said, "Four hundred ex-members of — Battalion South Wales Borderers, Sir. Unemployed."'

The King, the voice went on, was clearly and utterly shattered. And as the programme continued, I heard in musical Welsh tones, the 'No matter what they say, he was very popular down here. He still is.'

In Wellington Barracks that day in 1956 I knew perfectly well that whatever ill people had spoken of him, with whatever accuracy, this was a man for whom it would be easy to die. The fact, which I warmly acknowledge, that his brother made a greatly superior king, unselfish and dedicated, and that our country was fortunate in the way matters turned out, in no way diminished the intensity of the impression I received.

When I had been four years at Eton Neville Chamberlain flew, successively, to Berchtesgaden, to Bad Godesberg and to Munich, to see Hitler and negotiate – if the word is not absurd in the context – a European Settlement which would remove the risk of war. The price – the initial price – was the Sudetenland, a strip of Czechoslovakia adjacent to Germany and largely inhabited by Germans who had never in the least desired to be incorporated into the Czech State created out of the dismembered Habsburg Empire by the Treaty of Versailles.

Since Hitler tended to put the price up at each of these successive and disastrous encounters, and since there were, wrongly, supposed to be limits to what the world, and especially Britain and France, would swallow, war looked likely; and shortly after the beginning of the school year, in September 1938, we were assembled and told that anybody whose parents wished it could go home. For those who remained there would be no ordinary curriculum but a delightfully eccentric programme of filling sandbags (under instruction), learning something of how to deal with incendiary bombs, and the like. My parents were abroad (after commanding a Grenadier battalion, first at Windsor then in London, my father had recently been appointed military attaché at our Embassy in Paris) so I stayed at Eton. After a while we were told by Jack Upcott that various negotiations were under way, initially sponsored by Mussolini. War, he said, was now improbable.

My greatest friend in my House throughout my time at Eton was called Tom Miller. He was a charming, cultivated boy, hard-working, dark and rather Spanish in appearance, very good at games, and particularly interested in European history since 1870. We had together watched the flagrant dishonesty of the Nazi Government, the mixture of bluster and falsehood, with disgust. Worst of all, however, was the feeling that we in England were frightened: that we deliberately averted our eyes from evil, and that we chose to think well – or not too badly – of the Nazis, not through honest, if misplaced charity, nor even through stupidity, but through craven fear of the consequences of standing up for the right. I have had this feeling on more recent occasions, and it is the worst experience of all.

When the Munich Settlement was announced Tom and I felt utterly and irreparably miserable. We were allowed to go by bus to see Neville Chamberlain return – he arrived at Northolt Airport, and we in fact failed to see him. Tom and I had discussed whether to boo him as a futile gesture of loathing, but decided that it was a poor sort of act.

The majority were jubilant. The other members of our House Library stuck up a large photograph of Chamberlain – we at least got that down. We two were accused of being warmongers. I was told that because my father was a soldier I had no feeling for peace. We tried to explain the thing that stuck largest in the throat – 'Peace with Honour'.

We prophesied – gloomily and accurately. I have often been wrong in life, and often in a small minority – but I think I was right then, although I look back with a little compunction on our dismissal of that near-universal desire for peace as, mainly, cowardice. I realize now that there was honourable feeling there too.

I was a keen member of the Officer Training Corps at Eton, and found all aspects of military life – drill, shooting, Field Days, tactical instruction – very congenial. This was extremely unfashionable. Not only was it de rigueur to regard the 'Corps' (to which, although 'voluntary', almost everybody belonged) as a joke in bad taste; but the Regular Army itself was generally derided as a profession. It was held to be run on lines of archaic idiocy, where everything followed obscure and unnecessary laws alien to common sense. The same boys who took this view as a matter of course became enthusiastic and dedicated members of their Regiments within a few years. Etonian losses in the war of '39–'45 (all three services) were not as high as in the war of '14–'18, but they were not as comparably lower as was the national total. Eton lost 1,200 men in '14–'18 and about 750 in '39–'45.

We used to parade once weekly for drill, weapon-training, map-reading and so forth. Several times a year there were Field Days – a march to Windsor railway station: off to somewhere near Aldershot or Chobham: a march to some heather-covered *champs de manoeuvre*, and deployment (we constituted an entire and rather large battalion, of five companies) into tactical formation for some operation: wildly uncontrolled combat against the 'enemy' (on lucky days, another school), projectiles like pencils occasionally fired by our issued blank cartridges at Umpires' horses – a handful of regular officers were detailed to organize, supervise and umpire these manoeuvres; a return journey by train (behaviour disorderly), form up, march back to Eton behind the Corps of Drums of the Guards Battalion stationed at Windsor. Our commanders were masters holding territorial com-missions – and a number of them, hardly older than ourselves, were killed before 1945.

My letter home after my first Field Day gives something of the flavour:

. . . after about 1 mile over the heather we lay down on top of a small hill which commanded a very good view. Then we pushed on over a lot more heather and came to a wood. We found a section of No. 4 Company lost. Herbert, a Maths beak, commands our company. Coleridge* commands 4, a huge man, very strong. 'Please Sir, do you know where Mr Coleridge is?' 'He's doing something very extraordinary, somewhere amazing,' said Herbert.

---

* Fred Coleridge, a rightly celebrated Eton character, returned to it after distinguished war service, and ended as Vice Provost.

But although mockery was obligatory a sense was in the air that for at least some of us there might soon be a dramatic and unplanned change in our circumstances.

The summer Half of 1939 was a curious period. The general opinion, by then, was that war, sooner or later, was inevitable. A guarantee had been given to Poland, and as far as we could gather no secret was made in Germany that the Germans intended to settle the Polish question by force.

Conscription had been introduced in England, and the press began to take its inevitably renewed interest in the Army. The Corps paraded for the annual inspection, on that occasion by the Duke of Gloucester, and marched past in slow and quick time in columns of wavering half-companies. Corps camp, which normally started the summer holidays, was cancelled. The following Michaelmas Half was intended to be my last and I was due to return to be Captain of the House, with Tom Miller Captain of Games. Many friends left, some for Sandhurst.

But before the end of that Half, in July 1939, extraordinary scenes took place at the annual Eton and Harrow cricket match at Lord's. In earlier times – until, I think, 1920, just after the end of the First World War – there had been a great yearly rough-house between Etonians and Harrovians of all ages, all over the cricket ground at the end of play. There were long-ago stories of smashed tophats, broken noses, uncontrolled rioting. Then the MCC authorities had called 'enough'. If such disgraceful scenes were to happen the schools could no longer play each other on the sacred turf. In both schools, therefore, stern warnings were issued. The match continued at Lord's as an annual – largely social – function through the 1920s and 1930s, and when stumps were drawn people left without incident. In fact Etonians, and probably Harrovians, had largely left already (attendance was not compulsory) because the cricket took place – a two-day match – on the Friday and Saturday of our summer 'Long Leave', and boys were heading for home; or, if in London, for a family junket, theatre and so forth. During my time, therefore, 'Lord's' was a tame affair, not made less tame by the fact that the match was almost invariably drawn.

Until 1939. That Saturday there was electricity in the air. Harrow was winning. It looked as if there was actually to be a finish. They had not won since, I think, 1911. When the final run was scored the

Harrovians erupted. They had been making a good deal of noise – the Etonians, anyway fewer in number through early departures and defections, had been more subdued. Now, all over the ground, morning-coated figures of all ages (everyone went to the match in tailcoats and top hats in those days) were racing towards the Pavilion. We all joined in and in front of the rails the huge crowds massed, yelling to their teams to come out on to the balconies and respond to the shouts. '*Harro-o-w! Eton! Eton!*'

Then a top hat was smashed over its owner's head, then another, then another. Then the blows began, scrums were formed, carnations littered the grass, trousers were ripped from Etonian and Harrovian limbs. In the whole arena between the Pavilion and the wicket there were innumerable fights going on – groups, single combat, the lot. The noise was deafening. I was staying the weekend with friends, Reggie and Dolly Marriott, in their house in Eaton Place – their son Miles was an exact contemporary and friend and we were at the match together but got separated. We were due to go to a theatre – 'See you at Eaton Place, get a taxi!' were Miles's yelled words to me before we were separated by the mêlée. '*Harrow!*' '*Eton!*' I can see an elderly cleric, in top hat with strings attached in the senior clerical manner, gaiters on his legs, Harrow's cornflower in his buttonhole as he stood triumphant at the Pavilion rails, grinning, confronting us. '*Harrow!*' I brought up the crook of my umbrella – I was by the rails and could reach him – and smashed it through his top hat. It was an exquisite sensation.

Eventually I reached Eaton Place, clothes much damaged. The press – very naturally – attacked this loutish behaviour with energy. 'Our "Gentlemen" disport themselves!' was the evening paper headline. The attack was wholly justified. Nevertheless I enjoyed myself more than I would for a long time, and so did everyone else. I am sure that the imminence of war – sensed, even if not outwardly accepted, as highly probable – lay at the heart of much of this release of aggression. Violence and frustration were in the air. Nobody had been yet allowed to vent them on Hitler. For the moment, Harrow would do.

At the start of those summer holidays I spent several weeks in Brittany with my father and mother; 'home' was now a charming flat in Paris.

We played golf at St Briac, explored St Malo, Mont St Michel, Combourg (my mother was absorbed in reading Chateaubriand, once the chateau's inhabitant), Fort Lalatte, where Tristan once sang to Isolde. Sea, heather, heat haze. A very hot August. Little sense of doom. Everything seemed out of human hands. My father was determinedly optimistic. He had great – and, alas, unjustified – belief in General Gamelin, the French Supreme Commander, but he had spent a good deal of his time as military attaché pointing out to the British Government the futility and inadequacy of their own preparations for war. Chamberlain and his Government had been so determined not to have a repetition of the war that had ended only twenty years earlier that they refused to face the need for a 'Continental Commitment' for the (anyway tiny) British Army. They supposed that the only threat to Britain was from massive aerial bombardment (for which Germany was in fact not yet ready). They thought – or pretended to think – that the Alliance with France which was belatedly negotiated could be sufficiently honoured by the existence of the comparatively formidable Royal Navy. The idea, then and always, was futile. Sea power, whose effect is attritional and protracted, can certainly make the difference to the ultimate outcome of a long war, but it cannot defend the frontiers of a Continental Power from invasion by land. France was threatened, if at all, by the German Army.

I had arranged to go from Brittany to Scotland. I crossed the Channel, took the train north, and set out on a walking tour in the West Highlands, with Peter Balfour, another great friend. We tramped across Ross-shire from coast to coast, walked south across the hills from Ullapool, and spent two days at Kinlochewe with Tony Garton, shooting grouse over dogs and enjoying that lovely place. Then we shouldered our rucksacks and walked on west and south to reach Loch Carron at Strome Ferry. The innkeeper had a wireless set and the news of the German concentration of troops was sufficiently definite to make us decide to finish our tour and to make our several ways to a family base, to consider the next step. Peter was bound for Balbirnie, his home in Fife, and I for an aunt's house in Appin, Argyll.

The daughter of the innkeeper's family was planning to make her way somehow to Mallaig for a visit and a dance and was in tears since her father had forbidden this jaunt in view of the dangers of the general situation. 'Surely there'd be little harm in her trying to get to Mallaig,' pleaded her mother. There was a sound of noisy weeping.

'Mallaig!' roared her father. 'Why not go to Berlin and be done with it!'

The next morning, 2nd September, all public transport stopped: there was no particular reason for this beyond a natural Highland inclination to take the day off on so memorable an occasion. It was quite certain that to get from north to south (my Argyll destination) on the west coast would be impossible. I therefore crossed Scotland from west to east by thumbed lifts and saw few men sober; wars don't begin every day and Scotland was having a party. In Inverness, which I reached by a lift with a commercial traveller in wines and spirits (an unsteady run), I found that a bus was due to run along the Moray Firth coast which, with several changes and after many hours, would bring me to Fraserburgh. I telephoned Cairnbulg and spoke to my aunt Dodo Saltoun from the Station Hotel in Inverness. 'Come here whenever you like,' she said.

As I walked away from the hotel I saw the notice on the hoardings – 'Germans Invade Poland.'

TWO

6

Waiting in an Ante-Room

Perceptions of the passage of time differ greatly in the several ages of man. My childhood was dominated by the First World War, not because I remembered it but because it was spoken about as so extraordinary and tragic – yet glorious – an episode that it seemed to have drawn a heavy and impenetrable curtain across the century. 'Before the War' – the war of 1914–18 – behind that curtain, lay a different era, unimaginable to me but to my parents and elders golden. To me, of course, 'Before the War' was as remote as if they had been speaking of Waterloo; yet to my parents in 1939, when another war started, the First War had finished only twenty-one years before – they had been young then, they were young still. The twenties and thirties had represented my own childhood and youth, seemingly interminable. To them those decades were but a brief interval; an interval, as it turned out, between wars.

Thus to my father, a Regular soldier who had already been a young but battle-hardened lieutenant-colonel of 28 in 1918 and was now a colonel of 48 in 1939, the previous war 'seemed like yesterday'; seemed as if I, today (I write in 1999), were looking back at 1979 when I was already a full general and about to retire. 'It seems like yesterday,' and to my father's generation those wars, so close to each other in time, were, furthermore, against the same enemy and initially on the same ground. That perspective, that sense of a struggle simply resurrected after a twenty-year armistice, sheds a little light on the attitudes of some of our predecessors which strike us – in the military sphere – as reactionary, sluggish or perverse. To them it was, after a certain interruption, the same war.

It became of course, to an unimaginable degree, an entirely different war.

*

I have already described my uncle Alistair and Cairnbulg Castle, which was to be my home for the next three and a half months. I wrote immediately to my parents in Paris telling them my news, where I was and what I hoped – a fifteen-page letter. On page 13 –

Now about another matter. We gather that all people over 18 are going to join (and a lot under 18). Peter [Balfour] is going to the Scots Guards soon. Dougie [Graham-Campbell] is going to the Argylls and Uncle Alistair is, I think, going to try to get Master a commission in the Grenadiers as he'll be 18 by Christmas. Could I get anything like that, I wonder? . . . I am nearly 19. I travelled here in the bus with a boy who's just been called up (TA) who is only 17, so I *couldn't* go back to Eton . . .

Postal services were disrupted by the outbreak of war and I didn't get a reply to this for a long time. The atmosphere at Cairnbulg is conveyed by an earlier sentence in the same letter. 'Uncle Alistair . . . has just said something about war making people reckless, and given me a fiver, which has made me red with gratitude.'

My uncle, without having volunteered for it, was *in loco parentis*, and simply supported me in whatever line I thought right, after discussing pros and cons in a wholly adult way. I knew that my name was on the books of the Grenadiers. Although, when we discussed careers, my father had opposed the idea of my being a Regular soldier I would probably have obtained a commission in the Supplementary Reserve of the Regiment had we remained at peace. Since I had been scheduled for one last Half at Eton nothing had yet been done about a possible university place.

Uncle Alistair, of course, knew such details as addresses. I was, clearly, on my own. I wrote to the Grenadiers' Regimental Headquarters in London and obtained a letter from the Regimental Adjutant telling me what to do. My name was on a list called the 'Officer Cadet Reserve', and on the assumption that I had completed my education, was not in a reserved occupation and was ready to serve, I should attest for service at the nearest military station – join up, in fact. I would then receive further instructions as to when and where to report.

This was good enough. I had to make up my mind. I wrote to Upcott saying that I didn't intend to return to Eton, and went off to the recruiting office in Marischal College, Aberdeen. There I had a medical examination, enlisted as a private in the Gordon Highlanders, swore an oath, received one day's pay, and was told to go home until required.

I hoped that this would be shortly. In fact it was to be nearly a year before I was summoned by the Army. Nobody, it seemed, was very keen on my services. Meanwhile I had a series of telegrams from Eton, of which one ('Return at once. Headmaster') gave me a certain illicit joy. I had no intention of returning. I had made my choice – entirely wrongly – and once I have severed links with anything or anybody I always detest going back.

My Tutor later wrote to me, very nicely. He understood my actions, but thought them unnecessary. He had made Tom Miller Captain of the House, but would be prepared even at this stage (the Half had started) to have me back on a sort of 'dual consul' basis. I did not go. I had burned my boats. Tom was certainly a much better Captain of the House than I would ever have been. I was also about to become the junior member of Oppidan Sixth Form (the ten senior boys in the school who were not Scholars) and my place was taken by the next one down, Simon Phipps (later Bishop of Lincoln). He, also, was a great deal more suitable. My father was not pleased at my decision but took it pretty well. He was, I think, utterly wretched that his son might have to go through something like his own experiences of twenty years before.

I was now at something of a loose end, having acted with precipitancy and folly. My father, through fraternal letters, and my uncle were understandably anxious that I should not waste the next months in sitting idle without intellectual effort. A tutor from Aberdeen University, a friend of my uncle, was a charming Miss Taylor. She came to stay and set me to write history essays, having prescribed a course of reading. I also read a good deal of French. I did a lot of research into family history which I would never have found time to do thereafter and which gave me a solid background knowledge of Fraser genealogy, and of the connection between the very numerous branches of the whole Fraser tribe.

A contemporary, Sacha Carnegie, son and grandson of lifelong family friends, also came to live at Cairnbulg. His father was at sea, and together we played golf, shot, argued, played billiards and watched birds. He was a born entertainer and the best of companions. It was in many ways an excellent time, but of course marred by the lack of positive indication of when our services were likely to be required. The war in the west was, after the first few weeks, quiescent. Poland was conquered – Sacha had a Polish maternal grandfather. We chafed. The Germans had won the first, easy round against a Third Eleven. When were we going to have the chance to show them some real opposition?

The chafing was to some extent increased by a good many disagreements with my uncle. The most kindly of men, he had, as I have described, a well-developed (and often admirable) talent for taking a different line from most of his contemporaries, including his family. In 1939 he thought that we should not slam shut the door on the possibility of peace by negotiation at some later stage. He disliked chauvinism and blanket condemnation. He accepted that war had been virtually unavoidable – 'they deserve a damned good hiding,' he said to me sadly, late at night, after I had arrived at Cairnbulg off the bus from Inverness that September evening. But he felt throughout his being that the war was a tragedy and that its consequences would get worse and worse the longer it ran. Utterly patriotic, he nevertheless hated the idea of a younger generation going through it all again; and he thought, to a probably perverse degree, that we had been stupid in our dealings with the Germans – oppressive and vengeful when they were down, feeble and conciliatory when they were up. And he always thought the British obtuse about how other peoples think and feel. There was, of course, the matter of the German Government's internal policy – of oppression – still only known in part, but regarded by most people then as essentially a domestic concern. Uncle Alistair, on a London visit, discussed it with the elderly Lord Mancroft, a distinguished Jew whom he revered, and said, 'The hardest thing to tolerate is the treatment of *your* people – but I can't regard that as a sufficient reason for war.' 'My dear boy,' answered Mancroft, 'I agree with you entirely. Entirely.'

I, of course, felt very differently, and there were sharp arguments. My predominant sensation was of happiness and relief. We had watched, I reckoned, for several years, a bully get away with fraud, insult and cruelty. That was the way it appeared to me; and the fact that we were now committed on what seemed manifestly the right side had been long anticipated and was a profound release.

Inevitably, I over-simplified the issues. It is absurd to pretend that the Germans had no case for the rectification of frontiers; and equally false to imagine that the treatment of minorities by the Poles (and Czechs) had been invariably satisfactory. The British and French guarantee to Poland had thrown down a challenge to Hitler and, it could be argued, made war inevitable. Was this wholly responsible? The division of Prussia by the 'Polish corridor' was clearly unhistorical and a source of anger and trouble. The assertion by Germany of the traditional position of the Central Powers, armed, self-contained and formidable, was not in itself a cause for hostility – indeed in different circumstances it should have contributed to the stability of Europe. But no moderate and enlightened European mind, no Prince Bismarck, was controlling the government of the Reich. Hitler, it was obvious, was determined to achieve his objectives by the use of force, and he conducted affairs in such a way that force had to be used. That was the way it seemed to me.

After a while Uncle Alistair went south to a War Office job, openly exultant that he was back in uniform ahead of me. He confided to me the key of the well-stocked cellar, gave me a brief indoctrination, a few words of advice on certain vintages, told me how to complete the cellar book, instructed me on how to broach an enormous (I think thirty gallons) barrel of whisky he had ordered, correctly assuming that it would be in short supply before long, and went off to catch his train in high good humour. He wrote at Christmas (I had by then left Cairnbulg) to tell me how moderate he thought my drawings from the cellar had been.

My parents were to return from Paris early in the New Year. My father had been succeeded as military attaché by a Reservist officer, Lord Malise Graham, who had agreed to take over as sub-tenant our flat in the Rue Cognacq-Jay, our possessions, car and servants. The war seemed wholly inactive. People tried to find analogies with what had happened between 1914 and 1918 but they were perplexed. I supposed that at any moment I would receive the longed-for summons from the

Grenadiers to go somewhere for training, but it didn't come. There were no casualties, no fighting, no requirement for fresh officers. There was a superfluity.

A friend of mine, Dougie Graham-Campbell, of Shirvan in Argyllshire, had left Eton that summer. Intending ultimately to join the Argylls, his family and local Regiment, he had gone up to Oxford, to Christ Church. I wrote asking whether I could stay with him for Christmas before travelling south in this curious no-peace no-war era, and left Cairnbulg with most of my luggage, which had ultimately got there from both Paris and Eton.

Dougie – and his father – were superb pipers and very knowledge-able lovers of all Highland things. I was a novice at the pipes – I had started learning at Eton – but keen. It was a hard winter, very beautiful, with snow on the Argyllshire hills, and in between shooting over the rough ground at Shirvan, piping and exploring country new to me Dougie talked about Oxford. It was, he said, enormous fun. There was total freedom (I was, of course, still a schoolboy in experience, or lack of it). It was obvious, Dougie said, that nobody would want me in the Army for ages. Most of their neighbours and relatives were in the 8th (Loch Fyneside) Territorial Battalion of the Argylls and they were either on leave or doing absolutely nothing. Why not come up to Oxford?

I was already coming, reluctantly, to the conclusion that I'd behaved stupidly. I travelled south after Christmas and found that my father and mother had returned from Paris. They had been lent a house in Kent, temporarily, and when we all met there it was clear that my father was in a pretty bad mood. The reason for this was not – or not primarily – my own behaviour, but his own military life. He had been relieved in Paris by Malise Graham, and was hoping for active employment. He had (when we first saw each other) just been given command of a Home Defence brigade, a prospect which appalled him – the British Expeditionary Force was now in France and it was assumed by all that, as in 1914, north-west Europe was where the great encounters would take place. A brigade at home looked singularly unenticing.

But my father's dissatisfaction with life went deeper than the personal. He had watched with gloom and frequent expostulation what he had regarded as the unrealistic attitudes of the British Government towards preparation for war. He had fully understood – and represented to his authorities – the mistrust of the French about British policy, particularly British refusal to consider conscription (until March 1939, when it was suddenly introduced in an unpremeditated and cack-handed way). Now the war itself seemed likely to be marked by British muddleheadedness, as he saw it, about strategy.

The mental approach of the British to hostilities was distinguished by their prime faults – slackness of mind and wishful thinking. Because they had so strongly desired peace they had – by a superstitious rather than rational association of ideas – neglected and then delayed military preparedness as in some way likely to produce the evil they should have sought to deter. Then, having drifted like sleepwalkers into a war they had done little to make themselves fit for, the British decided that it was a crusade against the forces of evil. Crusades are hard to control. They involve arousal of the most vigorous passions – especially in democracies, which need a good deal of convincing that the whole thing is necessary. Once convinced, the people of democracies need to believe that good is opposed to evil – hence the spirit of crusade. All this, with its attempted arousal of vigorous moral and ideological passions, tends to work against that cool concept of war as a (doubtless regrettable) extension of policy defined by Clausewitz, an exercise with finite, obtainable objectives.

My father was more aware of – and more disgusted by – the character of the Nazi regime than many of his compatriots. He was, however, a well-informed European too, with a historical sense and a wide acquaintance in both France and Germany. He was also a well-educated soldier. He knew that the object of war, whatever the emotions aroused by it, should be a better peace. Aims should be clear and attainable – otherwise it is unjustified to start. The British and French aim (never, in the event, attained) had been to honour a guarantee of Polish sovereignty; Poland was now swamped by the brutal invasions of both the *Wehrmacht* and the Red Army. Another aim was to teach Hitler a sharp lesson and stop his nonsense – thus encouraging those elements in Germany which thought likewise. But the sharp lesson was being sadly postponed.

For the British (and in this respect the French), although at once embracing the war as a crusade, were by no means inclined to pay a high price for indulging in this righteous activity. The only conceivable way of honouring a guarantee to Poland was to conduct an offensive in the west as early as possible. Not only was this not done, but the very idea was regarded as impracticable (which it was not) and immoral. To the French an 'offensive' implied Verdun; to the British it meant the Somme and Third Ypres. To both it meant casualties by the hundred thousand. It was also unpleasantly warlike. Surely a peaceful people's correct tactical doctrine was to sit on the defensive and wait until the enemy (thus reaffirming his turpitude) himself launched an offensive? Then to destroy him in large numbers from what everybody knew to be the comparative security of entrenchments? Meanwhile we could, with superior forces in this sphere, conduct maritime operations – with luck comparatively inexpensive: no blood bath, no Somme. But, sadly, no instant lesson to Hitler. And no defence of land frontiers.

All this was, to my father, lunatic from a strategic viewpoint. The Allies, I knew that he knew, actually enjoyed a preponderance of material strength in the west in land forces and this preponderance had been very great when most of the German Army was engaged in Poland. To my father an Allied offensive in the west was a strategic imperative.

'Isn't their Siegfried Line very strong and hard to attack?' I asked. We went on a number of long walks through the icy Kent countryside that Christmastide.

'Then go through Belgium,' said my father curtly. He had, of course, plenty of contacts in Belgium as well. He was, I know, unrealistic in all this. There would have been an adverse international – particularly American – reaction to a breach of Belgium's neutrality; but the real reason against was the lack of moral readiness for any offensive at all levels of the French Army, and this my father, albeit a Francophile, was reluctant to accept.

Instead the Allies sat, trusting to an impregnable Maginot line, inactive and with the deteriorating morale which inactivity brings, and waited until the Germans were ready. My father was, a few months later and to his great pleasure, appointed to command the 24th Guards Brigade – a brigade whose Guards battalions were doing ceremonial duties in the West End of London, whose artillery and support services, such as they were, had never been combined with them for any sort of training or familiarization, and all of whose units, including the Brigade Staff, were first seen by their commander when they actually and unexpectedly embarked for operations overseas in April. Their fate reflected the attitude of the British to preparation for war. This lay in the future – in December I simply knew that my father was disgruntled and sceptical about the military policy of our authorities, although to me, of course, he spoke with discretion and restraint.

For me, the immediate question was whether to try to go up to Oxford – an idea strongly supported by both my parents. My mother's brother, John Maude, was a successful junior barrister with a flourishing practice at the Criminal bar. He had been at Christ Church immediately after the First War and had loved it. A telephone call from Kent, and two days later he and I were on an unheated train to Oxford.

I was, again, lucky. My uncle John was a witty and entertaining man. He had the reputation of being in the first rank of cross-examiners: colleagues told me later that nobody could more quickly scent a witness's lying, nor more adroitly find the questions which would expose it. He had a mellifluous voice, which probably owed much to his mother, Winifred Emery. Like some others I have mentioned he had the irresistible gift of agelessness – throughout life we talked unaffectedly, as contemporaries. Tall, handsome and untidy, he was extravagant, irreverent, lacked almost all practical common sense (like my mother) and was extremely funny. He was a chain smoker and I think invariably indulged whatever taste took his fancy. He had little self-discipline and all the charm in the world. At this time he was 38.

At Christ Church we first called on the Dean, a senior cleric – Dean of the Cathedral and Head of the College. The Dean was a Canadian who didn't know John, but he was not discouraging. He passed us on to Dr Russell, the Senior Censor, an official more in the executive chain of command, so to speak. The last examinations I had taken were the papers of School Certificate at sixteen, passed, as I explained to Dr Russell, with respectable results. Thereafter, at Eton, boys did not undergo the annual 'Trials'. I was asked to write a brief essay in the Senior Censor's dining room in the lovely Peckwater Quad – 'Peck'. I was already taken with Oxford.

'What about, Sir?' I asked. I didn't yet know that dons are not schoolmasters, to be addressed as 'Sir'.

'Anything you like,' Russell responded, affably. I wrote for an hour on some forgotten historical subject. I suppose it sufficed to show I was literate, and thereafter John and I paid some more calls on a few favourite dons of his who were in residence – it was vacation time, January 1940 – and returned to the Senior Censor, who told me to 'come up' on the following Thursday. So I did.

Having, much later in life, experienced the competition of the young for university places, the almost scientific precision with which colleges seek to select and balance their intakes, the care exerted not to have too many public school boys (especially too many Etonians) so that the social mix is beyond class-based criticism – having vicariously suffered all this for a later generation I feel somewhat abashed at the ease with which I was able to wander into Christ Church.

But it was wartime. At frequent and unpredictable intervals, and often with no notice at all, undergraduates were being called up for military service. It was obviously hard for colleges and academic departments to plan – and difficult to budget. New blood, even if unexpected, was surprisingly welcome. I found friends already at Oxford – Dougie Graham-Campbell had rooms in Peck and as I found my way around many Eton friends materialized, not yet caught up in the war. I had rooms in Brewer Street, moving into College and a set of rooms in the Old Library at the start of the ensuing summer term. I enjoyed, as Dougie had told me I would, the sense of adult liberty, the clubs (in my case the Carlton and the Grid) where we drank too much and pretended to be grown-up. In the summer term, to my delight and at my urging, Tom Miller came up to The House, as Christ Church was always called.

We had an unusually cold winter in 1939 and there was snow when I went up, snow which had not melted by the end of term in March; I first saw the grass round Mercury, the statue and fountain in the centre of Tom Quad in which unpopular undergraduates were sometimes ducked, at the beginning of the summer term. The College and University were, we were told, undergoing stringency which would make life very harsh by peacetime standards. It didn't seem so. It was, it was true, difficult to give luncheon parties in one's rooms in College (not that I could have afforded many) but a list of requirements handed in to the Junior Common Room ensured a delicious tea, for whatever numbers ordered, brought round at the time indicated – toasted tea-cakes, honey sandwiches (a speciality), fruit cake and so forth. This was a negligible privilege to the older undergraduates not yet in uniform, who grumbled furiously at their hardships and told us how much of the *douceur de vivre* we had missed. But vintage port was nine shillings a bottle, food in hall was uninspiring but adequate and the freedoms and friendships of Oxford were exhilarating.

I read PPE, Politics, Philosophy and Economics. A system had been inaugurated whereby examinations were held of 'sections' – parts of a number of syllabuses – since clearly nobody knew when or whether he would still be around to take finals. I soon discovered how much I disliked the study of economics, which seemed to have little bearing on the world at war, and I managed to give it up, throwing Alfred Marshall's classic on, I think, the 'Theory of Rent' out of my window with a sense of liberation. Philosophy – and political philosophy – on the other hand was much to my taste. My tutor was Gilbert Ryle, a distinguished philosopher. Dons acquired personalities through their views, actual or fancied. 'Have you come across — [a distinguished Christ Church don]?' he asked one day.

'No.'

'He's a Hegelian.'

But I acquired a new view and a different opinion every week and it was highly enjoyable. I still, of course, felt frustrated and a fool, who had bolted from school with inflated ideas of fighting. But since nobody was fighting and most contemporaries were in the same boat it was easy to live in the moment. And to make new friends and savour something like liberty, including the delightful if illusory sense of liberty produced by wine taken to excess.

During the spring vacation matters livened up as far as the war was concerned. I gathered from careful hints in my mother's letters that my father might not be around for a while, and we soon learned that the Germans had invaded Denmark and Norway.

The British Government (this, of course, was unknown until many years later) had planned to pre-empt a German invasion of Norway by a seaborne incursion of our own. The Allies placed great importance on Norway. German supplies of Swedish iron ore came, during the winter, by the sole usable route via Narvik. Because Norway was neutral German ships could move with impunity from north Norway to the Skagerrak, through Norwegian territorial waters; and – as a separate issue – the Norwegian western ports in German hands would seriously hamper the British blockade of Continental Europe. The Allies, therefore, reckoned that they should find a good reason to press unsolicited help on the Norwegians. It was thought that if we mined certain Norwegian waters the Germans would be bound to react, and we could react to their reaction and appear as the defenders of Norway – and in that guise occupy some territory vital to the conduct of the war. 24th Guards Brigade was one of the formations earmarked for this enterprise, destined to occupy Narvik in the far north of the country.

The elaborate plan, needing as it did the combinations of a number of military expeditions with readiness to fight a major fleet action in the North Sea, and with political manoeuvres of the utmost disingenuousness, was complicated by the Finnish business. Finland had been attacked by the Soviet Union in November 1939 and the Western Allies had, some months later, decided to send forces to help the Finns – including my father's Brigade. This was to have given us an admirable pretext to occupy Norwegian ports (with the advantage already noted) in order to ship an expedition to Finland; but in March the Finns had capitulated. It became more difficult to find a new pretext, and the mining option was chosen, to provoke a German move for which we would have the pre-emptive counter-move ready and forces already at sea.

Unfortunately the Germans, who also reckoned that Norway was important to them, decided to move first. They pre-empted the would-be pre-emptors, and on 9th April sailed in and occupied the major Norwegian ports, including Narvik, with troops in the south landing in the Oslo Fjord and marching into the capital, a band playing at the head.

The muddles which now arose on the British side, with troops needing to be returned to Glasgow and re-loaded – or unloaded, since it at one moment appeared that the Navy might fight a major fleet action, and didn't want ships crowded with soldiers and holds stacked with their equipment; the separation of units and formations from their own equipment; the confusion in higher planning, with large forces earmarked but ill-equipped for a major campaign in North Norway; the total absence of any understanding of the principles of combined land–sea operations, as well as the near-total absence of air support; the ignorance by each Service of the limitations and character of the others – all this was, of course, mercifully hidden from the British public, and I only learned it from my father, and from his excellent diaries kept during the expedition, a good deal later. Norway, including Narvik, was an inglorious episode, for which the British were unprepared – unfit, untrained and ill-equipped. My father, himself, was wounded by a shell-splinter in the throat during an early reconnaissance at Narvik, so that personal anxiety for him was, at the time, the chief impression of the Norwegian campaign. In France all still seemed entirely quiet, although at Oxford knowledgeable undergraduates explained that General Gamelin would undoubtedly launch a major spring offensive.

Having discarded Economics, and with it a tutor of left-wing views and unsympathetic personality, I found that Dr Ryle had moved into the Army and bequeathed me for the study of political philosophy to another Christ Church don with rooms in Tom Quad, by name Frank Pakenham. He had, it appeared, joined the Army but for some reason – perhaps connected to health – had returned to Oxford. 'He's a Socialist,' my friends said, 'but a gentleman, and rather nice although a bit soft in the head.'

I found that there was something in all these observations. Frank Pakenham had a large, high-foreheaded head, a vague expression, and the appearance of some short-sighted and absent-minded professor of caricature. He said that he thought I had better read some Marx, and go to one or two lectures on him. There was certainly no proselytizing in this, but a very proper instinct that my mind needed broadening. My first essay for him (on 'The Communist Manifesto') was, in academic terms, not very successful.

'It's quite a good sermon!' he said mildly, blinking. 'But I'm not sure you've really analysed very carefully what Marx is trying to say!'

He impressed me – it was impossible not to be impressed – by his goodness and kindness, as well as his erudition. But he also impressed me by what seemed a lack of realism about human nature. I remember him telling me that we, in England, had not reached a level of society where honesty could be taken very much for granted. He gave an example.

'I often go and ride, early in the morning, up on Cumnor hill. Last week I was wearing a new jersey. I thought it was going to be rather hot, so I took it off and hung it on a bush. Then I had a gallop, and half-an-hour later I rode back. It had gone.'

He seemed to find in this something sad about the condition of the country. I suppose there was, but the story left me unsurprised. Unlike, I fear, him. But tutorials with him were invariably agreeable – he was diffident, generous, friendly; perhaps – understandably – a little bored. Frank Pakenham showed even then a taste for unpopular causes – often with exemplary courage. His attempts to get decent treatment for the Germans starving and in destitution after the war (he was by then a Minister) were wholly honourable. He had known my American cousin, Jo Burden, who had also been at the House, and had liked him.

'He *might* have got a First. One needs originality for a First, but he might just have made it.'

I missed reading History – I supposed that PPE was a broad collection of disciplines, but time was so short – I might be at Oxford two? three? four terms? Surely I could somehow pursue my favourite study here, as well as political philosophy? I had just thrown Alfred Marshall out of the window, and I decided to go to see the Senior Tutor, whom I had met on my first visit with my uncle John Maude.

The Senior Tutor was the famous – and to become more famous – J. C. Masterman, renowned in the Second World War as Sir John 'Doublecross', manager of Counter-Intelligence and Deception. A historian and brilliant games player, he welcomed me to his rooms most charmingly. He was, indeed, a man of the utmost charm and distinction, in every sphere, intellectual, athletic and social. He had taken a First in History immediately before the First World War, throughout which, by ill-luck, he was interned in a prisoner-of-war camp in Germany. Later he represented England at tennis in 1920 and at hockey in 1925 and 1927; in 1937 he had toured Canada with the MCC. Tall, lean, sharp-featured and dapper, he looked a little like the Naval Officer he had once, at Dartmouth, been designed to be. He listened patiently while I explained my feelings about History, and about Economics. I felt I'd been wasting an opportunity, that I'd been put in the wrong box.

'Yes, of course,' he said.

'I don't like the economics –'

'Of course not. Perfectly dreadful.'

'I want to read some history, if it's possible –'

'Of course you must, and of course it's possible. Come with me.'

He led me to Peckwater Quad to meet another don, Tallboys. Mr Tallboys had been a master at Wellington; he was now living in Oxford and putting in time as a part-time Tutor at the House – at least I think that was something like the arrangement. He always took some pains to emphasize that he was somehow an irregular, a being from a slightly different plane. Masterman clearly thought the world of him, and introduced me with the briefest of explanations.

Tallboys had a much-imitated, mellifluous, rather sing-song voice. Tutorials with him were always enjoyable. We were reading the Napoleonic period. He detested it (quite rightly) when, as sometimes happened, I asked whether a particular aspect was 'likely to come up in examination' (at that time I still supposed my Oxford career might lead to a 'wartime degree').

'Oh dear, Fraser, please don't talk about things like that. You are NOT here to bother about examinations and marks and such matters. You are reading and thinking and talking about History, because it's worth doing. No other reason.'

'I just wondered whether it might help me if I concentrated on –'

'Help?'

'For the examinations.'

'I don't in the least mind, Fraser.'

I had written an essay mildly critical of Charles James Fox. My temperament led me firmly into the camp of the younger Pitt.

'Oh dear, Fraser, don't you *like* Fox?'

I muttered something pompous and disparaging.

'Fraser, I do hope you are going to *enjoy* life. Fox did.'

And so on. Conversation with him was civilized, mildly irreverent, a thousand miles away from the conventional exchanges of pupil and master. And he was always funny – a brilliant teacher while wholly disguising the fact.

The war went remotely on, with uncomforting stories coming back from our only active expedition, in Norway. The Allies, having committed an expedition to seize Narvik for a North Norwegian campaign, had also attempted to capture the important port of Trondheim. This led to disaster – our forces were evacuated from the Trondheim area, through Namsos, on 3rd May. These had been the northern wing of a force planned to move on Trondheim from both north and south. Untrained, suffering from the huge and unplanned expansion of the Territorial Army in March 1939, they had been landed without transport and without artillery. There was virtually no air support. In these circumstances they had met the German Army, the first British troops to do so in the Second World War, and had been worsted – outmarched, out-fought, out-commanded, outwitted. The best team had undoubtedly won.

The fate of the southern wing directed at Trondheim was similar. These met German troops who had been landed near Oslo and were pushing up the country by road. Their British opponents, plagued by contradictory and unrealistic orders, had been split into detachments and were soon swept aside. A Regular brigade was then brought in to reinforce and gave a good account of itself but it, too – with the unfortunate Territorial brigade first deployed – was soon forced to retreat. The troops of the southern wing of the 'Trondheim offensive' were evacuated through Aandelsnes the day before those of the northern wing, who had come out through Namsos. At Narvik, where my father, wounded, had already been evacuated, battalions of what had been his brigade were sent here and there by sea with minimal air cover and over enormous distances.

In the newspapers, therefore, we read what seemed perplexing news. To our generation it was simply inconceivable that the British could suffer even a serious setback, let alone a defeat. We had been brought up in the afterglow of victory. We had, from infancy, learned that we were invincible. When, a little older, we had heard anecdotes of what seemed the leisurely and unprofessional attitude to military matters of our leaders (not our fathers, but leaders of the inter-war generation) we took it as evidence of the splendid, all-conquering insouciance of the amateur. The Germans, on the other hand, were, we supposed, second-rate in fighting terms; their defeat twenty years ago showed it. They were humourless worshippers of professionalism and as such likely to be completely outclassed by the light-hearted brilliance of natural winners. But although, as yet, not much was known about the details of the Norwegian campaign, even the official communiqués were disturbing.

At Oxford the Communist Left opposed the war virulently, and, with several others, I was arrested for bombarding (with eggs, astonishingly) a Communist procession in the High, a procession marching with banners proclaiming 'Stop this Capitalist War'. To read some later politicians' accounts one might suppose that the further to the Left the more determined the resistance to Hitler. In 1940 the reverse was true. The two criminal regimes were having a temporary love affair, an affair which at least – mercifully, while it lasted – made our own position morally clear beyond doubts.

Then, on 10th May, the great German offensive in the west began. And immediately – with astonishing speed – it became clear that this was the climactic moment of our lives so far.

We bought maps and small paper flags on pins. Very soon – by 16th May – there seemed to be an extraordinary bulge in the line of flags. Not only were the Germans approaching Brussels, but south of it – far south of it – they appeared to be racing westward. I was familiar with the geography of the Western Front in the previous war, my father's war. Now – it seemed wholly incredible – places which had featured in the battles of 1918 were being overrun as fast as I could reposition my little flags. Cambrai, Arras, Béthune. It was utterly astonishing. What had happened? What was going to happen now? Strategically minded undergraduates said that the Germans were obviously walking into a trap. Soon there would be a great pincer movement from both north and south of the penetration.

20th May. Amiens, Abbeville. The Channel. Dunkirk. My mother had got a job working for what ultimately turned out to be MI5. My father, evacuated to England, was still in hospital from his Narvik wound. At Oxford we felt desperate. An enormous battle had been fought and it seemed possible that the next enormous battle would be for the defence of England. People still talked in terms of a new front being formed in France, but as news – heavily censored though it was – filtered back from the Continent the extraordinary possibility floated on the air like poison gas that the Allies, the victorious British and French, had actually suffered an irreparable defeat. And after that? Might we fail to succeed in applying the first rule of strategy – always fight a war in someone else's country? I wrote to my mother on 2nd June.

I don't really know what to do, as one feels pretty awful just sitting here doing absolutely nothing to help . . . almost all my friends, Dougie, Tom etc., are going down this term and going into this Home Defence Force until they are called up . . . if invasion comes it will come this summer, I expect. It seems that things aren't going too well, to put it mildly; not since 1804 has this island been so threatened – and yet I shall spend the long vac. reading history or moral philosophy or something. I'm afraid it is almost beyond my powers . . .

It was completely beyond my powers. I had written to the Grenadiers' Regimental Headquarters to ask whether I was about to be called up, and if not whether I was legally free to join what was publicized as the 'Home Defence Force'. This consisted of a large number of battalions, mostly 'Young soldiers' battalions', which could enrol men of an age group not yet called up for active service, if they volunteered. The only age criterion was to be over sixteen and a half (I think) and under nineteen and a half, when the regular call-up applied. One of these battalions was forming near Oxford and a number of us planned to go down, take a brief holiday, and then, reunited at Oxford, to join it at a date in June.

I went to the 4th of June at Eton. There were the usual crowds, and a large number of officers who had returned from Dunkirk in the previous few days.* Some of them were playing cricket for the Eton

---

* Operation 'Dynamo', the evacuation of the British Expeditionary Force from Dunkirk, ended on 3rd June.

Ramblers, whose annual fixture, with two elevens, always took place on that occasion. It all seemed rather unreal but somehow, also, rather glorious – Drake and his bowls. Talk was of much beside war: the Derby had been run at Newmarket and Miles Marriott, whose father was a knowledgeable racing man, was already in the Grenadiers and discussing form as if it alone mattered.

The Grenadiers answered by letter. There was nothing against my enlisting in the Young Soldiers Battalion of the Home Defence Force – it was 8th Battalion, Royal Berkshire Regiment. Our party lunched well – rather too well – at Oxford on 22nd June: besides Tom Miller and Dougie Graham-Campbell, I remember Julian Paget, Richard Fortescue, Peter Heslop. We then went to a centre near the Railway Station for a medical inspection and attestation. After that we reported to a drill hall somewhere on the outskirts of the city, were allotted to a company (all of us in the same very large platoon), drew uniforms, rifles, straw-filled palliasses.

By then, of course, the Germans had finished the business in France and the French had asked for and been given an armistice. The brilliance of the German operational plan, the energy of execution, the enlightened decentralization of control, as well as (seen on newsfilm in British cinemas) the obvious smartness and soldierly appearance of all ranks of the *Wehrmacht* were clearly marks of an Army superbly trained and led, with a tactical doctrine of high quality and presumably served by a magnificent staff. The campaign of 1940, in which the Germans defeated forces (including armour) of equivalent strength and conquered four countries in four weeks, was an incomparable achievement. Every preconception of ours needed revision.

I had first formally enlisted in the Army, in the Gordon Highlanders at Aberdeen in September 1939. I had a Gordon Regimental number. Now, with the same number (confusingly to the clerical staffs of successive Regiments), I was a private in the Berkshires, and three months later would be a Recruit in the Grenadiers. At last I was in the war. I had put on uniform. I would next be a civilian on 5th February 1980.

7

Uniform at Last

The debacle of 1940 had stunned us all. For some time it seemed probable that England would be invaded. There was a good deal of newspaper discussion (but keeping on the right side of the Defence of the Realm Regulations which forbade publications likely to lower national morale or help the enemy) about why and how our country seemed to have fallen so low and so suddenly. Yesterday at the top of the senior league, we now appeared to have been decisively defeated in a campaign which had undone the work of four years of war only twenty-two years ago: defeated and now mortally threatened, friendless and alone. All over the world, we read, various neutral nations were saying agreeable things to and about the Germans. Nobody seemed in the least to like us. The Italians had, at the last minute, joined Hitler in his devouring of the carcase of France. France herself had reached an accommodation with the enemy; Stalin had sent Hitler a message of congratulations. One or two heads of state – the King of Norway, the Queen of Holland – had escaped to England and we read brave words about resistance in the occupied countries but it didn't, surely, add up to much in terms of real power. Across the Channel a huge, efficient, menacing machine had subdued, it seemed, the whole European Continent.

Meanwhile the war went on in the air – the one ray of brilliance in the darkness. The Germans began their raids on England, and every day we read of their losses – inflated, no doubt, but it didn't matter. In the skies above England, if nowhere else, we were winning. It was an alarming, stimulating hour. And of course Churchill's great speeches – he had succeeded Chamberlain on 10th May shortly after the debate on the Norway campaign in the House of Commons – acted as a memorable tonic. His effect on England was magical, although to my father (who had known him well in the First War) and that generation there were always question marks ovre Churchill's judgement.

There were voices – not many and mostly subdued but a few eloquent and seductive – which questioned the wisdom of the strategic posture Britain had adopted. Not primarily defeatist (although, of course, accused as such) they pointed out that the Royal Navy had frustrated Napoleon's attempts at world domination and could do the same for Hitler. What had Britain to gain by involvement with the Continent? To wage war for fancied moral imperatives was absurd. Strategy demanded concentration on the facts of power. France and Germany could settle – had settled – their own destinies. Britain should simply concentrate on assuring her sea-borne supplies and 'look to her moat'.

This line of argument – beguiling in its historical appeal and apparently making the best of a bad job – was, of course, to ignore the fact that sea power (by then anyway largely dependent on complementary air power) might avert defeat for an island people but could certainly not produce victory. Nor could it do anything to help nations whose land frontiers were threatened – its effects are long-term and attritional, whereas invasion can be swift, brutal and decisive. Nor, for that matter, could it do enough to defend England itself: for that we needed the Royal Air Force's Fighter Command. Nevertheless, in times of trouble historical analogies, whether or not misleading, can comfort: some at that time found their comfort in recollections of the Napoleonic wars and quotations from Admiral Mahan's theses on the influences of sea-power in history.

The Royal Berkshires were an ancient and illustrious Regiment with an outstanding record. Life in the 8th Battalion, however, was full of shocks. After a brisk few weeks of drill and rudimentary weapon training we were deployed at various places in the Cotswolds – in my case first at Charlbury and then at Shipton-under-Wychwood. We had been under canvas at Oxford, and were then billeted in various lofts or halls, in most insanitary conditions. The officers were either elderly reservists – with a certain background of military knowledge – or middle-aged additions with none. The latter, very naturally, felt inadequate and bewildered. Their bewilderment was increased by the nature of the unit itself.

Some of the senior NCOs were reservists – generally reservist private soldiers, given rank on the spot, but familiar with the basics of drill and military administration. There were very few of these. The rank and file – all young like ourselves, or younger – contained a high proportion of criminals, although there were some very decent boys as well. The criminals mostly came from Birmingham, where the magistrates were generously advising youthful malefactors to join the Colours as an alternative to custodial or Borstal sentence: patriotism or punishment. Whole criminal gangs (as we soon discovered) joined together.

We – the ex-OTC members – were almost at once made junior NCOs and thenceforth had to run the show. We were naturally detested. The majority of our charges indulged only in petty pilfering, mostly from each other: they also, however, carried out acts of gang violence and boasted of periodic robbery and rape. They were hostile to society and they regarded the country as essentially organized by their natural enemies – the educated, the law-abiding, and the owners of property. They were totally uninterested in politics or the war. Such attitudes were in striking contrast to the picture of England fostered day and night by our own propaganda – of a country united in patriotic resolve. For these young soldiers Churchill was simply a noise on the wireless, to be turned off. Only Chamberlain – these were Birmingham boys – was beyond reproach. Generally speaking, they believed in little but violence, and from a moral point of view compared most unfavourably, in our view, with the youth of Nazi Germany, whose unselfishness, courage and idealism had all been enlisted with skilful appeals in the service of a detestable regime. Hitler might be – was – perfectly ghastly but it appeared that at least he had given the 'Jugend' something beyond themselves to believe in and defend. It did not seem to be so with us.

Of course we exaggerated. The first impact on ourselves – straight from Eton, Oxford and the much more segregated life of those days – of close and equal contact with the youthful illiterate, poor and criminal was inevitably harsh. We, the privileged, first encountered on equal terms the very underprivileged. We were naively surprised to find ourselves disliked. We were also amazed at the level of depravity. In fact, as ever, talk was greater than action with these young men. They loathed us and said so; they threatened us; but I only once remember an occasion when one struck an NCO, and on the whole we were (resentfully) obeyed. We stuck together; we had to. We got precious little support from anybody above us.

The members of our platoons were foul-mouthed and hostile. They were also, however, prone to fits of great sentimentality. They were intensely loyal to their own groups. They would steal from but never betray a friend. They thought – and they were quite right – that we were unbelievably innocent in the ways of the world. Their brutality and immorality shocked us, and they enjoyed shocking. They hated us – but, curiously, they trusted us. They confided their possessions to our care to save them from others. Their chief resentment was our education. We were 'College boys' and they had started work at fourteen. This was the uncrossable gulf, greater than any between nations. The German threat had not bridged it.

We managed to get the use of a room in the back quarters of an inn, where we – the hated 'College boys' – could meet and be by ourselves occasionally. There we could exchange horror stories from the jungle of our platoons, could laugh, could listen to a borrowed radio and could sometimes talk about the war and about what had happened to our country. We lamented the evidence all around us of inefficiency and indiscipline. We talked in a rebellious, often ill-informed under-graduate sort of way about the leadership of Britain. Despite Chur-chill's brave words, was our leadership any good? Were our ministers worthy of the hour? Were our generals, our military leaders, up to the challenge or were they futile and incapable?

Some of us had met generals. Two, in particular, were figures I had known myself, and impressive figures too. They were friends of my father, although slightly older than him. Both had been engaged in the fighting of 1940 – one in France and one in Norway. I had met both on several occasions at my parents' dinner table.

The first was General Andrew Thorne, 'Bulgy' Thorne, a Grenadier, already described. I had, furthermore, seen him again on my brief leave between going down from Oxford and returning to it to join the Berkshires. With my parents I had spent a few June days in the beautiful home of great friends near Frant in East Sussex. Thither had come – in uniform and pretty well straight from France – Bulgy Thorne. I can see him then, because he was wearing the regulation khaki knicker-bockers we wore in service dress in pre-battledress days, but with stockings (as in a shooting suit) rather than puttees – an irregularity, but more comfortable than either puttees or field boots and breeches, at that time more customary for senior officers. He seemed, I remember, almost boyish, affable, unperturbed, confident. He had been military attaché in Berlin and knew the German Army and many of its seniors particularly well. He was making light of the air raids which were already beginning, with German aircraft discernible from the house.

He had commanded, in France, the 48th Territorial Division (he had, immediately before the outbreak of war, been in command of the London District). His Division had taken part in the retreat as part of I Corps, having arrived in France in January. Long afterwards I learned – it was a characteristic experience – how untrained in the rudiments of tactics his subordinates then were. He had a defective machine, but I do not believe that he himself was anything but a thoroughly effective driver of it. Later he commanded Scottish Command, after command-ing a Corps responsible for the most threatened part of the English coast; he led the Allied Liberation Forces which took the surrender of the German Army in Norway in 1945. Never to command in battle again after 1940 was undoubtedly a disappointment to him. A good man was to an extent wasted.

The other figure very clear to me from those days is that of General Bernard Paget. He, too, was a family friend whose character and professionalism were, I knew, particularly highly regarded by my father. He had commanded the Staff College and had a name as something of a martinet. An officer of the Oxfordshire and Bucking-hamshire Light Infantry, he was large-nosed, dark-haired, sharp-tongued and – as as even at my age I had learned – extremely funny when he chose. I remember him at dinner at our house in London in Cheyne Gardens – I imagine it was in 1937. Paget was telling my father that some of the Staff College students had approached him asking whether it was really necessary to work on certain afternoons.

'I told them their leave for the rest of the year would be halved,' he said. The flat harshness of the remark was encouraging to remember at a time when so many seemed flabby. As with Bulgy Thorne it was impossible to believe that such men were greatly inferior to the generals of the *Wehrmacht* who had just inflicted humiliations upon us.

Bernard Paget, whose son, Julian, had been with me at Oxford and was now a fellow Lance-Corporal in the Berkshires, was in the news in 1940 during the Norwegian campaign. He was sent out to take command of the Trondheim part of that unfortunate expedition and, having arrived at Aandalsnes on 25th April (by which time the 'southern wing' of the Trondheim force was already withdrawing under great pressure), he had the melancholy task of overseeing the withdrawal by sea, complete by 2nd May. He later became Commander-in-Chief Home Forces – a key appointment but, since the Germans abstained from invading, not one which involved fighting. Although – after handing over to General Montgomery – he was ultimately appointed Commander-in-Chief Middle East the war, by then, had moved away.

A third figure, a general senior to either of these two, I had also met although he had very recently retired. Sir John Burnett-Stuart was an Aberdeenshire man, whose home was not very far from Cairnbulg. His brother and sister-in-law, with a lovely house on the Deveron, were great friends of my parents.

I had met Sir John – 'Jock' – Stuart at Cairnbulg. He was not instantly sympathetic to a young person, and I remember him as rather withdrawn. I suspect he was an anxious and disappointed man at that time – anxious because he had little faith in the leadership of the Army but was out of it and could do nothing about it; disappointed because he was widely regarded as the most intelligent officer of his generation, often tipped as a 'natural' for Chief of the Imperial General Staff. Both my father and my uncle Alistair felt affectionate admiration for him.

He had a name, however (as I discovered a little later), as a frank – too frank – critic of his superiors, and his wit gave acid to the criticism. Stories about him multiplied. About two Christmases before the war the War Office official Christmas card was a photograph of the three Military Members of the Army Council sitting on their horses after the King's Birthday Parade – in those days the Military Members rode in the Royal Procession. Jock Burnett-Stuart – commanding Southern Command at Salisbury at that time – stuck the card on his mantlepiece in a prominent position. Underneath he had written 'The three first reasons for mechanization!' Such things get around. Intolerant and too sharp-tongued he may have been, but he was very clearly a man of rapid mind and exceptional character. When thinking of the criticisms then being voiced of our higher commanders, these were the figures which came to my own mind, and I did not believe the Germans necessarily outclassed them except, no doubt, on the rare occasions when they produced a genius. The French divide senior officers into *'le grand chef'* and *'le bon general ordinaire'*. Perhaps we had few *'grands chefs'* but there were more *'bons generaux ordinaires'* than supposed.

There was also at this time, of course, much denunciation of the inter-war political leadership of the country. There was a good deal in this, but the leadership had reflected pretty accurately the mood of the people. Baldwin was attacked, in a vindictive, disagreeable way. It was said that he had not told the people the truth and that this accounted for our unpreparedness. In fact, as anybody honest could recall, the people were determined on peace, and befuddled by wishful thinking: and no amount of 'Telling the Truth' by Baldwin would have altered the fact. I have never understood what sort of 'Truth' was allegedly kept from the electorate anyway. If it was the fact of Germany's armament and preparation the newspapers were full of it and the whole world knew. Even Churchill, temperamentally generous, was less than large-minded in this regard.

But the public needed scapegoats. Criticism of our military leaders between the wars was popular and to a large extent justified, although it was seldom remembered under what political and financial constraints they had had to operate until the eleventh hour. It was true, however, that after 1918 we paid the price of victory in the complacency victory produces. It was supposed by too many that war, if it ever came, would take a similar form to that recently ended. Experimentation was expensive, and thus to be discouraged. And, of course there was – again until the eleventh hour – a stultifying failure to accept that war would mean large-scale operations on the Continent of Europe. It was exactly this that successive Governments were determined not to recognize, and their policy absolutely inhibited the military leadership from doing, or even thinking, anything realistic about it.

For whatever reason and with whatever justice or lack of it, the public were fed by the popular media a picture of an archaic British military establishment which had been worsted by the forces of modernity, represented by the German Wehrmacht. Our military conservatives – 'Colonel Blimps' in Low's cartoons, reactionary, class-dominated and ignorant of modern technology – had been shown up by German modern, mechanized man.

There was something odd about this diagnosis, and even lance-corporals in the Berkshires found it a little facile. It was true that the Germans appeared to have used considerable numbers of tanks in their astonishing campaign and that we, the British – as far as we could tell – had remarkably few. But the French – and everybody knew this because they had been frequently and impressively photographed before the war and early in it – had huge numbers of tanks (in fact more than the Germans, although we didn't, of course, know that; and many of high quality). Furthermore the image projected, of Modern Man in field-grey opposed to Colonel Blimp in khaki, was somewhat distorted by the photographs which reached our newspapers and newsfilms of German generals and German officers, immaculate uniforms, gleaming field boots, monocles in many eyes. These seemed more to reflect the men our fathers had fought against than the Modern Man we were supposed to emulate if we were to match him. Again – and stories from the brief campaign and newsfilm both bore it out – the German Army, apart from its panzers, seemed still to depend on huge numbers of horses. Our own horsed transport had, as far as we knew, all or virtually all been motorized, and our Cavalry had been or was in the process of being wholly mechanized. To those of us brought up to approve of tradition this seemed sad. Uncle Alistair, however, had remarked to me that 'anyone fond of horses must be glad of their departure from warfare'. But right to the end they were a prime resource in the German Army.

In the Berkshires we had no transport, horsed or otherwise, and didn't need it. But that there was something specious in the popular diagnosis I think we sometimes felt, and said to each other. For the truth was, of course, that we, the French and British, had been beaten not simply, not even primarily, by superior or more modern equipment, although the enemy had outmatched us in mechanized vehicles, in the air and in the emphasis he had clearly put on using air power as an adjunct and close support to land operations. Nor had we been beaten by superior numbers. We had been beaten by dynamism; by entirely traditional 'grand tactics' or operational doctrine; by excellent minor tactics, fitness and discipline; but *above all* by an army imbued with high, confident morale and the spirit of the offensive. We didn't appreciate such things at the time, but – particularly at the beginning of a war or a campaign – he who attacks has a priceless initiative. He can plan, rehearse, choose his place and his moment. For him who defends there is a two-fold penalty: he does not know what to expect because the enemy holds the initiative, and he does not know what to expect because the whole experience of war is new. By their absolute determination to stand on the operational defensive (drawing false lessons from partial perceptions of the previous war) the Western Allies made their defeat virtually certain.

What of the men, the people themselves? The popular image was of Germans intimidated by tyranny, devoid of initiative, obeying mechanically or through fear, opposed by free-born Britons, believing in their way of life, in democracy, in liberty. Surely the latter cause, so morally superior, would triumph? Surely men raised in liberty must, like Athenians facing Persians of old, prove superior on the battlefield? Our experiences with the Berkshires were inducing scepticism on this score (excessively so, I think) and some stories from Dunkirk were reinforcing it. It didn't seem that we had outclassed the enemy, to put it mildly. There were stories of indiscipline, of cowardice, of officers deserting their men, of positions abandoned without shame; and some of the stories were true.

There was one further, understandable but unattractive, aspect of the search for scapegoats for that defeat. The French and Belgians were everywhere blamed by the British for the disaster. It was said – and truthfully said – that the morale of the French Army had in many cases been poor, that they had not fought, that it had been clear even before the battle that they would not fight. France, it was said, was rotten. What could one expect? I think we were inclined to believe much of this.

The condition and performance of the French under arms in 1940 have been endlessly analysed. In too few cases have the heroic episodes of the campaign been remembered – the battles of small numbers against huge odds, the resistance to the death in hopeless circumstances, and the formidable tally of casualties. Too seldom remembered by the British has been the minuscule contribution made by ourselves, some of it of poor quality and equally poor performance. Nobody had much to be proud of in 1940, except the Germans; and they had a very great deal.

I have a clear picture in my mind of Ditchley Park, that fine house near Charlbury. Leaving our squalid billets in Charlbury – this must have been in July 1940, I think – Tom Miller and I went for a walk one beautiful evening. All signposts had been removed (to avoid helping the invader) and we had no idea where we were, but after a little we saw the splendid front of the house, with statues prominent on the roof. I had seen photographs of it and remembered.

'I think that's Ditchley.'

The road runs quite near the house and we stood and gazed at it for a little. There was absolute silence everywhere. Tom said, 'We've got to face it, you know.'

'Face what?'

'Unconditional surrender. We can see or guess enough to realize that that's what's coming if they invade. We're up against people in a completely different league. I know there must be better troops around than our bunch of criminal young thugs but it's obvious we couldn't win. If they come.'

'Well, let's hope they don't,' I said.

And they didn't.

I don't think Tom believed what he was saying but its clarity was coldly refreshing. He was wondering whether, if we ever got leave, he should marry in haste, although only nineteen, and try to leave a child – he was in love with a girl in Sussex. His occasional letters throughout the war were shrewd and perceptive, but I only saw him once or twice after we both left the Berkshires. He was commissioned in the 60th Rifles. His last letter to me in the autumn of 1942 described, exultantly, the successful defensive battle we fought against Rommel's exhausted pursuers in Egypt, after Gazala, before Alam Halfa. He was killed at Mareth in North Africa in March 1943.

We were at Shipton-under-Wychwood when I was sent for to the Company Office – we were billeted in a large school. Rather remarkably considering the many matters the British Army was having to arrange at that time, a piece of official paper had arrived with my number and name on it. I was to report to the Guards Depot at Caterham for Recruit Training on 20th September 1940. Laden with full marching order, dressed as a Corporal in Royal Berkshires uniform, in crowded buses and trains without hope of a seat, I made my way.

The Guards Depot was in a Victorian barracks on the top of a hill outside Caterham. Next to it and very visible was a lunatic asylum of not dissimilar architectural style, subject of innumerable wry sallies. The Depot had been hugely expanded when war came and a hutted camp, an additional enormous parade ground and a large number of temporary roads – muddy and undrained in winter – had been constructed. Many thousands of recruits for the Foot Guards were processed every few months, before moving to the Training Battalions each Guards Regiment maintained as pools from which to feed Service Battalions or in which to hold the unfit, the wounded, the returned for whatever reason. The Grenadier Training Battalion – also huge, because there was now no fighting since we had been expelled from France, no casualties, and Service Battalions were full of both officers and men – was at Windsor, both in the barracks and in billets all over the town, including in the Mews of Windsor Castle itself.

At Caterham each Regiment maintained its Company; and each Company was composed of a large number of squads, each with about twenty recruits. Each Regiment also maintained, as one of the Depot squads, a 'Brigade Squad' of potential officers. This segregated us from the rest of the recruits and has been criticized for that reason. We were, after all, taking part in a great innovation in the British Army, started in 1939, whereby every officer must have 'gone through the ranks'. By segregation at the Depot stage we were, it was said, going past rather than through the ranks; and the practice was perpetuating the class divisions which the system was, in theory, meant to circumvent. All this was true – again in theory. The country, however, now needed officers without unnecessary delay, and brigade squads did a shorter recruit course before sending their products on to an Officer Cadet

Training Unit for longer indoctrination. Recruits in other squads could be – and were – selected for officer training as well. Meanwhile a 'batch' of potential officers were conveniently handled together. To us, of course – quite apart from any advantages or disadvantages of principle – it was a great blessing. We were with our friends. The most important thing in a war is to spend it with one's friends.

Each squad was in the hands of a Lance Sergeant or Lance Corporal Instructor. A number of squads were grouped under a Superintendant Sergeant. The squad lived together in a barrackroom or hut (even in the old barracks every square yard had been used for the erection of additional huts). Within these quarters the squad was in the care of a Trained Soldier – a Guardsman not holding non-commissioned rank but nevertheless a superior, to be addressed and treated as such.

'Leave to fall in, Trained Soldier.'

'No. Get out and march in again properly. And stand up straight when you're talking to me.'

'Yes, Trained Soldier.'

'Well, get on and do it, then. And – CHRIST, CLOSE YOUR HEELS!, you're meant to be at attention!'

'Yes, Trained Soldier.'

And so on.

First arrival at the Guards Depot was certainly intimidating. I was at a disadvantage being already in uniform – and with the stripes of a Corporal on my arm, quickly removed – so that while the others were making a fresh start in military life amidst a good deal of hilarity, my kit and various necessaries were expected to be present and in good order. After the Berkshires they weren't. But a great joy was to discover many Eton friends in the squad – and a great many others who became fast friends thereafter. The experience of the Depot was physically exhausting but was also a tonic. And seldom in life have I laughed more, or in better company.

It was a tonic, and a much-needed tonic because now, at last, I was part of an organization with really high standards, really strict discipline and really good morale. From the moment a recruit arrived at the Caterham barrack gate and was marched off by a picquet sentry to join his squad, feet moving so fast that he seemed to be flying, there was not a moment to relax: through the first haircut (a shaven head) to the first and subsequent drill parades; through the sound of reveille blown by bugle at six o'clock, with all recruits tumbled out and standing at attention by beds one minute later; through the occasions when it was decided (on principle) that we had been 'idle' and needed sharpening up – HALT! Stand at ease! 'GAS'! (old-style respirators on – most uncomfortable from a respiratory point of view) – Squad shun! Squad will fix bayonets – FIX! (this was the old, long sword-bayonet, with a tricky fitment to the rifle for the inexperienced or maladroit) – BAYONETS! Slope Arms! Quick March! Left – right – (what seemed thirty miles an hour) – Break into double time, Double MARCH! Mark TIME! Lift Knees, Up, Up, Up!

Through the shining parades, when we sat astride our beds in the evening, a tin of boot polish and duster in hand, and answered questions on Regimental history, Regimental personalities and so on – the progress of shine on boots was a matter of unceasing anxiety.

'Those boots are below standard! Unless you get a move on them you'll find yourself back-squadded, lad!' Official shining parade only lasted an hour but we kept at it until lights out. And it was in the unofficial parts of it that we could wander a little, laugh, gossip, make friends. Smoke. Although if a matchstick fell to the floor at the wrong moment –

March down the barrackroom. Stamp to attention.

'Leave to fall out, Trained Soldier.'

A nod. A turn to the right, a march back, a retrieved match stick, its disposal, another march down the barrackroom.

'Leave to fall in, Trained Soldier.'

Another nod. The bugle for Lights out. Sleep on three wooden trestles placed on two wooden stretchers and surmounted by three 'Biscuits', square mattress-like objects. Two blankets.

Through all these experiences the impression was indelible. We were in a bit of the Army quite unlike any other. And it worked.

But this was 1940, and already the Guards Depot had been bombed and a number of Irish Guards recruits killed. At frequent intervals on most days the sirens would go. Then, from nearby Kenley Airfield, the fighters would scramble and take off over the Depot within, I suppose, a half-minute. Hurricanes. When it happened by day – this was the season of the Luftwaffe's great daylight raids on London – there was always a chance that we would be mercifully dismissed from drill on the square, but this didn't happen often. The anti-aircraft guns made an incessant clatter during raids but only rarely did we simultaneously hear the wonderful, welcome 'Disperse' blown on the bugles, which meant a squad being fallen in and dismissed to the air raid shelters for a brief respite on the damp benches before physical activity began again with the damnable blowing of 'All Clear'.

It was, of course, necessary to give us the Air Raid Precaution orders from the start and on our first evening the Squad Instructor and Trained Soldier formed us up in the barrackroom. On the blowing of the Alarm (this was done by the drummers, bicycling rapidly through barracks, handlebars controlled by left hand, bugle held to mouth by right) all recruits were to move instantly by day or night to the nearest shelter. The shelters were trenches dug (in our case) on the cricket ground and roofed over with corrugated iron and plenty of earth atop. They were very damp and muddy. The way down to them in darkness was particularly slippery and treacherous.

I can see our squad instructor, something of a wag, as he gave out the orders to our astonished and apprehensive squad members.

'Get this clear. On the alarm being sounded every recruit will move in double time to the shelter and will take steel helmet, respirator, rifle, bayonet and his bandolier of twenty-five rounds of ammunition!'

So we were ready for anything. We soon, what is more, learned additionally to take candle, matches, duster, bootpolish tin and boots in the hand, so that we could continue shining and not waste precious minutes. On occasion the alarm went several times in one night, although I never remember the fact being accepted as excuse for the slightest lowering of standards required in the morning.

It so happened that the alarm was blown soon after we turned in for our first night at the Depot – puzzled, laughing somewhat nervously, ignorant of exactly where our designated shelter was, in most cases completely new to the Army and its ways. Then the bugle – insistent, unmistakable. The 'Alarm'.

'That's it!'

Out we tumbled in the darkness. Somehow we found the bits and pieces we'd been ordered to bring. Somehow we found the doors, the path, the shelter. The Depot, naturally, was under total blackout, with no light anywhere.

'This way, this way!'

We pushed into the trench. After a while laughter, chatter, began. Suddenly the blanket hung over the entrance to the trench was pushed back and a senior NCO materialized (very obviously; we couldn't see him, we could only hear him, which was enough) – 'Pay attention, all Recruits in here! There is a raid on!' As if we didn't know. Both bombs and guns were noisy and, it seemed, not far distant.

'Recruits will remain here until the All Clear is blown. Thereafter Recruits are to return to barrackrooms fast. Any recruit returning to the shelters without orders after the blowing of the "All Clear" will be shot for cowardice!' He disappeared.

It seemed pretty definite. I don't expect anyone believed it. But there was a general feeling that we were in the Army now, and no mistake. After the atmosphere of insubordinate laxity and indisciplined malad-ministration in the Berkshires (inevitable given the circumstances) the Guards Depot was a superb experience. Training was confined, of course, to the basics of drill, personal weapon-training, physical training and Regimental indoctrination. More sophisticated and tactical training came later, at Windsor, in Service Battalions. The object of the Depot was to make a Guardsman – for on 'passing out', inspected by the Commandant and approved, a man bore that proud title.

Sometimes a squad had particular fatigues or duties. One of these was 'Passive Air Defence' when, instead of going to the shelters when the alarm blew, we doubled to some other particular point in barracks. On one such occasion my own duty was to double with our Trained Soldier to man a sandbagged embrasure at the corner of the parade ground, steel helmet on and eye-shields (anti-gas) at the ready. It was a beautiful morning, we had raced away from drill when the bugles sounded, and now the air was full not only of gunfire and bomb explosions but of the droning of huge numbers of aircraft.

I looked upwards. A fanntastic sight, high in the heavens, hundreds of German bombers with sunlight glinting on their wings. Circling round them like sheepdogs could be seen their own fighters, protective, apparently infinite in number. They were flying north, towards London. We were meant (I can't remember why, or, indeed, what our function was) to remain uncomfortably below the sandbagged parapet. Suddenly the Trained Soldier hissed, 'Get down!'

It sounded urgent and I did. After a moment I said, 'What is it, Trained Soldier? Bombs?' One could often see bombs, black and falling.

'Fuck bombs!' he said, shortly. 'It's the Drill-Sergeant-in-waiting!' Drill Sergeants in the Foot Guards were Warrant Officers, two per battalion and two at the Depot, who acted as eyes and ears of the Regimental Sergeant Major, and generally harried lower forms of life.

All this, laugh as we often did, was superb human and moral rather than technical training. The Guards Depot was the indispensable manufactory of the soldiers of the Brigade of Guards. A man was changed by it, reborn. Its system – easy to smile at in later life, in quieter circumstances – lay at the heart of whatever successes the Foot Guards achieved, whether in peace or war. Furthermore its fame was widespread and it set a standard, recognized even if reluctantly, for the entire Army. Questionable counsels have more recently led to its abolition. I do not believe the virtues it produced will be so certainly attained by other means, and perhaps not at all.

We 'passed out', after eight weeks, inspected by the Commandant, Lieutenant-Colonel the Earl of Romney, Coldstream Guards, who had a black patch over one eye and spoke to each recruit, mostly about the standard attained for his boots (mine were indifferent). Then we went in a body to the 161st Officer Cadet Training Unit (OCTU) in the buildings of the Royal Military College at Sandhurst. There the regimen was also arduous, with ferocious warrant officers and unceasing drill, physical training, weapon-training, inspections; but there were also lectures, tactical training of an elementary kind, and instruction in the rudiments of military administration. At Sandhurst, however, we were living in a much more relaxed way than at the Depot. We each had a small room. Those with radios or gramophones could play them. Food, although not very appetizing, was served in a dining room by the former Military College Staff. It was all a contrast, and an enjoyable one.

The greatest blessing of Sandhurst lay in the discovery or rediscovery of friends. Since I had left Eton – unexpectedly – a little over a year before there had been a sort of diaspora of familiars. Now it was possible to find what the war had done to friends, where it had deposited them. And a good many were here, at Sandhurst. By word of mouth I learned more of my friends from Upcott's and from Eton. From our old 'Library' in Keate House I had, of course, been with Tom Miller until recently. Patrick Nugent – from both St Aubyn's and Upcott's – had gone to Caterham on the same day as I, destined to be a Grenadier. A good oarsman and a charming, fun-loving Ulsterman, he had been part of my life since 1930. (He would be killed in Tunisia.) Jock Russell, another from Upcott's, was, I learned, about to become a Gordon Highlander. He was a competent and enormously enthusiastic cricketer and follower of cricket – a sort of Brian Johnston in the making – and an equally enthusiastic painter of wildfowl. He had an irresistible, chuckling sense of humour and of the ridiculous. Later he was taken prisoner by the Japanese when Singapore fell in early 1942.

I next saw him in London, on leave very shortly after the war. He looked a bad colour – unsurprisingly. I took him to tea at the Guards Club and we caught up with a little of life – we had been close friends. I asked him, tentatively, about the Japanese, his gaolers.

'Oh well,' Jock said, in the easy, *dégagé* way I remembered so well, 'all those people, in that part of the world, are the same. You simply can't expect them to behave like you and me. They don't know any better!' It struck me then and strikes me now as a marvel of fundamental generosity, and if it is also as patronizing as we all were, the generosity surely far exceeds the patronage. Jock became a very successful stock jobber with Wedd Jefferson.

Returning in spirit to Upcott's Library I was able to learn of the Neville brothers. The younger, Robert, had been a friend and contemporary: eccentric, reserved, witty, unathletic, avowedly intending to be ordained in the Church of England. His elder brother, Dickie (by then Lord Braybrooke), had been in College, a scholar and a good medium-pace bowler. Both brothers were extremely clever and cultivated. Dickie, slightly older than me, I had not known but soon would – he became a Grenadier, was with me at Windsor, and would be killed in Tunisia in January 1943, while Robert would die at sea as an Ordinary Seaman in the Royal Navy in 1941.

The Nevilles were academically gifted, scholarly, precise in speech, rather old-fashioned in outlook and with quirky and highly individual senses of humour. They both needed knowing and were shy – they were originally an acquired taste but an enjoyable one. They lived in a famous and beautiful house, Audley End near Saffron Walden in Essex. They were a family with a considerable gap between generations – their father was born during or immediately after the Crimean War, in which his uncle, a Grenadier, had been killed at Inkerman. They were distant relatives of mine through the Maudes on my mother's side, and had a hereditary connection with Magdalene College, Cambridge, of which Lord Braybrooke was Visitor. It was good to hear of them once again from friends who had come from Cambridge to the Army.

But a figure ubiquitous, memorable and deeply impressive from those Sandhurst days was our Company Sergeant Major, John Lord, Grenadier Guards. When we first arrived at the OCTU from Caterham we found ourselves standing in a queue ready to march up and report to a man seated at a table in one of the ante-rooms. Peering round the queue we could see an exceptionally ferocious, black-moustached face beneath a red-banded Grenadier forage cap, and could hear an equally ferocious voice. 'Stand up straight, Sir, and give me your number and name! Now turn about, go out and tell the next Cadet to report. I SAID TURN ABOUT, SIR! COME BACK!'

Malcolm Strang-Steel, a tall, gangling, wholly delightful fellow-Grenadier from Caterham, gazed rather anxiously towards the door. He turned to me and muttered,

'I'm not sure I like the Company Sergeant Major, David!'

Most unusually, Malcolm* was not only wrong but utterly wrong. Lord was one of the great of the earth, and the greatest figure to impinge on the Sandhurst landscape. He was a man of imposing appearance and with a personality which immediately dominated an assembly or a parade ground. Smart, upright, physically masterful, he exuded strength, indomitability and – when he removed the mask a little, as he often did – humour and kindness. He was intelligent, a

---

* Malcolm Strang-Steel, like Tom Miller and many other friends, was killed in the 6th Battalion Grenadier Guards at their first battle, at Mareth in Tunisia in March 1943; a battle in which, of the Battalion's twenty-nine officers, fourteen were killed and ten others wounded or taken prisoner, most of the latter wounded as well.

thoughtful and articulate man who understood the world. Now, as our Company Sergeant Major he was, quite simply, the most formidable man most of us had ever encountered: nothing in the next four months (the length of the OCTU course) changed our opinions.

After the war Lord, by then a Regimental Sergeant Major, became a famous Academy Sergeant Major back at Sandhurst, where he influenced – for good – large numbers of cadets, including future generals, Ministers and Kings. But my memory produces an image from April 1945. The war was approaching its end and the Guards Armoured Division was advancing rapidly through Northern Germany. We halted for a night and a morning near a place called Fallingbostel where, it was rumoured, there was a prisoner-of-war camp. Somebody said that a number of British prisoners taken with the 1st Airborne Division at Arnhem were interned there, 'including Sergeant Major Lord, it's said'. Lord had volunteered for the Airborne Forces when the British Parachute troops were formed, and had been a Regimental Sergeant Major with one of the Parachute Battalions. We were not due to move for some hours. I was at our Battalion Headquarters and asked my Commanding Officer if I could take a vehicle and go to investigate. I arrived at an enormous, barbed-wire-surrounded camp. At the gate was a British sentry, armed, immaculate. He might have been on a barrack guard in London. An NCO was with him.

'Can you tell me if a Sergeant Major Lord is here?' The corporal nodded and indicated. I walked down the long line of huts and outside one I heard a familiar sound of boots stamping on floorboards and an equally familiar bark from long ago. 'Number, rank and name?'

I went in. Lord – immaculate as ever but with maroon beret rather than the Grenadier forage cap – was busy recording prisoners' names, beginning a process of bringing strict administration out of disorder. When I saw him he stood, grin immense, salute as perfect as ever. To keep him from the Germans, who, he'd learned, had planned to deport him as a dangerous influence, he'd been hidden under the floorboards of a hut for seven days. I was the first British officer he'd seen and we had a memorable reunion. He gave out, as he always did, an aura of reassurance and vigour. From the whole landscape of my memory I treasure that figure above most.

Because 'call-up' was staggered by age for most of the population,

I found at Sandhurst fellow-cadets who were years older than I. Some men had been deferred or exempted as over age but had applied to join despite their years. This meant that there was also a huge range of differing experience. I and most of my immediate colleagues had come virtually straight from school or university; we were children. Others had already begun – or in some cases experienced for a considerable time – professional lives. They were extraordinarily tolerant of us, their juniors in age, who must often have been irritating with our immaturities and callow enthusiasms. Two figures, who both became particular friends, stand out from the Sandhurst scene.

I have written elsewhere* about William Douglas Home, who had joined our company at the same time as us, from service as a lance corporal in the Buffs. He was exceptionally entertaining and, with the cadets, popular. He had a delightful wit and made light of life in a way which seldom endeared him to the authorities, but enchanted us. He had, for us, a certain glamour which came from his association with the stage, and he enjoyed learning of my connection to Grandpa Maude. He was kind to others, friendly, funny, and although we could not foresee the great success as a playwright which came to him later, we would not have been in the least surprised. His younger brother had been a contemporary of mine at Eton.

William made no secret of his opinions. He was a rebel. He was critical of the war, which he thought unnecessary; and believed that we had not sought peace when it might have been had, with intelligence or understanding. We had blundered ahead without comprehension, and had then got angry. His natural humanity made him loathe the idea of war; and his inborn dislike of self-righteousness always made him quick to see an enemy's viewpoint. He was very alert to the ease with which men apply to themselves different standards from those which they expect in an adversary.

I did not at the time agree with him over the war, and do not in retrospect. The evidence was, and is, that Hitler sought to obtain his ends not peacefully but by violence: and the campaign in the east was not forced upon him. However, William's views later impelled him into a vigorous demand for some definition of our war aims, and in

* *Will* (David Fraser, Andře Deutsch, 1995).

this he was surely right. He condemned an attitude to the war which made the waging of it an end in itself. War, he said, is detestable: and if ever justified it must be for some finite and comprehensible political object. Otherwise it becomes an exercise in killing – unlimited, insensate, and inevitably creating more problems than it solves. These opinions ultimately brought him to protest, and prison. It is ironical that they uphold principles of sanity which have been most consistently and cogently pressed not by the most vociferous apostles of peace, but by the most intelligent students of war. War is a political instrument, one in which political warfare, psychological action, propaganda and combat operations must all be woven into one pattern. At Sandhurst William and I argued passionately. He regarded me as reactionary and obstinate. But we became great friends and the friendship lasted throughout life. And I always much admired the best of William's play-writing. It has so much of his character in it – light of touch, inventive, entertaining and invariably generous.

The other figure from a slightly older generation who occupies the foreground in my memories of Sandhurst was Robin Fyfe. Robin had been in our squad at Caterham as a slightly improbable candidate for the Grenadiers and we had all taken him to our hearts, albeit somewhat perplexedly. He had a huge head, very fair hair and at that time a fair and luxuriant moustache. He had gone from Cambridge into the Indian Army, inspired by an ineradicable romanticism – 'ineradicable' because to my knowledge he never lost it. He saw himself sitting in some Himalayan pass with a rifle across his knees and a volume of poetry – he could quote and recite ad infinitum – also to hand. He loved song, women and (later, although not at that time) wine. He had a beautiful, gentle and enchanting wife, similar in temperament to himself.

Robin had been invalided out of the Indian Army after falling off a horse on to his head, and he undoubtedly suffered thereafter from the effects of this accident, which left him damaged, although the damage was not always detected. He was not only a romantic to the core of his being but an incorrigible exhibitionist. He loved the character and works of Sir Richard Burton and would read them aloud, squatting on the floor of the canteen at Sandhurst in Pathan clothes (he had served during his brief Indian military service with the Pathans), reading with vivid miming from Burton's bawdy and brilliant edition of *The Arabian Nights*. Sergeant-Major Lord viewed him with tolerance and a wide grin masking the severity.

'Come along, Mr Fyfe! That'll do!'

Robin was perhaps the kindest and most generous person I have ever known. He had enormous wells of affection inside him and he dispensed it freely. He was wholly unworldly, and was incapable of thinking ill of anyone – a characteristic he shared with William Douglas Home. He was not destined by providence to be a soldier – he was not destined for any profession. His humour was irresistible and irreverent. His tastes were literary, but he had little of the self-discipline writing demands. His genius – and it was genius – was in personal relationships. Because he was so extraordinarily sympathetic he made improbable people feel valued. He touched with his friendship and affection large numbers who had, perhaps, seldom known friendship or affection before. He took an interest in the lives of all, and the interest was sincere. For the world at war he was unsuited – he could only see it through a generous cloud of illusion. He was disorganized and in the ordinary sense totally inefficient. But he made a great many people happier.

We were quartered in the 'New Building' at Sandhurst – a huge, red-brick adjunct to the noble, classical 'Old Building'. One evening a bomb was dropped on it – I expect that a German bomber returning from some slightly more worthwhile target area like London had jettisoned its bombload before going home. I was in one of the glass-roofed lavatories and got away with part of the glass roof coming down on my head, which sent me, blood streaming, to the temporary hospital set up in one of the Sandhurst houses, but with no serious damage. Several of our friends, including two from our Caterham squad, were killed and we were drilled at the next opportunity with particular ferocity – 'chased', in soldiers' parlance – by the Regimental Sergeant Major, Brand, a Grenadier. It was supposed that this treatment would be good for morale and drive away any tendency to melancholy. It probably wasn't a bad idea. We buried our comrades with full ceremony, following the Sandhurst Military Band, our officers and the coffins.

Eventually we passed out from Sandhurst. The final parade (which

I missed, having broken some bones in my foot) took its traditional form, with the Adjutant riding up the steps of the Old Building on his charger. My father was now Brigadier General Staff at the Head-quarters of an Army Corps, quartered at Taunton, and I stayed for a short leave with him in the Senior Officers' Mess. At the beginning of April 1941 I joined the Training Battalion of the Grenadier Guards at Windsor as a Second Lieutenant – known in the Brigade of Guards as an Ensign. It was a great day and I had, for eighteen months, been impatiently awaiting it. Initially, of course, I had been concerned that the war might end before I could participate – like most generations at the start of most wars. By now it was clear that I needn't have worried.

8

Time of Preparation

Everybody who joins the Grenadier Guards owes a considerable debt. I owe more than most. My Regiment gave me happiness, friendship and firm military principles. The love and admiration which it rightly commands is unbounded, and the longer his service with it the more involved with its fortunes a man becomes. Its good name is a matter of very personal concern, while any fault, inadequacy or departure from standards is felt in the individual's heart. So it is with every distinguished Regiment, Corps or Service and so it must be – as was impressed on me and all my friends from the first day – with each of us. Because we were British no attitudes were struck, inner feeling was lightened with humour, a little amiable mockery and self-mockery were indulged. But in all of us this feeling was present, and it deepened with time.

The first gift bestowed by the Regiment was the sense of high standards. Nothing but the best would do – a lesson already vigorously taught at the Guards Depot. No detail was too small to be exempted from the demands of perfection. Since the Regiment, like all others, was composed of fallible human beings these standards were not invariably maintained, but the important thing was and is that they exist: beyond argument. Strict attention to detail was the passkey to the standards required. This exactitude – finding its most obvious and ubiquitous expression in matters of drill and dress on formal occasions (and, at least in peacetime, less formal occasions also) – was sometimes thought unnecessary or overdone. It reflected, however, the traditional belief in the Regiment that by insistence on strict obedience and observance at the most simple level more serious derelictions become less likely. As with every traditional belief, application of principle to practice needs constant thought to ensure that it does not become a matter of mindless and irritating pettifoggery, but if common sense – that superb and particularly British solvent – is injected into the veins of principle at regular intervals I believe that our traditional belief in this regard was and is sound. Demand attention to detail and you will have less misbehaviour, and less necessity for punishment.

The next gift the Regiment conferred was the sharing in its history and traditions. I knew something of these from family connection – I was the fourth of my family to hold a commission in the 1st Guards and I was proud of the fact that the first of us had gained distinction as the defender of the orchard at Hougoumont in the Battle of Waterloo. From the first day I enjoyed reading – and giving periodic lectures to the Guardsmen – about the campaigns of the Regiment, about the complicated history of the Regiment's Colours (which I learned with fascination but without practical application, since all Battalion Colours had been removed from Battalion care for the duration of the war), about the origins of Regimental customs and their observance. All these things worked their way into the bloodstream and became a part of the background to life. Every institution is the stronger for a vivid and well-recorded tradition, history and assemblage of 'family habits'. Tradition, nevertheless, should not become the enemy of efficiency, and only does so if it is misunderstood. It should not become a brake on progress. It should, instead, add depth and a certain wisdom to developments – those who lack the knowledge, sense or humility to look well back in time seldom look far forward. Obsessed with the immediate, they lose sight of the fact that tomorrow today will become yesterday.

My Regiment, as I have said, had its origin in 1656 when Charles II, in exile, formed a personal guard from loyal fellow-exiles in Flanders. At the Restoration the King formed another Regiment of Guards at home, and then amalgamated the two. This – the Royal, later the First – Regiment of Foot Guards won distinction on the battlefields of Europe as the wars against France of the Spanish and Austrian Succession, and the Seven Years' War, formed and tested the new British Regular Army. By the time of the Napoleonic Wars the Regiment, after a hundred and forty years, had acquired certain characteristics, a certain 'style' which remained constant, an emphasis on exactness, precision and conscientious observance of orders. In reading contemporary letters and diaries of those times one is struck less by the expected and vivid differences from our own experience than by how much produces an echoing ring.

In the Peninsular War the Regiment earned Moore's commendation at Corunna, as an example to the army of discipline and good conduct amid the frightful ordeals of the retreat. The example was to a significant degree re-enacted at Dunkirk nine months before I joined. At Waterloo the name 'Grenadier' was won when the Regiment was made 'a Regiment of Grenadiers' after the battle, in honour of the final defeat of the grenadiers of the Imperial Guard.

At Inkerman in Crimea, in 1854, the 3rd Battalion had won immortal renown for their tenacity. In the First World War four battalions had formed part of the Guards Division, eighteen thousand Grenadier recruits had passed through the Regiment's ranks and some fifteen thousand officers and men had been killed or died of their wounds. Now, in the Second World War, all three Regular Battalions – 1st, 2nd and 3rd – had been in the British Expeditionary Force commanded by Lord Gort, a Grenadier, in the recent campaign in France and Flanders which culminated in the evacuation from Dunkirk; while three new Battalions, 4th, 5th and 6th, had just been formed. History was a living thing.

The last great gift every Grenadier inherits is fellowship. Writing of standards, of discipline, it is easy to strike a formidable, unbending note. The image can be misleadingly severe. The reality – in all ranks – was of abounding laughter, friendship, trust and happiness. This was the happiness of shared experience, shared loyalties, shared hardships. It took time to enter fully into this inheritance, but this was the family I had now joined.

On reporting to the Grenadiers' Training Battalion to undergo the usual Young Officers' courses and to indulge in the usual young officers' escapades in nearby blitzed and exciting London, I was posted to No. 1 Company, stationed within Windsor Castle itself. The Company was responsible for the immediate protection of the Royal Family if there were to be an airborne assault on England, presumably as part of a general invasion. Since we officers had rooms in the Lower Ward we were made members of the Equerries' Mess and often dined in it. Lunch for two officers (there were five in the Company) was taken as guests of the Royal Family if we were not out on training, and very kind, hospitable and friendly to us they invariably were.

The Equerries' Mess was congenial and educative. Most of its regular members were of our parents' generation rather than our own. One who became a particular and treasured friend was the King's Private Secretary (at that time Assistant Private Secretary), Sir Alan Lascelles. 'Tommy' Lascelles had a thin moustache, a spare, elegant figure, and was especially good at talking to the young – one of those often met in these pages who seemed oblivious of age. He talked of sport, books, history, philosophy, war – he had served, of course, in the First War, like all his generation. He was an admirable companion, with broad experience, his reading wide but unobtrusive, his memory good, his turn of phrase sharp, his comments on personalities pungent. There was little equivocation. His charming son, John, was an Eton and Grenadier contemporary of mine who became an especial friend after the war and died tragically young, from illness rather than the hand of the enemy.

Tommy Lascelles was the prime agent in a turn in my own life many years later. In 1973 I wrote an article in *History Today*. I was surprised to receive a letter from him recalling our talks in Windsor days and asking me to lunch – he lived in an apartment in the Old Stables at Kensington Palace. We had occasionally met and corresponded in the intervening years . . . At lunch he reminisced about the Second World War and the leading figures in that drama. He spoke with great admiration of the Chief of the Imperial General Staff, Alan Brooke.

'The most formidable of our military men in that war! I'd hate to have been told off by Brookie – I never was, but I'd have hated it. Has his life been written?'

I said that as far as I knew Arthur Bryant had edited selections from Brooke's diaries but it was not a full biography.

'There must be one done. Why don't you do it?'

I made the usual noises. Unqualified. Busy (I was Vice Chief of the General Staff at the time and there was a good deal to do). And so forth.

'Well, I think you should. Think about it.'

Tommy Lascelles had latterly grown a luxuriant grey beard and looked like a figure from the Old Testament. I said I'd think about it, and from that conversation came the first book I ever wrote, although it would not be published until 1982.

When I had been about three months at Windsor and was about to go at last to a Service Battalion, the German Army invaded Russia. 'Barbarossa', the huge operation which Hitler believed would smash the unstable edifice of Stalin's Communist empire, was launched on 22nd June 1941. Churchill immediately proclaimed that any enemy of Hitler's was a friend of ours. The war became a very different sort of struggle.

The immediate consequence, of course, was that the Germans had taken on a new and enormous adversary. 'One kick at the door and the whole rotten structure will collapse,' Hitler had remarked, and as the German spearheads advanced deep into Russia and the Ukraine on three divergent axes, while reports came in of hundreds of thousands of Russian prisoners, of whole armies surrounded and surrendering, it seemed to the watching world as if Hitler might have been right. In the autumn the divisions of General von Bock's Army Group Centre were in the outskirts of Moscow. Then the weather and numerous reinforcements brought from the eastern provinces of the Soviet Union turned the tide.

The military, the political and the moral situations were all trans-formed by 'Barbarossa'. In his biography of Sir Stafford Cripps Colin Cooke remarks of it, 'There was no one in Britain who did not welcome the new Alliance.' This is untrue. There were a number, and I was one of them. Of course it was strategically advantageous, although by then Hitler's attention had turned away and any direct German attempt to invade Britain was improbable. Nevertheless it was certainly hard to see in the summer of 1941 how we could actually win the war – or, rather, how Germany could fail at the least to produce a favourable draw. 'Barbarossa' provided an answer to that. Another answer – clinching the ultimate result of the war – came in December that year when Japan attacked the United States and British possessions in South East Asia, a move immediately followed by a declaration of war on America by Germany. This was probably the most foolish of Hitler's many follies. The strategic tide turned at the end of 1942 when the great Soviet victory at Stalingrad and the great Anglo-American victory in Tunisia took place. From late summer 1943 the war news in military terms became excellent and the Soviets swarmed across the frontiers of Poland, Romania, Hungary, ultimately Germany. Strategically 'Barbarossa' was a watershed in the European war. Politically, however, it did not take great insight in and after 1941 to see that if the Continent of Europe – or the centre and east of it – were not dominated by a victorious Germany it would be dominated by a victorious Soviet Union. There seemed little reason to rejoice at this.

There was even less reason to rejoice as the war went on and it became clear what sort of regime the Soviets were likely to impose on lands they occupied and equally clear what the unfortunate inhabitants of those lands could expect from the Red Army. They were in most cases exchanging one ferocious oppressor for another. There was widespread knowledge of this, although the official line in Britain was sternly opposed to any denigration of the Soviet ally. There were in Britain, however, large numbers of Poles (for instance), soon joined by many others who had been prisoners in Russia since Stalin's invasion of Eastern Poland in harmony with Hitler in 1939. There were many sources of information from eastern Europe later in the war and they all told the same tale – barbarity, mass murder, the elimination of non-Communists, the deportation of thousands, perhaps millions, to unknown destinations in the far reaches of the Soviet Union. This had already been the fate of many in the Baltic States. These things were not unknown, and some periodicals in England – notably the *Tablet* – were able, cautiously, to refer to them since, of course, persecution of the Church was an invariable facet of Soviet policy.

Nobody argued – or should have argued – that the Nazi regime in the occupied countries was not evil; but there was considerable reluctance in Britain – encouraged by official policy and censorship – to face the fact that it was likely to be replaced by something equally repulsive. This became increasingly clear. The bright, clean ideals which had shone in 1939 and 1940 when Hitler and Stalin had been allies and, from June 1940, when it was Britain *contra mundum* – these ideals seemed increasingly tarnished. We were in bad company. The political and strategic inevitability of this – or most of this – was clear, but any sense of triumph at victory when victory came was overshadowed, and the shadows lay long.

The domestic political effect in Britain of 'Barbarossa' was remarkable. Until then the Communist Party had opposed the war as a 'Capitalist struggle'. Now the Party line from Moscow changed – naturally and instantly. Soon we were told by everyone on the political Left that only the Soviet Union had in the past seriously opposed Hitler or was now serious in fighting him (Hitler, recipient of Stalin's congratulations after his victories in 1940). The British Communist Party increased its numbers very significantly, particularly in the factories. The general – and justified – sympathy British people felt with the Russians, resisting the German onslaught with undoubted valour, was transmuted as far as could be managed into a sympathy, qualified perhaps, with the system for which the brave Russians were apparently fighting and dying. To criticize that system became subversive, almost pro-German. Such was the general burden of official publications and propaganda, although, of course, many people were sceptical – the resistance of the British to belief in what their authorities tell them is undoubtedly their noblest virtue. Nevertheless, cheerful admiration for 'Uncle Joe' Stalin, depicted as a rough, tough, magnanimous son of the people, standing up to Hitler and doing the bulk of the fighting (this, of course, was largely true), presiding over a people united in classless, unselfish comradeship – this picture coloured most of the popular press and a good deal of the public mind.

At about the time 'Barbarossa' began I was, to my joy, sent to a Service Battalion – the 2nd – which was, on and off, to be my home for more than six years. The Battalion was stationed in billets in Sherborne, and I joined it, with several others, at a moment of extraordinary transformation.

The 2nd Battalion had taken part in the brief and disastrous campaign in France and Belgium in 1940 and had been a good deal shaken by the extraordinary and unexpected superiority shown by the enemy, whether in equipment, numbers, enterprise or tactical skill. Our elders, therefore, knew things about war which we, the newcomers, did not. They had been 'in action', been blooded. But now we – and they – had to learn completely new tricks.

In May 1941 it had been decided to form a Guards Armoured Division. Six – later seven – Guards Battalions were to be equipped with tanks. Others became 'Motor' – mechanized infantry – battalions, while Armoured Car cover was provided by a Household Cavalry Regiment, itself drawing on both of the two Regiments, the Life Guards and the Blues; another composite Household Cavalry Regiment was in the Mediterranean theatre. One of the two Armoured Brigades, which included the 4th Battalion of the Grenadiers, later left the Division to become an independent 'Guards Tank Brigade'.

The Guards Armoured Division was a magnificent formation in which to serve. All Regiments of the Household troops were represented. Everybody knew everybody else and it was like a huge family. The Divisional sign of the Guards Division in the First World War, the Ever-Open Eye within a shield, was readopted as our symbol. The senior officers of the Brigade of Guards had signified their endorsement of the change. The King had approved. There was a general sense after the disaster of the 1940 campaign that the British had been slow to adapt to modern ways of warfare and in particular to Army mechanization (although, in fact, most armies retained horse cavalry and horse transport, not without logic, well after the British; and the Germans and Russians, in particular, did so until the war's end). The view, however, that the British were out of date, although they had invented the tank and blazed the trail of armoured theory over twenty years earlier, was reinforced by the lack of progress in actual implementation. Only one armoured division – and it was split up before deployment and arrived anyway too late to affect the main battle – had formed part of the British Expeditionary Force in 1940. Now, it was reckoned, the conversion of those pillars of tradition, the Guards, to an eminently twentieth-century role would provide additional evidence of determined modernity. There was, therefore, a political element – and understandably so. On objective military grounds there were, however, reasons to question the wisdom of the step, although it was probably wise to give other factors priority.

Firstly, it was generally, and I think fairly, held that the Guards Regiments were excellent infantry. At the tactical level their field training was not, initially, all it should have been: but their steadiness and discipline were renowned, and these qualities had recently proved themselves during the retreat to Dunkirk and the embarkation of troops. Discipline and morale had been by no means universally high among the British Expeditionary Force. In a few cases, as noted earlier, arms had been abandoned, officers had deserted their troops, and a general spirit of '*sauve qui peut*' had prevailed. The example of a battalion of Grenadiers marching perfectly in threes down the Dunkirk Mole with their weapons, halting and dressing by the right before embarking, had become a legend: a very salutary legend. The prestige, as infantry, of the Foot Guards stood high. There must be compelling reasons to convert such infantrymen to another role. Furthermore, as the war proceeded, good infantry became very scarce. The Guards were not only of high quality but were to some extent protected by the privilege under which they had, by Regulation, to serve together in Guards Brigades under their own officers. The consequence was that, unlike the rest of the infantry, Guardsmen were not posted indiscriminately to wherever reinforcements were required. The unfortunate Infantry of the Line were too often exposed to the pernicious practice of being treated as impersonal numbers, so that a man, after wounding or some other incident, could find himself in the ranks of a Regiment of which he knew absolutely nothing – not once, but, on occasion, several times. Thus the morale and cohesion of a unit, which essentially depends on groups, particularly small groups, knowing each other and developing human bonds and trust, frequently needed rebuilding from near scratch. This particularly hit the infantry, where casualties were generally the highest and where the need for such cohesion is, arguably, most acute – and most difficult to attain. The result, especially in the latter stages of the war, was sometimes disastrous. Fault lay not with men but with the system of the authorities. The Guards were lucky – and the luck was, reasonably, resented – in being spared this. Now, however, a large part of the Brigade of Guards were to be lost to the infantry role.

Secondly, mechanization itself was by no means so taken for granted as it has since become. The conversion to armour was a more revolutionary change of style than it might be today. This meant that to a large number of senior non-commissioned ranks in particular it was so unfamiliar as to be almost unassimilable. Warrant Officers who had grown up in the strict, competent, but admittedly rigid tradition of the

Brigade found the difference in skills and attitudes difficult, and in some cases impossible. They were wasted men, who either suffered an unsatisfactory existence in the Armoured Battalions, seeking to impose an unsuitable system of discipline and confused by what seemed to them a sudden collapse of standards; or they were posted to other battalions, and their virtues – very real virtues – were missed.

Thirdly, and closely allied to the second point, the system of the Brigade was not particularly suited to the armoured role. The tank was a fitting war chariot for the Cavalry Regiments, with a traditional master/groom attitude, a shared responsibility towards the horse, and a more relaxed relationship between ranks. It was not so naturally adopted by the Brigade, whose method of achieving results and dealing with people was less suitably demonstrated in small spaces enclosed by armour-plate. It could be done and was done but it was not certainly the ideal use of resources.

None of this is to say that the Guards Armoured Division did not become a formation of which all could be, and were, intensely proud. But I do not believe that the general level of mechanical knowledge was as high as in some other formations: and I think that some outstanding infantry were wasted. When the war ended the armoured and mechanized battalions reverted instantly – within weeks – to the infantry role, and, inevitably, there was once again a great deal to learn afresh. That part of the Brigade of Guards which had not formed part of the Armoured Division had largely served in North Africa and Italy – campaigns very different in terrain and type of fighting from that in north-west Europe. Officers and soldiers who had experienced the Mediterranean theatre knew a great deal that those in the Guards Armoured Division had to some extent missed but which would have more enduring relevance in the post-war years – 'to some extent', because, of course, there was plenty of infantry-type fighting in the Armoured Division. The armoured role may, too, have made us a little quicker on occasion, given a wider perspective: swings and round-abouts. These considerations lay far in the future but they have a certain effect on the way some of my generation of Guardsmen view the past.

For the time being we, in the Division, were billeted all over the West Country, with all officers and soldiers undergoing an extended

1. *The East front of Philorth House*, 1851, by James Giles RSA.
The tenth Fraser of Philorth, through his mother Margaret Abernethy, became tenth
Lord Saltoun in 1668. He built a new house in 1660 and called it Philorth House.
It was there that my father and his brothers and sister were brought up.

2. Cairnbulg consists of two towers, one round and one – the older and taller –
square, with a connecting centre between the two.

3. My father, dressed as he usually was by day in the uniform of a major in the Gordon Highlanders.

4. My mother was in many ways the exact opposite of my father – impractic when he was immensely practical.

5. My father, a grenadier now – he had exchanged from the Gordons in 1927.

6. *(Above left)* My grandfather, aged sixty-three, had returned to the Army in 1915 and was about to take command of a home brigade stationed in the south of England.

7. *(Above right)* My paternal grandmother was born Gratten-Bellew. The family's homes were Mount Bellew in Galway and Tinnehinch in Wicklow.

8. *(Above left)* My uncle Alistair was a man quite unlike all others.

9. *(Above centre)* My cousin, from 1933 Master of Saltoun, was a year younger than I, a noted scholar, musician and athlete who excelled at anything he did.

10. *(Above right)* My aunt, small and bird-like, carried herself as erectly as a guardsman.

11/12. My maternal grandfather, Cyril Maude, was a very successful actor-manager of the late-Victorian and Edwardian era.

13/14. In 1888, without much security in life or prospects, he married my grandmother, Winifred Emery. Aubrey Beardsley drew her, rather effectively, for an edition of *The Yellow Book*.

15. *(Above)* The seventeenth-century house of Leith
Hall was built somewhat in the French manner.
16. *(Right)* 'Old Charlie' Leith Hay of Rannes,
one of the most delightful and entertaining men
who ever lived.

18. My uncle John Maude,
a witty and entertaining
man.

17. Aunt Dolly Marriott, with her son
Miles and (on right) the author.

19. *(Left)* My father's German colleague, and friend, Colonel – soon to become General – Leo Freiherr Geyr von Scheppenburg.

20. *(Below)* From older officers' conversation it was clear that views about the higher command were less than universally complimentary. The exception seemed to be the Divisional Commander, Montgomery. Montgomery, they said, seemed to know exactly what he was doing.

21. At Sandhurst William Douglas Home made no secret of his opinions.

22. The 2nd Battalion's senior subaltern was Peter Carrington.

23. Sir Allan Adair was much loved. When he talked to men, of any rank, he made them feel that they were important – and important to him.

24. Farewell to armour.

programme of conversion courses. We also, of course, had an anti-invasion role, should the Wehrmacht decide to interrupt the programme by staging an invasion. We were still organized as infantry and there were new faces to learn, new colleagues from whom, with luck, to win approval.

The senior subaltern in the Company I joined in that summer – and commanding it in the absence of most of the seniors on courses – was Robert Cecil. He was a striking personality, large in physique and heart, generous in his friendships and endowed with massive common sense. To me, whether fancifully or not, he seemed a near-replica of his great-grandfather, the Prime Minister Lord Salisbury, surely one of the most sensible holders of that office although perhaps handicapped – or, on occasion helped? – by a somewhat melancholy temperament.

Robert Cecil's temperament was by no means melancholy but his shrewd sense in response to any circumstance, military, political or human, was exceptionally impressive. Some years older than I, he was extremely well-informed. Politics were, of course, in his genes, but his reaction to any development was the reverse of partisan. He was invariably objective. He formed strong views but they were his own, and more often than not they derived from a good deal more knowledge – and, already, personal experience – than most of us possessed. With a wry, mildly cynical sense of humour, he was first-class company and his comments on anything were always reflective and often memorable.

Later in the war he was badly wounded and injured by accidental circumstances and spent a good deal of his life in much pain. After the war was over he went into Parliament and married the extraordinarily beautiful and talented Mollie Wyndham-Quin. At their lovely houses, Cranborne in Dorset and Hatfield in Hertfordshire, they created or developed gardens of international renown and were as hospitable and generous as it is possible to be. Everything they touched they made delightful.

Soon it was my turn to be sent on courses to learn about tanks, gunnery, wireless. These lasted some months; in that autumn of 1942 I returned to the 2nd Battalion, now formally entitled 2nd Armoured Battalion Grenadier Guards. New impressions, new personalities. One in particular.

His voice was rather high-pitched, not least when he indulged, as he periodically did, in a flow of exceptionally violent language at some behaviour which he found inadequate. His figure was tall, burly, commanding. His memory for detail was extraordinary, and his stamina no less so. When not enraged by obtuseness or lack of spirit detected in some subordinate (or superior) he was kind and encouraging, particularly to the young.

To those of my generation of Guardsmen who joined one of the battalions of Foot Guards converted in 1941 to some mechanized role – in tanks or motor battalions – he was a memorable figure, whether or not there was much personal contact (on the whole dreaded, albeit unnecessarily so). He was Major-General (later Lieutenant-General) Sir Oliver Leese, Baronet, sometime Coldstream Guards, first commander of the Guards Armoured Division; later to be a Corps Commander – a very good one – under Montgomery in the Western Desert and Italy; later, again, to succeed Montgomery in command of Eighth Army; and, lastly, to be Commander Land Forces under Mountbatten in South-East Asia Command, a position from which he departed in unfortunate circumstances, taking blame which only in part belonged to him.

Oliver Leese was an enthusiast. When the decision was taken to form an armoured division from the Guards he threw himself into it with tempestuous energy. There was everything to learn about their engines for those who would soon be driving these mechanized monsters, the scarce and wholly strange armoured vehicles available to the British Army at that time; and everything to learn for those who would be shooting their main armament (which changed frequently, as did the tank types themselves). There was everything to learn about radio communications – in those days a mysterious art with a strange and esoteric language. These technical matters were handled by huge numbers of courses for officers and soldiers at every level, run by the schools and training establishments of the Royal Armoured Corps. Perhaps equally important, however – and not, I think, very successfully managed – were the concepts of tactical handling of armour; or (as it perhaps should have been, but seldom was, expressed) the tactical handling of forces of all arms, of which tanks constituted one.

Any failures in concept lay in the command of the British Army itself, which then, as earlier and later, was not at its best in matters of operational and tactical doctrine. There was an insufficient core of doctrine – general doctrine, not specifically mechanized – deriving from history as well as current experience. The result (in tactical matters) was a sense of an Army clutching at the latest reports from the only active theatre in which the British were engaged, the Western Desert, and drawing hasty lessons as if they must have universal application. They often didn't. It was a confusing time for those responsible for tactical leadership.

Oliver Leese showed no signs whatever of feeling confused. He was a well-educated soldier and he probably had as good ideas as anyone in the Army about tactical doctrine. His main initial concern, however, was to make the entity – the Armoured Division – work. This involved not only an immense diversity of individual training, but the tireless exercising of all parts of the Division – staff work, movement, supply, communication and so forth. He was determined that when we went to war our *systems*, at least, should be impeccable. This was less easy than it sounds, and in this sphere he built a strong foundation. The Guards Armoured Division functioned splendidly as a machine. Oliver Leese had bothered himself personally with every part of it, large or small.

Nothing escaped his interest or his attention. I see him standing on the stage of some cinema in a country town in the West Country – the Division formed in the Salisbury Plain area, moved to East Anglia in early 1943 (by which time Leese had left us) and on to Yorkshire that autumn before concentration on the South Coast prior to D-Day in the spring of 1944. At the end of any one of the innumerable large-scale exercises we performed, *all* officers of the Division would assemble. There would be a narrative recounted by the Chief Umpire telling us how the mock battle – probably a four- or five-day affair but sometimes considerably longer – had gone. Then the Divisional Commander spoke. Memorably.

He was always immaculate: service dress jacket, Sam Browne belt, sometimes knickerbockers and puttees, sometimes gleaming field boots and breeches. And then, in that high-pitched, rapid voice – and without, as I recall, many, if any, written notes – he started to talk. Logical sequence. Not a detail omitted. Not a fault in any unit or command undetected or unmentioned. March discipline; speed and distances (and it must be remembered that on the line of march an armoured division probably occupied about two hundred miles of road); the alertness and appearance of all ranks in or out of vehicles; the initiative, or lack of it, shown by individual commanders at every level in particular, specified, situations; Air Defence sentries and precautions; digging, whether for protection, defence or both, to the prescribed dimensions of trench; radio procedure; the smooth working or resupply between the various echelons; the promptness and efficacy of vehicle repair; the Medical Services; the efficiency or otherwise of the Military Police; the meticulousness (or the reverse) with which junior officers had ensured that their men were informed, at every stage, of what was meant to be happening. It was not unusual for Oliver Leese to go on for three hours or more, enumerating errors, drawing conclusions, exhorting, condemning, ultimately encouraging. These were magnificent performances, and he was a magnificent Divisional Commander.

After the end of the North African campaign I remember that he spent a few days in England before the Italian business began and was invited to talk to the Division's officers once again. He was as compelling as ever – and, rather untypically, spoke with obviously sincere admiration of the confidence everybody in Eighth Army had had in their Army Commander, General Montgomery – 'untypically' because the last quality associated with Oliver Leese was any sort of deference or sycophancy.

His last military days were sad. After going from Eighth Army Command in Italy to south-east Asia he formed the view, at the end of the Burma Campaign, that the Fourteenth Army Commander, General Slim, was tired; and that for the next step in the Far East (planned to be an invasion of Malaya) Slim should hand over his Army to General Christison and himself command another army of occupation to 'clean up' the difficult situation in Burma. Slim, to whom Leese mooted this idea, was outraged, and so were most of Fourteenth Army, to whom 'Bill Slim' was an icon. Slim now said he would prefer to retire.

Oliver Leese had undoubtedly been in error. He had acted with a certain precipitancy – a failing of his. Huge enthusiasts, as he was, are seldom consistently wise. The energy of enthusiasm tends sometimes to drive out balance. In this case there had probably been unwisdom. Army commanders were only to be replaced with very high-level approval, notably by the Chief of the Imperial General Staff in London, the formidable Field Marshal Alan Brooke – and probably by the Minister of Defence, Winston Churchill, himself; and in this case nobody outside South East Asia Command had been consulted. But before flying to visit Slim at Fourteenth Army Headquarters, Leese had called on the Supreme Commander, Lord Louis Mountbatten, and told him his ideas. Mountbatten had agreed that Leese visit Slim to 'discuss' his proposition, which he did with such unfortunate results. The responsibility for putting the idea to London, of course, had thereafter been Mountbatten's, and since he had not done so but had tentatively acquiesced in Leese's ideas he at once exchanged a sequence of extremely long letters with Brooke (long, that is, and nervously self-exculpatory on Mountbatten's part; Brooke's were terse), following a furious signal from the CIGS. Leese was then removed, Brooke's displeasure having been made ruthlessly plain.

To some commentators – both military subordinates at the time and military historians with hindsight – Oliver Leese has been marked as a failure: ponderous, unimaginative (paricularly in the Italian campaign) and tactless in human relations. I expect there is something in this – the record makes it hard to deny – but there is a great deal more to this considerable figure. To us juniors he was not only impressive but, as we used to say, he 'knew his stuff'; that was what mattered.

After return to England Leese reported to the CIGS in July 1945. Brooke wrote later:

That interview has remained vividly impressed on my mind owing to the wonderful, manly way in which Oliver faced up to the blow that had hit him. There was not a word of abuse from him against anyone, or any suggestion that he had been roughly treated. And yet at the bottom of my heart I had a feeling, and still have a feeling, that, although he may have been at fault, he had a raw deal at the hands of Mountbatten.

I agree. Leese was what we always called 'carted'.

*

One of my contemporaries in the Grenadiers at Caterham, Windsor and other places was John Hawkesworth, later a distinguished producer of film, especially of various series for television, in which he made a great name. His father was a general and on one occasion in early 1941 – perhaps when we were at the Training Battalion at Windsor, waiting to join Service Battalions – John took me to visit his family in Camberley, where his parents had taken a house. I think his father was Director of Military Training in the War Office at the time, and I remember that there was in progress at Camberley some huge assembly of generals – a CIGS exercise or some such. General Hawkesworth drove John and myself in to the Staff College grounds, where senior officers in red hats were coming and going on all sides. As we sat in the car he said,

'There goes somebody you'll hear a lot more about before this war is over.'

He indicated a small, dark-haired man with a narrow face, a thin moustache and (I remember clearly) a curious atmosphere of solitude around him. Nobody was with him. He seemed detached from his surroundings. I don't think I saw his eyes – he was wearing an unbecoming shape of khaki Service Dress cap, with no 'set-up'.

John said, 'Who's that?'

'Montgomery.'

General Montgomery had been commander of the 3rd Division in the campaign of 1940, the Division in which the 2nd Grenadiers had served. From older brother-officers' conversation, eagerly attended to by their juniors like me, it was clear that views about the higher command were less than universally complimentary. The exception seemed to be the Divisional Commander. Montgomery, they said, had seemed to know exactly what he was doing. Unlike some. A story later became current that he 'didn't get on with the Brigade of Guards'. That was not our experience – nor mine when, years later, I actually talked to him. I remember at our luncheon table he was asked his opinion on the relative merits of British troops. 'Best troops?' he answered – 'The Guards. No question. You can rely on them. They do what they're told.'

Later, in 1940–41, he had been Commander, in England, of the Corps in which our Battalion was serving in its counter-invasion role.

As Corps Commander (the post he probably held when I set eyes on him at Camberley) he acquired particular fame by insisting on everybody, of whatever rank, carrying out a five-mile run once a week (or so it was said and so he seemed to believe). I next saw Monty when the war was over and victory had been won. As Commander of 21st Army Group he took the salute at the farewell parade of the Guards Armoured Division in the summer of 1945. Long, long years later I found myself, with a family, living only a few hundred yards from him in Hampshire.

Many books have been written about this strange and, I think, misunderstood man, a man who often seemed almost to encourage misconceptions about his own character. He has received his mead of praise – there are some 950,000 words in the Authorized Version of the Bible and significantly more – mostly celebratory – in the authorized version of the life of Field Marshal Viscount Montgomery of Alamein, a statistic 'Monty' would have accepted with equanimity.

The adverse side, on the other hand, the flaws of personality, have also received plenty of attention – and, on the whole, deserved it. He was, or became, obsessively conceited. He supposed his military judgement was near-impeccable, and he refused to accept or under-stand legitimate criticism. His conceit was that of a bumptious school-boy – immature, insensitive, often rather ignorant. He was needlessly unkind to and about other commanders unless they served him and he could gain some reflected light. He was – it was a facet of the same characteristic – suspicious and jealous of contemporaries unless, like Alan Brooke the CIGS, they dominated him: in others he saw only competitors, to be denigrated and despised. Sometimes this lack of generosity was rooted in shrewdness, often it wasn't. He was thick-skinned and tactless, with Allies in particular; so that most Americans disliked him heartily and for entirely understandable reasons. What-ever the rights and wrongs of particular cases – and most were and remain contentious – this tactlessness resulted in deplorably bad manners and harmed his country's cause. He was unscrupulous on occasion in getting his own way.

All that is bad. As a soldier, however, Montgomery was thorough, tough-minded and professional. He thought things through. He was not in the least original and his battles largely – and by no means unwisely – became affairs in which massive bombardments by air and/ or artillery would be followed by the well-organized advance of greatly superior forces. For manoeuvre, opportunism, speed and ingenuity he had little instinct. He believed, like Ludendorff, in the big battalions – if you need a Division for a job, use three and thus win more cheaply and more certainly; if you haven't got three, wait until you have. His victories were gained by the orthodox and, some would argue, ponderous deployment of numerically predominant force, intelligently used. They were also – a crucial factor – greatly assisted by the Allied achievements in the field of Intelligence and cryptographic penetration.

But Montgomery's achievement was much greater than is conveyed by enumeration of his somewhat pedestrian military virtues, just as his personality was a great deal more attractive and compelling than his very obvious faults made evident. His human touch was sure and sound. He immediately recognized, later, people who'd once served under him – remembered their names, made a connection. That is a talent beyond price. His huge quality – needed in the war as seldom in history – was his ability to give confidence. Because this curious little man, with his spare frame, his rather high-pitched, jerky speech, his penetrating eyes, so obviously believed in himself others believed in him too. He showed his troops that he knew what he was doing and that all would be well. He made sure that they understood his intentions – in simple, sometimes simplistic, generally unadorned language. He enjoyed difficulties – his reaction to the disaster which ended in Dunkirk was to learn, criticize forthrightly and start again. Because he reckoned, rightly, that war and soldiering are too serious a business to be unduly affected by social considerations he was impatient with the sort of kindness which can excuse a poor performance. I once remarked to him that so-and-so was 'a very charming chap'. 'Oh, yes,' he said dismissively, 'I agree. But I know a great many very charming chaps who are absolutely no damned good, and so do you!' *Touché*.

Monty took over command of the Eighth Army in Egypt in 1942 with a number of preconceptions (some of them erroneous) but was determined that he would not allow the impact of his will to be blunted by the tired knowingness of the 'old desert hands' – in spite of the fact that the 'old desert hands' were sometimes right. He meant to show who was master, for the Montgomery will was of steel, the sharpest weapon in his armoury. He knew that in war will often matters more than skill. He never expressed it thus, of course, because to him his skill, too, was almost beyond the reach of criticism. His temperament was ideal for war and he dominated the consciousness of the British Army. Clausewitz remarked that 'determination proceeds from a special type of mind, from a strong rather than a brilliant one'. Whether or not brilliant, Mongomery's mind was indeed strong.

And despite his much advertised churlishness with contemporaries, his intolerable lack of generosity with allies, his periodic vindictiveness and self-aggrandizement, Montgomery could be kindly, charming and, above all, amusing in private company. His own childhood had been harsh, dominated by the unsparing discipline of a mother who showed little love to this probably difficult, obstinate and rebellious child; and he clearly needed affection, very deeply. He could – with great enjoyment – laugh, and even laugh at himself. He could be charming with young people, with children. Some of the stories told of his bragging miss the point that he often bragged with a sceptical eye cocked on his companion to see if the point, the joke, was being taken; as if saying, 'I'm a naughty fellow, aren't I, to be as cheekily self-confident as this?' And the tales of his quiet, understanding kindness on occasion are a great deal less well known. I only met him, in human terms, long after the war was over, when he was eminent in retirement; but his personality still somehow teases across the years. His views still provoke contradiction. His voice – thin, sharp, nasal – still echoes, finding relish in the outrageous comment, the sometimes immature judgement, the often unfair verdict; while he, himself, like an impish schoolboy, still seems to be grinning a challenge. I am glad to recall that figure in the dark landscape of 1940 or 1941, when all lay before him. We needed him; we needed him very badly.

9

The End of Waiting

At about the time I rejoined the 2nd Battalion (now stationed in billets in Warminster) the Japanese attacked the American Fleet at Pearl Harbour and invaded American and British possessions and associated states in Asia. Hitler then – immediately – declared war on the United States – an action absolutely insane. Henceforth the final act would, we presumed, be a return to Europe in strength. Anglo-American strength.

The chief effect of being in the Guards Armoured Division was that we were, as was clear from at least the middle of 1942 if not before, being kept in England for this ultimate – as we supposed – act in the war against Germany: an Anglo-American invasion of north-west Europe. Our comrades in other battalions of our own Regiment were serving in the Mediterranean theatre of war from the winter of 1942 onwards. We learned of their doings, we mourned their casualties; we were unblooded until 1944.

Although, obviously, a matter of selfish gratitude this was by no means easy, and in terms of morale the keeping of a huge army in England with fighting apparently postponed *sine die* was also by no means easy. Training, of course, occupied us all the time, and the longest part of the war years was dominated by particular areas of England, where it was decided to assemble and manoeuvre large armoured formations. First was Salisbury Plain, where we conducted a considerable number of manoeuvres from one end of that great, haunted expanse to the other and back again. It was always difficult to tell exactly where one was on that featureless sweep of rolling grassland. The isolated clumps or ancient barrows provided fleeting landmarks, gratefully noted but then quickly becoming invisible as one's tank slid into some shallow valley and all directions were suddenly uncertain. Ignorance of where one was constituted – rightly – a serious military crime. It was also, as I had discovered commanding a platoon in the pre-mechanization days, the failing in an officer which most provoked the insubordinate mutterings of his men. They could stand a lot – they were remarkably tolerant of incompetence – but if their leader, who was paid to understand such things, showed weakness in map reading they felt badly betrayed, and showed it. They were right. Their lives would depend on this one day.

My own squadron commander was a brilliant map reader, the best in the Battalion. Arthur Grant – Sir Arthur Grant of Monymusk, an Aberdeenshire laird whose house I'd visited once or twice as a boy in the Leith Hall days – was very small, neat, strict, taciturn, efficient and alarming. He had served as a Regular officer in the 3rd Battalion in the 1930s, and resigned his commission to look after his property. An exceptionally good horseman (in a battalion which had boasted several such), he was a born soldier, decisive, quick-witted and inventive. He was autocratic, showing no disposition to discuss his or anybody else's orders, and to a young officer joining his squadron he was formidable – sharp-tongued, distant and austere. After a little his inner nature could be (carefully) discerned. He was intelligent and sensitive. He had schooled himself to be harsh, but he had remarkable understanding and this showed when it mattered. He walked like an active small boy, his usual expression was unsmiling, he could – and did – quell unwanted intimacy with paralysing silence or an abrupt, dismissive word. The soldiers of his squadron had absolute confidence in him, and they are always the best judges. Arthur Grant was killed in Normandy in July 1944, in the first big battle fought by the 2nd Battalion after landing. No loss was greater.

Joining, or in my case rejoining, a Service Battalion of the Regiment was always daunting. One was again a new boy, ignorant of much and particularly of personalities, all knowing each other as a close-knit family with shared jokes, nicknames, experiences. Early signals of friendship could mean a lot. I was lucky – as so often. On the first evening back with the Battalion I found I had been posted to Arthur Grant's squadron. His reputation was intimidating, and he was about to hold a conference for his officers and senior NCOs in his squadron office, in the main street of Warminster; we were billeted all over the town. I found where to go – I had been met by a truck at Westbury station and had arrived in Warminster only minutes before. When in the Battalion at Sherborne in the summer I had served in a different company. I was at sea.

The other officers, distant in manner, mostly unknown to me, were gathering, awaiting our commander. Somebody said to the senior subaltern in the squadron, 'This is David Fraser. He's just arrived.'

The senior subaltern – I cannot sufficiently convey the agreeable shock of this – smiled warmly, and said to me, 'How absolutely ghastly for you!' This was Peter Carrington, already Lord Carrington, having succeeded his father while at Sandhurst before the war. Known as 'The small Peer', he was shortly afterwards, sadly for me, posted to another squadron, which he ultimately commanded, having taken the leading half-squadron of the Guards Armoured Division across the Nijmegen bridge over the River Waal in September 1944.

For me the meeting held another echo. At the start of my first summer at Eton, in May 1935, I had gone to the cricket field called 'Sixpenny' to play in the appointed game. To my disappointment, because I loved cricket although certainly no star, I was down to be scorer – perhaps doubling as 12th man, unlikely to get an innings. Sitting next to me was a boy, slightly older, whom I'd never met and from another House. He had grinned at me with instant friendliness and a smile with real humour in it. He was co-scorer.

'Hello, my name's Carrington.'

Again, such unreserved *kindness* – for that was what it was – had instant effect. Because he was a little senior to me I hardly saw him again at school and when I had served in the 2nd Battalion in the summer of 1941 he had been undergoing the armoured courses which lay ahead of me. Now, at Warminster, here he was again. The remembered smile, the same sympathetic humour in the eyes and voice.

'How absolutely ghastly for you!'

Peter Carrington showed the same qualities throughout a life which took him to the highest reaches of British politics and international diplomacy. He was shrewd, pertinacious, courageous, funny, enormously charming, utterly honest and honourable, and above all kind. When, long years afterwards, the Conservative Party was to be categorized and divided he was generally depicted as on the Party's Left (a futile definition) or as on the 'wet' wing (again futile and misleading) in Margaret Thatcher's day, despite her own considerable reliance on him and trust in him. To some extent this, where true, lay in his essential moderation, his temperamental aversion to dogmatic certainties in politics, his cautious pragmatism, his huge common sense. Nobody with his well-developed sense of humour could confidently hold extreme views, of any description, a characteristic which certainly did not imply lack of conviction about right and wrong.

But above all, I think, his views derived, more than many supposed, from his simple kindness of heart. He knew and acknowledged that he, and many of his friends and colleagues (and, in the Army days, his brother-officers), had been fortunate in life, and he felt with more sharpness than most that others had not. He believed – probably with more passion than he would have acknowledged – that the former owed something to the latter, that duty and patriotism involved generosity as well as self-sacrifice. Indifference to misfortune or tolerance of brutality revolted him, and the amused friendliness which had warmed my heart from the age of thirteen was a significant part of a man whose other qualities were legion. His two most evident moods were explosive anger and equally explosive laughter: often manifested simultaneously. Nobody aroused more loyalty in those who served him. Like Robert Cecil, he married a lovely wife whose genius in the creation of a garden gave joy to thousands.

We were, therefore, fortunate in our Battalion. Probably the best officer, in military terms, was another of the squadron commanders, Jock Gilmour. Sir John Gilmour of Craigmillar (whose father had commanded the Grenadiers and was a much admired friend of Uncle Alistair) had joined the Regiment as a young officer soon after the First World War, for which he had been just too young. He had then retired to become a successful stockbroker, and was now back in uniform as a fairly elderly major.

The soldiers deeply revered him. A strong, forthright, impressive man, he had great charm but above all a sort of irreverent, twinkling common sense which quickly deflated pomposity in no matter whom, and which went straight to the heart of a problem or a situation. During 1943, when Jock Gilmour was second-in-command of the

Battalion, we had an unhappy time when the Commanding Officer – who was, I think, unlucky – was replaced very suddenly. The men were puzzled and restless. Jock spoke to the whole Battalion (I was acting as Adjutant). He stood on top of a scout car so that he was audible and visible, and he found the perfect words – direct, absolutely honest, simple and uncompromising. He quoted to us the very critical words recently used to him about our Battalion by our Brigade Commander, simply adding, 'I don't expect you like that any more than I do!' Everything was perfect thereafter.

Sadly, the authorities decreed that Jock Gilmour was too old (and not a Regular soldier) to take over command of us, to the universal disappointment of every Guardsman: 'All we want, now Sir,' they said, 'is Sir John to command us.' During an interregnum which followed we had one very big exercise, all over the Yorkshire Wolds, and Jock Gilmour was commanding the Battalion. A sham battle it may have been (but one lasting several days) yet I remember the *intoxicating* energy which this temporary commander infused into our manoeuvres, and with what skill he did it. He was a born soldier, and everybody knew it and felt it. Soon afterwards he was removed for other tasks of a less active kind.

I have said that I was a tourist everywhere in England. One of the benefits of wartime service in England was that England itself could sometimes be explored a little. Very few friends had cars – petrol was rationed and unless some generous parent had a little to spare the ration pretty well excluded motoring for pleasure. Public transport was the universal means of movement, particularly after the war had been going on a few years. Buses ran in the country districts, however, and branch lines on the railway were still essential to life. I bought a motor-cycle – unreliable but economic on the tiny petrol ration.

While the Guards Armoured Division remained in the West Country I could, when and where possible, visit places in Dorset, Wiltshire, Somerset when not on duty. There was a curiously adventurous aspect to travel because of the removal of all signposts, already referred to. There was, also, blessed calm in a countryside almost entirely free of motor traffic except where huge military convoys were on the road. War meant peace. The war years, of course, coincided with my own years of early youth so that everything was discovery, and every new place – name disguised but perhaps recognized from remembered book illustrations or identified by more knowledgeable friends – could be a source of excitement. A disagreeable facet of war was that most houses of any size or distinction had been requisitioned by the Army or for some government purpose, the owner temporarily dispossessed. People were not where they belonged, so that the effect was of a dream from which one hoped one day to awake. But the countryside itself gave joy – more, perhaps, than at any other time.

The scale of training was huge. When our Division moved from the West Country to East Anglia, the move itself took place as part of an enormous troop exercise. This was in March 1943, and I think about fifteen armoured and infantry divisions took part, advancing across southern England. Except in built-up areas tactical movement off roads (no doubt hedged by certain restrictions) was allowed. A good deal of realism was achieved. Damage done was enormous. Casualties, including fatalities, were not inconsiderable. I had been away at Pirbright for a few months, instructing recruits at the Guards Armoured Training Wing, and I (once again) rejoined the 2nd Battalion after the end of the exercise, when they had reached their destination, a hutted camp in Didlington Park, Norfolk. I can see the Regimental Sergeant Major, when I discovered the Battalion Orderly Room hut and moved towards it to report; he was wearing plastic eyeshields.

He saluted. 'Have you got your eyeshields, Sir?'

'No, of course not.' Then I saw that every guardsman within sight was wearing them also. I supposed there was some sort of extraordinary Gas Alarm practice going on. Eyeshields were meant to protect from mustard gas spray.

'Part 1 orders, Sir –'

The light Norfolk topsoil was producing ferocious dust-storms which continued with positively North African intensity for several hours, and which caused many men to report sick with severely inflamed eyes. This hazard was new to us, and I happen never to have met it in England since.

We now trained not on the barren miles of Salisbury Plain but on the Stanford Training Area near Thetford, and a very realistic training area it was. At that time most calibres of ammunition could be fired there. There were plenty of features of a more European type than at Salisbury – rivers, small woods, ruined buildings left *in situ* – and the extent was considerable. There could be a variety of tactical situation simulated: no area could have been better for us. The only limitation was that really large-scale formation movements – requiring, as they do, many hundreds or thousands of square miles – could not be arranged. For that we were sent, in the autumn of 1943, to North Yorkshire, where a number of exercises were to take place in the Yorkshire Wolds. Periodically we moved to a practice camp to fire the main armament of our tanks and take part in 'Battle Runs', firing on the move and in a series of different positions over a course of considerable distance. One of these practice camps was at Linney Head in Pembrokeshire, and another in Kirkcudbrightshire. We went to both, loading our tanks on warflats and enjoying ourselves a good deal.

The Battalion's move to North Yorkshire took us to a hutted camp – there were three, adjoining – in the woods of Duncombe Park at Helmsley. (The great baroque house was a girls' school.) The convoys of tanks used to move from their concrete standings under the trees on the high ridge which skirts the park, to reach the road towards Malton, and ultimately to deploy on some area of Wold, probably near Sledmere. Movement across country was virtually free of regulation or inhibition. The damage done to crops and hedgerows was vast, but deemed worthwhile. Whole armoured divisions were ranged against each other in mock battle. One such must have taken place in mid-February 1944, because I can see a number of the officers of Battalion Headquarters sitting round a table in a huge farmhouse kitchen, arguing with a great deal of passion. I think the exercise, which had probably lasted a week or more, was just concluded.

The argument arose from the bombing of the Benedictine monastery of Monte Cassino, which had just taken place. The bombing had been demanded by the attacking (British) Divisional Commander, and the demand was understandable because the great Abbey – a place of historic and international religious importance – seemed so to dominate the area that nobody could believe it was not being used by the Germans for military purposes. In fact the Germans scrupulously avoided this (the local German Commander, General von Senger und Etterlin, happened to be a lay member of the Benedictine Order) and although a considerable number of civilian refugees were killed by our bombardment, no German soldiers were there. Therafter, of course, the Germans could occupy the ruins without scruple and militarily profit thereby; while the bombing was a gift to German propaganda.

The issues are complex. Right or wrong, the attacking commanders and soldiers believed the Abbey was in German hands and threatened them, and if men are to go forward and hazard their lives such beliefs matter. The general guidance in such cases, particularly in Italy, was that such shrines should be regarded as sacrosanct unless military necessity demanded otherwise. I can see the emotion on the faces of some friends in that Yorkshire farm kitchen, as they demanded whether those who opposed them would think it right to risk their men's lives to spare some ancient building; while, on the other side, other friends argued that in any war or any circumstances there must be some actions from which it is morally imperative to abstain, even at the cost of operational disadvantage. Was not the destruction of one of the most venerable shrines in Western Christendom just such an example? It was a hot debate, until new orders arrived and we mounted our tanks and drove away. As in most hot debates there was a good deal of ignorance of the circumstances on both sides. I was on the side of those who found the bombing appalling, and said so – but I had no responsibility. General Freyberg – who supported the request for bombardment and said that it was a military necessity – had.

On the first evening of our arrival at Helmsley I climbed down the steep incline to the Rye valley and walked along the river through beautiful, sun-streaked woods. I had seldom seen anything lovelier – there was absolute silence, peace, beauty, a sense of suspension between earth and Heaven. Quite unexpectedly, as far as I was concerned, we rounded a bend in the valley and saw the magnificent ruins of the Abbey of Rievaulx. It caught the breath – it never failed to do so – and those two names, Cassino and Rievaulx, remembered from 1943, found an echo in Ampleforth, Benedictine Abbey, famous school, where a number of my friends and brother-officers had been educated and where they sometimes took me if a Sunday evening were clear of duty. Benediction. A simple supper in silence, with a reading by a novice. Laughter and good company and beer among the genial and civilized monks thereafter. Above all, I think, the library, with its magnificent collection of illuminated manuscripts, shown to me with a quiet flow of gentle, erudite conversation by the Librarian, Father Barnabas Sandeman: thoughtful, companionable, finding the right words to engage the sympathies of a young Grenadier officer wondering what, quite soon, battle would be like.

Wartime Britain has been depicted as a political Elysium, despite the hazards and menace of hostilities, with a grand coalition of Parties forming the Government under a leader of genius, a spell-binding orator and the patriotic embodiment of the battling nation; with all classes united in eschewing selfish ends or quarrels, with a united aim, victory. There is something in this, but not as much as nostalgia and the entertainment industry represent. Of course most families had close relatives in the Armed Forces, so that bereavement or the threat of it bonded people. Of course in the cities, or some of them, there had been air attacks, destroyed homes and workplaces, civilian casualties. Of course there was general – almost, if not quite, universal – support for the war itself. And of course there were deprivations, scarcities, meagre and boring rations, the uprooting of families. But it is mistaken to suppose that there were, for instance, no industrial disputes. On the contrary, production – despite energetic propaganda – was sometimes seriously disrupted; while on several occasions the vehicles and equipment of military formations moving to a theatre of war could not be loaded on ships for some time because of refusal by dockers to work until some grievance was settled. There were also coal strikes, just as there had been in the First War.

During one of these I talked to my Troop Sergeant. I was commanding a troop of Sherman tanks. An outstanding soldier and man, a tank gunner of particular skill, and a quiet, firm disciplinarian respected by all, he had been a miner in the Midlands. I mentioned the strike. He looked grave.

'I don't, myself, agree with what the miners are doing, Sir.'

'Good.'

'But I understand them, Sir. They're wrong in this, but they think it's their only chance. They know that at this moment, because of the war, the Government is likely to give them what they want. After the war it won't. The country won't be in such difficulties, so their –

the miners' – hand will be weaker. And they remember what that can mean. They've got long memories, Sir, and a lot of the memory is of life on the dole.'

'Blackmail,' I said.

'Perhaps, Sir. But they'd call it more a matter of their families' survival. In the longer term.'

Whether from Warminster, Thetford or Helmsley, short weekend leaves were occasionally obtainable. My parents were homeless – my father was somewhere in the Army in England and, as I have said, my mother joined MI5, serving with it (enjoyably) in a sequence of bizarre locations which included Wormwood Scrubs and Blenheim Palace. Our flat in Paris, with all our possessions, was in a German-occupied city. Cairnbulg, through the kindness of my uncle and aunt, was always open to me but was beyond the reach of a weekend: and, of course, bright lights beckoned. A curious thing to recall is that under these bright lights – or, to be more exact, when going round London at night in wartime from one restaurant or nightclub to another in the inky darkness of blackout – we generally wore uniform, for such was the order. Yet I never remember a case of trouble or embarrassment, let alone assault, molestation, insult. The world was, or seemed, on our side.

In London, my surrogate home was with the Marriotts at 59 Eaton Place, a house which provided a wonderful London base for me on countless occasions; a place where I left my clothes, mostly now recovered from Scotland; a place of welcome. My friend and contemporary, Miles Marriott, was also serving in the 2nd Battalion and we sometimes managed to go to London together during those war years.

Reggie Marriott, Miles's father, had been a solicitor, and had a reputation as an enormously shrewd financial operator. He was also a dedicated racing man and although he was much too prudent to offer many tips, if he gave one it was wise to take it up. I remember an occasion immediately after the war, in 1946. I was on leave from Germany and was going north by train to stay with friends in Yorkshire for Doncaster races. I found 'Uncle' Reggie, as I called him, on the platform. I'd not yet seen him during that leave, and he was obviously going to be travelling in more comfort than I. I hurried up to him.

'How are you, Uncle Reggie? And what's going to win the Leger?'

'Airborne,' he said with total confidence. That was a rare communi-cation, and although the price was short Airborne carried my small wager, and won.

I remember dining at Eaton Place in late 1941 when the Germans were in the outskirts of Moscow.

'What odds on Moscow falling before Christmas?' Miles said to his father. The Russian situation certainly seemed desperate.

'twenty-five to one against,' Uncle Reggie said with his usual snort. I felt sure he was right.

Reggie had a rather nasal voice and a sceptical laugh. He knew a great deal about the ways of the world in general and of the City of London in particular. He had been extremely successful in his pro-fession and was entertaining about an earlier generation of lawyers, but money and financial advice and arrangements had been his real field of expertise. He told me, in his snuffling, rather sardonic way, that the way to lose a good case in the Law Courts was to brief Sir John Simon, because everyone so disliked him, and the way to win with a bad case was to brief Lord Robert Cecil for the opposite reason.

Dolly, 'Aunt Dolly' Marriott was a remarkable woman. The Marri-otts had married late – they were a good deal older than my own parents – and her health was never good. Nobody ever heard her complain although she spent a good deal of time in her bedroom, which became something of a salon. She always dressed in the same way – a 'uniform' – with a white silk shirt, pearls, a hat with a chamois brush *à la Tirol*, a skirt somehow reminiscent of a riding habit (she had been a dedicated horsewoman), Grenadier cypher brooch. She had an irresistible sense of humour, was totally uncompromising in her views (not one of which would today be within a thousand miles of the politically correct) and was the most generous person I have ever known. There were small gestures, but not small to the impoverished schoolboy or Grenadier ensign.

'Darling, you're going to play golf tomorrow, I do hope you will, Reggie will love it.'

'Splendid.'

'I managed to get two boxes of Dunlop 65s, darling, they're in your room. And I found some rather nice woollen cardigans in stock from ·

before the war at —. They had one or two left and I *do* hope you'll like one.'

Aunt Dolly was fiercely patriotic. The slightest backsliding or luke-warmness towards the war effort received short shrift. There was a terrible occasion, learned about afterwards by me from Miles, when, at the outbreak of war, the young footman, an elegant youth in livery, reported as ordered by the Ministry of Labour to some Depot for induc-tion into the Royal Navy. Two days later he was back at Eaton Place.

'I explained about me feet, Madam.'

'Your WHAT?'

'Me feet, Madam. They've always been a little flat, and they were a very nasty, rough lot there –'

To say he was pitched out on his ear would be to make what happened sound altogether too gentle. The staff at Eaton Place almost exactly approximated to the cast of the television serial *Upstairs, Downstairs* (on which my wartime brother-officers, John Hawkes-worth and Freddie Shaughnessy, were respectively producer and script editor), although William, the butler, left for the duration and the footman was not replaced. They adored Aunt Dolly – without reser-vation or sycophancy. She was the centre of their world, kind, fiercely protective of them, sternly demanding the highest standards, uncom-promising in her attitude to right and wrong. They knew her bravery under any circumstances (I have watched her when bombs were falling near and noisily, and admired how there was barely a flicker of an eyelid: she visited the cellar-shelter extremely rarely); her pride in her family; her love of her country.

Dolly Marriott showed the same spirit after the war. Miles was severely wounded a few days before hostilities ended and died shortly after VE Day. He was an only son and to his parents the blow was, of course, bitter, but Aunt Dolly remained entertaining, generous, affectionate, unbowed. By then she knew she was dying – she died in 1949 – and she was in constant pain, keeping to her bed much of the time. I can see the figure of Rose, the parlourmaid, a sweet, quiet, gentle person, undemonstrative and unchanging – Rose in the cemetery at Putney at Dolly's funeral, falling to her knees and letting slip a terrible cry of anguish. Her sharp, uninhibited call of grief did duty for all of us.

The virtual disappearance of traditional domestic service has had a bad effect on the manners of the employing classes. This is not because of the absence of the servants' labour – with a few exceptions machines and simpler life-styles have filled the gap. Nor is it the enforced self-help undertaken by families who would once, as a matter of course, have kept a number of domestic servants – without whom, indeed, in former times, no middle-sized or large house could run. Although this has led to routines which earlier generations would have thought appalling most people would now dislike a reversion to earlier ways – who would today relish the almost invariable presence of one or more servants hovering in a dining room at mealtimes, as Tomlin did? Clearing dishes, washing up, gossiping and laughing the while, is now an often agreeable part of our lives.

The bad effect, however, has come from the removal of the un-spoken, unacknowledged scrutiny of employers, of their families, and of their guests, by the employed. Punctuality; correct dress; a degree of restraint in conversation; these things were the outward signs of a certain consideration towards others, and they were absolutely neces-sary, and rigorously observed, when domestic servants were there – to watch, to serve, to scrutinize. Of course there were unpleasant, snob-bish and unfeeling employers, just as there were shiftless or disloyal servants; but far more often than not the relationship, with regard deserved by, and accorded to, both sides, was far from the caricature sometimes presented. It was enjoyable, honourable and rich in human dignity. Certainly the Marriott servants moved in a well-ordered rhythm of efficiency, affection and respect.

It was while at Helmsley that I heard my cousin, the Master, had been posted as missing. He was in the 6th Battalion of the Grenadiers in Italy and had not returned from a patrol. It was presumed that he had been seriously wounded and was perhaps a prisoner in German hands. This was in February 1944. He had earlier, in September 1943, also been recorded as 'missing' but had turned up two days later. He wrote excellent letters, which were circulated within the family, but there were no more letters after the February incident and he was never seen again: the only Grenadier officer whose fate was impossible to discover with certainty.

He had gained a high reputation as a soldier, as I was always sure he would – thorough in everything he tackled, quick-witted and extremely brave. His loss – and, particularly, the uncertainty – was a fearful burden for my uncle and aunt, and for several years after the end of the war Uncle Alistair attempted, very understandably but in vain, to find out more than official records showed of what might have happened. This led him to discover the names and present whereabouts of certain quite junior German Regimental officers who had been opposite the Grenadiers at that time, in the valley of the Garigliano – itself no mean effort of deduction and pertinacity. I remember – it must have been as late as 1950 – the astonishing feats of memory shown by some German (I think company) commander and his good-hearted assiduity. He drew, from memory and with great tidiness, a sketch map of all his unit's minefields and sent it, with what he could recall of a diary of incidents, to my uncle with sensitive apologies that he could not do more. Such things deserve record as well as gratitude. Meanwhile we mourned.

Our time in Yorkshire ended. Much of it had been tedious. By now the sense that the war was going on elsewhere and that we were permanently waiting was often oppressive. Of course we were fortunate, but to keep huge numbers of troops in a state of anticipation is hard. Men could get passes for weekend leave, and they were sometimes late in returning. Short absences were frequent. Discontent and boredom became harder and harder to counter. The censorship by the officers of the men's letters – an odious task, bad for human trust between ranks, inherently undignified even if necessary – started as 1944 began. We knew that it could only be a matter of weeks before we received orders to load our tanks and entrain for some other destination. Presumably in the south.

The Archbishop of York, Dr Garbett, came to talk to the Battalion at Helmsley – rather well, I thought, as he expressed an intelligent critique of the Christian position in simple language. I doubt whether it meant much to many of the Guardsmen. Robert Cecil compared him to the Archbishop of Canterbury, Dr Temple, whom he knew – I think to the latter's advantage. Robert said that William Temple, who had the reputation of being something of a Socialist at that time, was impressive, although the greediest man who had ever stayed at

Hatfield. Cecils inherit an aptitude – or at least a tendency – to appraise bishops and Archbishops like some sort of confidential secretaries who have arrived with references of perhaps questionable reliability.

Then, one day, we found ourselves packed into a number of trains and when they ultimately halted after long hours (the destination had been kept secret) we had no difficulty, despite the absence of station signs, in realizing that we were in Brighton. We dispersed into various streets of Hove, tanks parked along the roadway in front of stuccoed villas and boarding houses, soldiers billeted in large numbers of requisitioned houses and halls, Officers' Mess in a villa a short way behind the seafront. The vehicles had to be 'waterproofed', a laborious, evil-smelling task, and there could not, of course, be any movement to training areas – in fact there could be no movement of anybody, anywhere. The entire south coast was cut off by regulation from the outside world. We were again waiting. At night we heard the drone of bombers, flying south and east as part of the mighty 'Pointblank' aerial offensive to soften up the Germans' defences and paralyse their communications. One night, lying on my camp bed, I heard a peculiar, uneven aircraft sound, something wholly novel, rising and falling rather like a child's clockwork toy in need of winding. I was sharing a room with a brother-officer.

'What on earth was that?'

We knew it was something extraordinary. It was, in fact, the first V1, 'Flying bomb', 'Pilotless plane'; and we had heard it going over towards London. Soon the south of England was again swept by casualties and destruction from these weapons, and from the rockets, the 'V2s', which followed them.

I dined in a restaurant with a friend to meet Rex Whistler, at that time a troop commander in the Armoured Battalion of the Welsh Guards. We argued – we were talking about what might happen in England after the war and I was propounding some fairly nonsensical views about how on earth our country might recover spiritual greatness in defiance of the prevailing materialism.

'Instead of which,' I said, 'we simply seem to want a world in which every family, in every situation of society, should, as its ideal, have a swimming pool.'

'Well,' Rex said, 'what's wrong with that?'

'It's no great thing to aim for –'

'I asked "What's wrong with it?"' Rex said. 'Why shouldn't they have swimming pools?'

'I don't –'

'*You've* got a swimming pool!'

'No, I haven't!'

'Well, you *should* have! So should "they"!'

'I don't *want* a swimming pool.'

'Then you *should* want one! I INSIST,' Rex shouted, 'THAT AFTER THE WAR YOU HAVE A SWIMMING POOL!'

Later we returned to our Battalion Headquarters Officers' Mess, where Rex propounded ideas for an officers' party he thought the whole Guards Armoured Division should give in the Pavilion at Brighton. He accompanied his ideas with tiny sketches on pieces of 2nd Armoured Battalion Grenadier Guards writing paper, showing what the party might be like, with vivid, recognizable caricatures of particular figures in various stages of inebriation and atrocious behaviour, the shade of the Prince Regent watching benignly. Each tiny sketch took him seconds only. I wish I had kept those pieces of paper! Rex was killed in Normandy in July, in the Division's first major battle.

One day we were lined up in the various streets of Brighton, where our Battalion and its tanks were quartered, for inspection by an important personage. General Eisenhower had no time to do more than walk down the ranks, and as we were standing to attention it was hardly a human contact. Nevertheless I have a vivid mental picture of the general as he passed, and the effect was surprising. Ike had never photographed particularly well in the British press and I was not expecting an impressive figure. I caught, however, a clear and ineffaceable sense of greatness. He was taller than I had supposed and he exuded something almost physical. Nor was this the ordinary reaction to almost anybody who has actual power, as he had. On the contrary I was slightly resistant to the possibility of being impressed – there was a general view among much of the British Army that Montgomery should be in real charge and that compared to him, or Alexander (of whom Guardsmen, in particular, tended to have a high opinion),

Eisenhower might be something of an amateur. Then he strode down the ranks a few feet from me and I was perfectly certain that a great man had passed.

One morning soon afterwards I went to the street where our tanks were parked, for our morning parade. The news had just come through that the Allies had landed on the coast of France. I threw my beret high in the air. The waiting – four years of it – was over.

10

Norman Summer

A July morning in 1944. We were gathered in a green sun-speckled orchard, in Normandy, a great number of us, sitting on the grass and awaiting an address from our Divisional Commander. We had landed in France some weeks earlier, and moved inland pretty well unmolested as far as our own Battalion was concerned. Assemblies like this in the Guards Armoured Division were immensely social occasions. Friends not seen for, perhaps, weeks, months, even years suddenly materialized for snatched, treasured exchanges of conversation, immediate reminiscence and – always – laughter. The imminence of battle, danger, the unknown, greatly heightened every sense and every perception. Eyes were bright, talk charged with unacknowledged emotions. And because this was to be our first major battle there was as yet no weariness, no sorrow. In modern terms, we were on a high.

I found myself sitting next to a group from the Irish Guards. Ned Fitzmaurice, an Eton acquaintance not seen for several years, was sitting by me, full of laughter and memories, seeming to glow with vitality. He was killed in August, just before the end of the Normandy fighting – his elder brother fell in Italy a week later. Everybody at that moment, however, was caught up by excitement, confidence in (as we reckoned) our magnificent Division, and the sense of culmination, of imminent climax. I suppose the gathering was only part of the Division's officer strength – perhaps only our 5th Armoured Brigade – but all Regiments seemed represented.

Then our Commander began talking. Sir Allan Adair was much loved. He was slight of build, neat at all times in his appearance and his movements, elegant, fastidious. When he talked to men, of any rank, he made them feel that they were important – and important to him. A word from him left any soldier happier. There was about him a certain serenity, in whatever turmoil, under whatever pressure. It had not been easy to succeed the massive, formidable Oliver Leese and although the Adair charm, kindness and rapport with all ranks struck instant chords there were some who wondered – in my view unnecessarily – whether the bruising tone which all had respected with awe in his predecessor was sufficiently present in Allan Adair; but of the Division's devotion there was no question. His voice, much imitated, was high and often interrupted by a gentle, beguiling giggle. He talked, however, with absolute clarity; and when he vocally changed gear from the more personal to the public and oratorical mode his tones became musical, resonant and memorable. No man read the scriptures better in church and his military addresses had a comparable, almost prophetic, sort of eloquence.

Thus it was that morning. General Adair told us about the forthcoming battle. Three British armoured divisions and an infantry division were to cross the River Orne north of Caen, and having deployed on the east bank were to move south over the open country between Caen (in which the Canadians were to carry out a parallel operation) and the wooded and slightly rising ground of the Bois de Bavent, some five miles to the east of Caen, where the 3rd (British) Division were to attack. The armoured divisions were to advance, therefore, through something of a funnel – a wide funnel. Ahead of us (a large diagrammatic map was erected beside the general) would be the Bourguebus ridge, some high ground lying south of Caen; and our centre line would cross a road running south-east from the city, through small places called Cagny and Vimont. At that point the leading echelons were to turn south-east on the general line of that road. Allan Adair told us that the Army Group Commander (Montgomery) had seen him and said, 'Above all, we *must get Vimont*!' That stuck in my mind.

We didn't.

The morning of 18th July was perfectly beautiful – a brilliant blue sky, clear, calm, visibility superb. We had moved out of our bivouac area east of Bayeux during darkness and had halted on some high ground immediately north of the city of Caen, where there was time for the life-giving brew of tea made on the small tank cookers. From that vantage point in the exquisite light of very early morning we watched what seemed a never-ending procession of bomber aircraft from England, circling Caen, and the country east of it over which we were to advance, then flying home again, their deeds done. Occasionally we saw one tumble earthward, a victim of German flak. I remember no German aircraft that morning. From Caen itself came an unbroken, unceasing roar of exploding bombs – and, I suppose, anti-aircraft gunfire, but the dominant noise was the deep, unceasing rumble of bombs, blowing into pieces much of what still stood of Caen and its suburbs from earlier visitations and (we hoped) the German troops who would be contesting our march. For the fearful destruction being wreaked on the historic city, or the hideous suffering inflicted (and nobody supposed Caen was empty of French civilians) I recall no particular concern. War deadens human sympathy. Over one thousand heavy and medium bombers took part. When they had done their work and before our advance was resumed the great guns of warships – I remember that one was the massive 'Rodney' – started sending their huge shells into the German positions, succeeded by further waves of bombers.

Our own movement – divisions were advancing in succession, the Guards Armoured Division second in the order of advance, following the 11th Armoured Division – seemed mostly marked by long and frustrating delays. The whole attacking force had to cross a limited number of temporary bridges over the Orne, and the inevitable traffic bottlenecks were doing far more than the Germans to slow matters up. Eventually we reached the east bank, swung southward, shook out into formation and were on our planned axis of advance. At about the same time I became conscious of the first German soldiers I had yet seen in the war, as a significant number of dazed-looking and hatless men in field-grey uniforms made their way past us, heading northward. These were, for the most part, the survivors of the bombardment. It had been so devastating that some of those not actually killed or wounded had broken down and gone off their heads.

We moved onwards over open farmland, deployed in extended order. Far to the left I could see the Irish Guards – our neighbours in an advance on a frontage of two armoured regiments. The whole thing was a fine and dramatic sight – tanks moving through the standing corn, smoke and flames from the occasional farmstead or village still burning from the earlier bombardment, the dribble of pathetic enemy prisoners passing us in the opposite direction to our triumphant progress. Then the visible irruption of enemy shells – brown earth spurting all around us. 'Visible' but largely inaudible from an unforeseen (by me) and rather merciful circumstance. In those days we wore large earphones, clamped to the head on a flexible steel frame, through which the radio transmissions reached us; and the effect was largely to blank out all other sound. German gunfire and the explosion of German shells tended, therefore, to be almost entirely obliterated by the irate tones of some superior asking where the hell I thought I was going.

There was a good deal of German fire. Rommel, the German Army Group Commander, had visited this sector frequently in the preceding days, having been perfectly sure that it would be the scene of the next British offensive. What he knew of British deployments, his reading of the situation and his knowledge of Montgomery had all convinced him; and although he, personally, had been wounded by a British air attack on the previous day he had largely devised the German defensive plan, imposing it by frequent visits to the Corps and Divisional commanders on the ground. Rommel knew that there would be a great mass of Allied tanks and where they would be. There was a certain amount of restriction imposed on an Allied advance by the suburbs of Caen on the flank, and by the Bois de Bavent. The only German hope would be to deploy in very great depth, soaking up successive waves of attack, inflicting casualties, holding on to the more defensible ground of the Bourguebus ridge and doing the best possible, by digging and so forth, to survive the inevitable preliminary bombardment – although in the event this was so enormous that it caused surprise; the only thing which did.

We, therefore, were advancing over ground where every coppice, every farm, every village, held skilfully sited and concealed anti-tank guns or camouflaged tanks. The Germans only mustered about a hundred tanks, the British some eight times as many, but some of the German were Tigers, mounting the devastating 88 mm gun which dominated all opponents in open country: and this operation (named

GOODWOOD) was fought in open country. The German anti-tank guns, too, were lethally effective, whether the 88s, the 75s or 50 mm. And where their crews had not been killed or disabled all these were manned with courage and skill. They were deployed, furthermore, through a depth of some eight miles.

The first indication that we might not have too easy a run was given by a large number of British tanks on the crest of the gentle, almost imperceptible, ridge towards which we were advancing. These tanks were all on fire, blazing fiercely. They were, presumably, some of those of 11th Armoured Division. Like ourselves, 11th Armoured was equipped with American Sherman tanks – by that stage of the war the standard armoured workhorse for both British and American armoured formations. The Sherman was in some ways a good tank; it was mechanically robust, which counted a great deal. Its short-comings, however, were much in evidence if one went to war in it against the Germans. First, its main armament was a shortish-barrelled 75 mm (quite low velocity) gun; this gun could fire either high ex-plosive or armour-piercing rounds. Firing high explosive (and there were also two Browning machine guns, one mounted beside the driver and the other co-axial with the main gun) it was a most effective supporting weapon for infantry/armour cooperation. In spite of the excellence of our artillery it was useful to have a weapon of that kind which could blast enemy positions or suspected positions with direct fire. Firing armour-piercing rounds, however – in tank versus tank encounters – the Sherman's gun was outranged and outclassed by the German anti-tank weapons, whether 88 or the 'long' 75 mm. This was a reflection of most indifferent British (and American) tank design in the Second World War, which led us loudly to criticize the understand-ing of our authorities. Of course we over-simplified the complexities but it seemed to us that they failed sufficiently to appreciate the commonsense relationship between thickness of armour (both one's own and the enemy's), penetrative power of the tank gun and range. Against most of the German weaponry we felt like a man with a rapier facing a spearman; and a spearman with an exceptionally strong breastplate.

This was soon exemplified during GOODWOOD. The country had few obstacles to vision so that the Germans could – and did – open fire at their own chosen ranges, dependent on the gun manned; and the second shortcoming of the Sherman tank was soon evident. When hit it burst into flames with alarming instancy – exploding like the striking of a match. There were many theories about why this was particularly so with the Sherman, but it was. When a tank was hit by an enemy anti-tank round the crew were only too likely to be burned to death: or, at least, very badly.

The hazard was worsened by the design of the Sherman. The turret was round and very tall. In order to quit the tank the turret crew – three persons – had each to climb out of the round hatch, about two foot in diameter, which was approximately six feet above the turret floor. This climb was assisted (or somewhat impeded) by the working parts of the gun, which left little space between gun and rear wall of turret. The tank commander could get out first – indeed he had to, if others were to stand a chance. The gunner, in a small seat on the right of the gun and in front of the commander, had an awkward movement of extradition because there was a back to his seat. The loader/radio operator (the radio was on a shelf behind the gun, on the rear wall of the turret) had the worst chance since he had to climb under the gun. The driver and co-driver, in a separate compartment in front, had individual hatches. They were often, however, the most exposed to frontal fire, and felt it. More modern tanks have often got even more laborious ways of ingress and egress, but the Sherman always posed problems and its proneness to instantaneous combustion made these problems very vivid to the crew.

We rolled forward. It was easy actually to see the flash of a German projectile as it passed or crossed one's front. Here and there one of our own tanks was stationary, sometimes burning, sometimes not. If a tank was disabled, perhaps by a shot to the tracks immobilizing it, the crew – quite legitimately – got out as fast as possible. The next round would probably ignite it. And at some time in the early afternoon I saw an extraordinary sight.

I was commanding the Battalion headquarter troop of four tanks. About two hundred yards from where I was perched looking out of the turret of my own tank I saw another tank, I think from Arthur Grant's No. 2 squadron, hit by a German round as I watched. It did not, or at least did not immediately, burn. The crew baled out, knowing already (we learned quickly during GOODWOOD) that seconds could make the difference between reaching the ground and incineration. Adrenalin flowed fast. I watched – it took less time than to tell or write – as first the commander, then the gunner, then the radio operator, scrambled through the turret hatch and jumped to the ground; but the radio operator, the last and the man with least chance of beating the explosion, came out of the turret hatch, before my eyes, *vertically and very fast with his hands at his side*, his body moving upwards as if impelled by some extraordinary spring or dynamic force, until his boots cleared the turret and he – still vertical – landed on his feet beside the tank. No athlete could achieve anything like this, nor (I think) could it be explained by an exploding round within the turret. Long afterwards, and late in the campaign, I heard a Guardsman who had been wounded during GOODWOOD (but later rejoined us from hospital) tell some others of that incident – the only corroboration I ever heard. He had seen it too and he described it exactly as I remembered. I believe the Grenadier in question was killed subsequently so it was impossible to investigate his personal experience. I conclude, on reflection, that it was an extreme example of the way acute fear can lend near-miraculous agility to a man's limbs; we all know the adage that anybody, however unathletic, finds that he can vault a five-barred gate if a bull is in pursuit. This, too, seemed near-miraculous and that figure, describing a great and inexplicable parabola from tank to earth, remains firmly lodged in my memory.

GOODWOOD ended, or in our case fizzled out, to the accompaniment of unusually heavy rain. On the first evening I was sent to see the Irish Guards on our left and arrived just as the commanding officer of their 3rd Battalion (infantry, rather than tank) was finishing giving out orders for some rapid attack. They had been moving behind us in unarmoured lorries, as part of the 'lorried infantry' of our Division; they were now 'debussed' somewhere on our eastern flank; and had been ordered (I think) to advance towards and through the village of Cagny, earlier the objective of our own 1st Battalion (King's Company) supported by our tanks. It was nearing dusk and I remember the sense of extraordinary vitality which the Irish Guards Commander, Joe

Vandeleur, emitted. The situation was confused, nobody was sure where anybody else was (or where they themselves were), night was approaching, there was a great deal of noise. Joe Vandeleur – a red-haired, red-moustached, red-faced man of immense personality – seemed to me, an ignorant and uncertain visiting subaltern, to exude confidence, energy and decision.

Ultimately Cagny, Fenouville and other places which had featured on the map we had watched while Allan Adair had talked in the orchard a few days before were in our hands. But we did not reach Vimont. That evening we counted the cost. Arthur Grant had been killed during the early part of the day, Johnnie Corbett and Oliver Ruggles-Brise a little later. Tony Jones (an officer of extraordinary courage and pertinacity who had almost single-handedly with his carrier platoon restored a dangerous situation on the retreat to Dunkirk four years earlier) had continued in his tank after it had been hit and actually ignited until he had knocked out the German tank confronting him. We had lost over twenty tanks and many good men, including several of our best NCOs. My American cousin, Joe Burden, serving at Divisional Headquarters, had been killed by a shell. The Germans held the commanding Bourguebus ridge. They could – and did – observe and send shells over when they felt like it to wherever the battalions of the Guards Armoured Division were laagered during the ensuing days.

GOODWOOD was described by Montgomery in his memoirs as successful in the terms he had conceived it – that is as designed to make the Germans shift their armoured strength eastward, to the country south and east of Caen, thus weakening their western flank for the ensuing American *schwerpunkt* (point of main thrust). He dismissed the idea that GOODWOOD had at any time been intended to lead to breakout. One can accept that the concept of pressure rather than breakout – consistent with earlier operations near Caen – had been at the heart of GOODWOOD, and most historians have echoed the Montgomery thesis. Nevertheless I do not believe that he shut out the possibilities of the battle going better than it did, leading to the chance of a major offensive; a chance he would have taken. Mongomery wrote to the CIGS on 14th July, several days before the battle, 'The possibilities are immense; with 700 tanks loosed to the south-east of Caen and armoured cars operating far ahead, *anything may happen.*'

And on a map he sent with this letter he sketched arrows directing the army on Falaise, sixteen miles south of the battlefield of GOOD-WOOD. He wrote that his aim was to destroy 'all possible enemy troops in the general area Caen-Mezidon-Falaise-Evrecy', which, if achieved, would have so stretched the German defences as to make Allied breakout almost inevitable. Certainly we, before the battle, supposed that it would be the precursor to something decisive.

Montgomery merits no criticism for having alternate or overlapping objects in mind. Very reasonably, and as part of his overall strategy, he wanted to exert pressure in the east of the bridgehead, around Caen. He knew this would draw German panzer forces, and it did. But he surely also reckoned that this pressure – which he did not intend to get out of hand or 'unbalance' his forces overall – might lead to further and dramatic possibilities. If this happened he would exploit the ensuing situation. There was nothing amiss here. Montgomery's mistake – as on other occasions – was to claim that everything happened exactly as he wanted and expected. He reacted vigorously afterwards to any suggestions that he had intended, at GOODWOOD, a breakout by the armour of the British Second Army. Because it didn't happen, such suggestions, he reckoned, implied personal failure. But his earlier words showed that he had been ready – and probably hopeful – for more tactical success than actually came: both the readiness – and the hopes – showed perfectly good generalship. When things went less well than they might, he dealt with the ensuing situation as it actually was, and very ably. Only his obsession with pretending all events had conformed exactly to his will constituted his personal flaw in GOODWOOD.

The other main flaw in the operation was tactical. Within the armoured divisions of those days the armour – the tanks – were organized in a separate brigade from the infantry (except for one mechanized infantry battalion). This meant that in most battles, and certainly in GOODWOOD, there would be an imperfect balance of arms. GOODWOOD had represented a virtually all-tank charge against Germans in well-reconnoitred and prepared positions – a doubtful concept, only given a chance by the weight of air power used to saturate the enemy defences. The infantry – the arm needed, with artillery, to deal with the German strongpoints *in conjunction with* tank fire – were following separately.

Most battles require the intimate cooperation of tanks, infantrymen, engineers and artillery; and it is in the infantry that shortage is generally most apparent, and earliest. In the majority of the battles which the Guards Armoured Division fought until May 1945 infantry were in shortest supply – and suffered most. After GOODWOOD each of the armoured battalions, like ours, formed a permanent affiliation with one of the Division's infantry battalions, constituting an all-arms, two-battalion group; an arrangement which, while arguably not always the most economic use of resources, at least ensured that tanks and infantry moved, lived and fought in intimate proximity. The arrangement, given the British Regimental system, was facilitated by the fact that four Regiments of the Foot Guards each had both an armoured and an infantry battalion represented in the Division. Thus there were a Grenadier Group, a Coldstream Group, an Irish Guards Group and a Welsh Guards Group; our Group consisted of the 1st (Motor) Battalion, Grenadiers and our own 2nd (Armoured) Battalion. Tank squadrons and infantry companies were similarly twinned.

The repair and recovery of damaged or broken-down tanks played a large part in our lives, and its organization lay in the hands of the Technical Adjutant, who had to move around the battlefield in a lightly armoured scout car inspecting the vehicle casualties, assessing the damage and the best treatment, arranging evacuation or recovery. Our Technical Adjutant was Brian Johnston, a memorable figure, exactly the same man and personality who would one day delight television and radio audiences with a huge range of outrageous programmes and initiatives and – even more – enchant BBC radio audiences with his unique commentaries on first-class cricket.

Brian had an inexhaustible fund of absurd, irreverent, bawdy but never ill-natured anecdotes, expressions, puns and verbal absurdities. He attached nicknames to almost everyone, of whatever age or rank. He disclaimed a great deal of technical knowledge (although he certainly came to possess more than he pretended) but his great common sense and readiness to use the experience of others made him our

Battalion's incomparable general practitioner rather than specialist in the field of mechanical fitness. More than all his professional contribution, however, Brian Johnston was – throughout the campaign – like a human tonic to every one of us. His genial laughter and irrepressible comments on everything which happened, his deflation of pomposity, his unabashed desire to get the war over, get out of uniform and do more congenial things – these raised our spirits at even the most disagreeable moments. The soldiers loved him.

After GOODWOOD we were moved westward to take part in the battles later called Caumont and Mont Pincon. For the next weeks, we fought in the bocage country of Normandy, until that moment in mid-August when we were told of the great advances launched from the west of the bridgehead, the American Operation COBRA; the moment when – as we only slowly appreciated – the battle of Normandy was over. Won.

Meanwhile there were the battles in the bocage. The bocage resembles much of Devonshire. It is country of small streams; small fields enclosed by hedges atop high, steep banks; small, wooded hills; narrow, winding roads. It is country of great beauty. In the summer of 1944 it was also country marked by sickening devastation. The towns, or most of them (there were merciful exceptions: Bayeux, Balleroy, a handful more), were shattered ruins, all life extinct. The villages, if featuring in the fighting, were the same. Because, again like Devon, Normandy is a country of dairy products, the fields were speckled everywhere with dead cows, lying stiffly on flank or back with legs outstretched and rigid, resembling a child's discarded toys on a nursery floor but smelling a great deal worse. Dead horses, alive with maggots, were everywhere – farm work was, of course, entirely by man and horse and the German Army, anyway, was supported in the main by horse-drawn transport, and, often, guns. And there were a great many dead men. The exquisite bocage stank of death.

Because our two Grenadier Battalions fought as one group, command was exercised jointly by the two commanding officers, equals in rank. This did not alternate, like the Roman system of dual consulate, but depended on joint agreement on overall plan, and executive orders to his own subordinates by each; sometimes there were combined 'Order Groups'. The arrangement produced remarkably little discord or confusion, largely because personal relationships were so close. We knew each other well, at every level: we were all Grenadiers. So it was from Lieutenant-Colonel commanding, to Lance Corporal section or tank commander.

The commanding officer of the 1st Battalion, our infantry, was the senior of our two Lieutenant-Colonels and thus, by an unspoken and informal understanding, assumed the leading role in the Grenadier Group. This was Colonel Eddie Goulburn and he is ever present in my memory's eye when I recall the Norman landscape. Tall and extremely good-looking, Eddie Goulburn had been a very smart and formidable Adjutant at Sandhurst until early in the war. He had a seemingly gruff and alarming manner, a downrightness which threw any nervous companion or emissary back on his heels, a short, decisive way of speaking, occasionally interrupted by a curiously infectious chuckle resembling a horse snorting. Behind this brusque exterior he had the kindest heart in the world, and enormous charm, which he took trouble, unsuccessfully, to conceal.

Eddie also had huge common sense and an instinctive 'feel' – Rommel, who also possessed it, called it his '*fingerspitzengefuhl*' – for tactical situations and for terrain. He knew what the enemy were thinking, would try to do; and he knew how to frustrate it, pre-empt it, get in first. He was trusted absolutely by his entire battalion, and, indeed, by the whole Grenadier Group. His care for them was exemplary, and also had about it something instinctual, like his tactical sense. 'I'm not too happy about –', he would say or think, and would investigate the situation of some outlying company or detachment, generally by personal contact; often with reason, although nobody had known why. Sometimes, perhaps, he interfered too much with his subordinate company commanders – he had a fine team and they never let him down. His brother commanding officer, our own Colonel Rodney Moore, differed in this – he also had an admirable team of squadron commanders but he gave them their heads, supported them with whatever they needed and trusted their judgement in tactical decisions completely. Eddie Goulburn, however, was in very firm practical and personal control of every movement or action within his command. All had whole-hearted confidence in him. Above everything he had character – strong, brave, memorable character.

Battle, because of the terrain, was generally at close quarters and resembled our training exercises remarkably little. One morning I accompanied Rodney Moore to a mixed tank and infantry group which had been pushed up on to a wooded hill, south of the valley of the Souleuvre river, the evening before and which had been incessantly attacked by the Germans throughout the night. The tank squadron (of our Battalion) was commanded by Alec Gregory-Hood. There was no commander we more admired. A Regular soldier, he affected a certain dandyism, a studied nonchalance, a calmness and apparent detachment from the sordid realities which battle produced. All this was combined with great yet unobtrusive personal courage, enormous charm, an irresistible sense of humour and an inner will of steel. His men believed in him wholly; they trusted and appreciated his competence, they enjoyed his personality, they knew he both understood and loved them. I never remember him other than composed, courteous and, more often than not, amusing.

On this particular morning we reached the crown of the hill near a place called Drouet, on which Alec and his group had spent an eventful night. His colleague commander from our 1st Battalion was Rupert Bromley, with his company. Rupert was a dark-haired, dark-visaged man, like Alec very calm in all circumstances, apparently disdainful of the inconveniences to which the Germans had had the effrontery to subject him and his men for hours on end, both in daylight that morning and the evening before – and throughout the hours of darkness. I can see him now, as he stood with Alec and they explained how things had gone and what their tactics had been.

The hill was crowned by an oblong of hedgerow, below which the slopes in all directions fell away steeply. It was certainly not natural tank country – ranges of fire or of observation were minimal and one of the greatest enemies to the tank was likely to be the German hand-held bazooka, which fired a lethal projectile from close quarters. Rupert pointed to the defended area – the corner of the hill, perhaps two hundred yards long. Attacks after attacks by infantry, often supported by tanks, had come from all directions and for much of the time the Germans had been inside this perimeter. Shell and mortar fire had been incessant.

Rupert's eye was shot with blood. A German mortar shell had gone off in or just beside the slit trench in which he'd been standing. 'Alec and I agreed,' he said in his slightly drawling voice, 'that his tanks would deal with anything and anybody coming at us from outside and my company would handle everyone inside the perimeter.' And so it had been. Throughout those long hours, when the ground was alive with Germans, opening up with their machine pistols, their carbines, their bazookas, throwing their excellent stick grenades, all at close quarters; sniping at opportunity targets; or climbing the slopes of the hill to smash a way into our positions from without; throughout that time the 1st Battalion men had concentrated on killing every German inside the perimeter, swarming between our slit trenches only yards away, while Alec's tank crews had concentrated their exhausted eyes, their gunsights and their attention on the various approaches from without. With success. No tactical exercise we had ever undertaken or studied had resembled this.

Sometimes we were warned of impending Allied air attacks which might inadvertently threaten us, and we all had yellow smoke dischargers to show we were on the right side. There were, nevertheless, periodic mishaps, attacks by aircraft aiming at the enemy but hitting us. And sometimes – not, as I recall, in our Battalion – these caused significant casualties.

This can happen in battle, and there were also plenty of cases of ground fire hitting our own people. In the climate of split-second decision which modern air operations (in particular) necessitate this may well be even more of a hazard now even than it was in 1944. A more recent instance has disgusted a good many of my own contemporaries. A Coroner's Court in Oxford brought in a verdict of 'unlawful killing' when asked to enquire into the deaths of British soldiers apparently killed in battle by fire from American aircraft during the Gulf War of 1990/91. This seemed to have been regarded by the soldiers' families – and their lawyers, needless to say – as a matter for jubilation; television showed nauseating scenes of champagne bottles squirting from the grip of the triumphant bereaved. That such errors, whether culpable or not, should be made subject of legal proceedings, of clamour for a civil court to name the 'guilty' and so forth, is shaming, and an indication of the sort of people we, or some of us, have become

– ignorant (for nobody could suppose such incidents uncommon in any war), self-pitying and self-righteous as well as wholly unimaginative. Such antics mock honourable bereavement – 'Poor England,' some of us felt, 'what must America think of her!' Fortunately there were, I believe, no examples of this sort of reaction in the Second World War.

Many prisoners of war are seen by memory in the Norman landscape. Some of these were pitifully young – mere children. Some were veterans of the Eastern front, often grizzled, prematurely aged, sardonic, glad to be out of the whole frightful business for a while, perhaps for good. Many – we were surprised by this – were of a bewildering number of ethnic origins: Russians, Poles, Balts, Mongolians, men from every Balkan country. Some were members of *SS Volksdeutsch* units, but the Germans, very short indeed of manpower, had recruited wherever their writ ran.

I recall one young Pole, taken by our 1st Battalion early in the Normandy campaign. His name was Anton; he was short, sturdy, fair-haired. He spoke adequate English and had easily persuaded the good-natured Guardsmen of 1st Battalion Headquarters that he had served most unwillingly in the *Wehrmacht* and was now only anxious to join in the discomfiture of his former comrades, preferably in the uniform of a Grenadier. He was quickly fitted out with a British battledress, a beret and a grenade cap-badge; and made himself extremely useful around the armoured radio cars which constituted Battalion headquarters, taking cups of tea or plates of food to Eddie Goulburn when the latter returned from his travels at any hour of day or night. I can see a group of Guardsmen with Anton in full flow: 'He's just telling us about various places in France and Belgium, Sir. Places where he can show us where to go, where he and his mates used to have good time!' No doubt.

Burials took place as convenient – often near the Regimental Aid Post, wherever that was established. Our Battalion Medical Officer was an Irishman, Paddy Anderson, a large, brave, robust, good-natured man who understood the Guardsmen (standing no nonsense or malingering) and was thoroughly respected by them. His medical specialization was, I believe, gynaecology but the medical authorities looked on these things with broad minds.

Wooden crosses were carried in the medical vehicles, records were made, graves – sometimes, inevitably, multiple graves – were dug, French civilians often covered them with flowers, such obsequies as were possible were said, and ultimately, of course, all were gathered – as from the First World War – into those melancholy and beautiful cemeteries, large and small, which constitute the British Armed Forces' legacy to the landscapes of Holland, Belgium and Northern France; and many other places further afield. Similar treatment – but, it must be admitted, sometimes more cursory – was given to the enemy dead; and when, later in the campaign, I came on instances of German dealings with our own dead I found that their conduct had been most scrupulous, as was their handling of our wounded – often under difficult circumstances because of the ubiquitous threat of Allied air power.

I can see a particular small field in the Normandy bocage, near a place called St Charles de Percy. Our Battalion Headquarter tanks were placed round the hedges, camouflage nets spread, trenches dug for protection. We were in reserve, awaiting orders, and we hoped to be left there before the next operation for as many hours as possible. There was shade there and in different days it would have been a beautiful place. There was little enemy shelling – I think this was in early August when Allied pressure on the German lines was already increasing daily, until by mid-month they broke. The most troublesome circumstance in this place was one of our own heavy artillery pieces – an enormous gun – which was in the immediately neighbouring field and which was firing some sort of timed programme. This meant that every fifteen minutes there was a mind-shattering explosion from across the hedge, some thirty yards away: predictable, and irritating to the nerves. I was given a task. There were, it seemed, a number of German dead in the next small field, across a ditch from the gun and its crew. I was to take a party – and a tank fitted with bulldozer blades, which we used for all sorts of rapid, shallow excavation – and see to burial.

'But watch out! There's a report that the Germans have been booby-trapping bodies. Don't get blown up!'

I never heard an authenticated report to substantiate this but was prepared to go somewhat gingerly. In the field in question, perhaps a hundred yards from our own bivouac area, there were indeed a number of enemy soldiers lying dead, along a hedge which they had presumably been manning as a firing line. I took suitable precautions to see that the movement of any of them, if followed by an explosion, should do us minimum damage. None occurred.

There were orders about these things, including the removal from the dead of documents and identification, and recording of burial place. I did what needed to be done – they had been dead long enough to make body search somewhat difficult. But I can see very clearly the face of one young soldier. He was completely unmarked (some of them were terribly mutilated but this one showed no outward sign of wounding). He was wearing a camouflage-type smock – I think this was a Parachute Division, excellent troops. He was very young and very dark; black-haired, swarthy, giving a southern European or possibly southern Russian impression. A handsome lad, his brown eyes were open and slightly bloodshot, the only physical thing amiss. His expression was determined and a little angry. His Spandau machine gun was beside him. I do not know why of all the enemy soldiers I saw dead his face comes most vividly to me. A friend of mine has told me that on every day of Remembrance he says a prayer 'for all the men I killed'. This is absolutely right. In most wars one is closer in spirit to the enemy than to non-combatants on one's own side.

Sleeplessness and the desire for sleep are some of the outstanding recollections of those Norman days. It was summer – and for the most part beautiful weather but with all-pervasive dust when military columns were on the move – and the hours of darkness were few. We slept when we could – by roster. Tank crews dug a large hole and ran the tank over it, sleeping under it with considerable protection against shell and mortar fire (this practice had originally been forbidden as likely to lead to tank subsidence and crushed crew, a disturbing idea, but the ground in the fine weather, despite periodic showers, was so hard that in Normandy men slept under tanks as often as not). When I was moved from my tank and was made, for a while, a sort of liaison officer and general dogsbody at Battalion Headquarters, I was often mounted in a scout car. I acquired a small tent/bivouac cover and erected it over a slit trench in which I slept; very snug and convenient, since the ground between trench rim and tent bottom gave me on each side of my earthen coffin a narrow shelf for personal possessions.

Sometimes, of course, the night was filled by alarums and excursions, the sounds of battle. Sometimes it was devoted to movement and the huge effort to stay awake. But even when we were stationary, hours in the slit trench were all too short, brought to an end even on the least eventful nights by periods on duty in the Command Post, an excavated square with a canvas cover run between tanks, and with the radio headphones from two sets – one the forward, one the rear link – run into the square by extension leads. And before dawn everybody 'stood to' for a while until it was light, and time to wash, shave and enjoy a mug of tea and breakfast in a mess tin.

After a month or so of this it was difficult to think of sleeping happily anywhere but in my slit trench and under my tent cover; and the height of luxury would have been to be told that there was to be no 'stand to'. 'Now I sometimes feel,' I wrote home on 17th August, 'that I will never be happy except sleeping beneath the sky with no possessions but a pistol by me!' All this made my experience at the end of the Normandy campaign particularly bizarre.

We had been told that the campaign was going suddenly very well – not only very well but dramatically. The Americans, we learned, were advancing 'a good way'. We – the whole Guards Armoured Division – were to have a little time in reserve and resting. This was good news. Even better news was the rather astonishing order that a few officers could be given a day – or, rather later, several days – leave from duty and could take a military vehicle for local exploration and recuperation.

Almost immediately I was able to set off in a jeep with Robert Cecil. We had heard that the Americans had not only broken out of the Normandy bridgehead but had sent strong forces into Brittany. This was VIII US Corps, and although Brittany seemed a long way away we decided that we should aim at it. We had plenty of petrol jerrycans in the jeep and we reckoned (rightly) that the American Army would be helpful in that respect if required. To me the name 'Brittany' had an incredible, a remote, a magical aura of that last summer holiday of peace, of golf with my father at St Briac, of Fort Lalatte on Cap Fréhel, of my mother immersed in Chateaubriand. All this was only five years but seemed a whole lifetime away. Would anything seem reminiscent? What about four years of German occupation? What about the destruction of war?

We wove our way along roads thick with American columns, past Avranches, Pontorson, Dinan. It seemed virtually clean country, unscarred, wonderful. Everywhere British uniforms were welcomed with ecstasy. Although we hardly knew it the battle of Normandy had finally ended two days earlier with the taking of Falaise. The great German retreat was already under way.

As we drove I remembered, very vividly, an evening from that August holiday of 1939. Together with some friends also staying at St Briac I had gone with my father and mother to dine at a restaurant overlooking a bend in the Rance river. We had dined – deliciously – in an arbour. Another world.

We set out to find it.

And we did. I can see the *patronne* vividly. Madame had survived the war pretty well, but had had German soldiers billeted in the house and had disliked them. There were, as the French put it, '*Collaborateurs de Coeur*' and '*Collaborateurs de Porte Monnaie*', and I should say that she had been neither. A charming woman, she insisted that she would produce luncheon for us, as her guests. I told her of my family's earlier visit and we identified names in her visitors' book. Then she told us about the last four years. They had not been too bad in terms of physical deprivation, or fear, or harassment, but she was a Frenchwoman of dignity and it was clear that she had felt her home contaminated.

She brushed aside our protests and after an hour's wait and absorbing conversation she produced as good – and as large – a lunch as I ever remember. The food may have been straightforward – I can remember a noble omelette, river fish, cutlets – but it was superbly cooked and served by her charming young daughter. Robert and I had been existing on compo rations, bully beef, ration biscuits for seven weeks. This – which was better than anything on offer in England since many years – was rapture. And the *patronne* – I think the restaurant was called La Landriais – stands out as a most blessed and benign figure in my memory of 1944.

We drove back to Normandy, stopping on the way at Mont

St Michel, which I had also visited in 1939 and which was now packed to bursting point with American troops. We found ourselves in the small town of Balleroy. The town itself had escaped serious damage although St Lô, a few miles to the south-west, was completely obliterated. At one end of the main street is a chateau, standing on raised ground, behind high gates, handsome. We stopped in the street, where a number of French were about. For some reason there seemed few Americans in evidence although we were in the American Army sector. A child, a girl of perhaps ten or eleven, was standing on the pavement. We always carried some chocolate for these encounters and I offered her a piece and pointed back along the streets to the chateau gates.

'*A qui ce chateau?*'

She looked at me gravely, obviously finding such ignorance odd.

'*A Monsieur le Marquis.*'

'*Le Marquis d'où?*'

Again a grave look of puzzlement. Could there be any possible different answer?

'*Le Marquis de Balleroy.*'

I thanked her and looked more carefully at her face. It was perhaps the most beautiful face I had ever seen, and with the most beautiful expression – gentle, serious, composed; a thin, delicate face beneath straight, golden hair; an atmosphere of grace and serenity, shaming the externals of war. Other-worldly. Unrepeatable. A Leonardo, perhaps. I felt an extraordinary sense of goodness. We drove on and I said to Robert, 'I rather think we've just seen an angel.'

He agreed.

But the most memorable of these end-of-campaign pictures came a few days later, days in which we had continued to rest, clean ourselves and our tanks and our clothes, bivouacked in some lovely country near Flers. The horrors of the Falaise pocket and its immense count of carnage and destruction were some miles away. We knew that the Americans – so far it seemed only the Americans – were starting an extraordinary, unprecedented advance. The name of their General Patton was on everybody's lips; his army seemed to be moving to completely new parts of the map. Indeed, we had no maps ourselves which showed much beyond Normandy and Brittany and supposed ourselves confined to the north-west indefinitely. Then we heard the astonishing news that the Allies were actually approaching Paris! Paris! At the same time I and three others were told that we could have two days off (as several others had already taken) to go for a short break (destination unspecified) to 'bathe and relax'. Furthermore our Commanding Officer had somehow acquired a second staff car (such acquisitions were already becoming quite frequent) and we were given the loan of it.

We stuffed it with jerrycans of petrol, our sleeping bags and bivouacs, spades (it was surely probable that wherever we found ourselves it would be prudent to dig, to get below ground, as had been obligatory for the last few months), and set off with a huge sense of holiday. Once clear of the Battalion area we held a quick council: 'we' were, beside myself, Peter Carrington; Teddy Denny, an uncompromising, black-moustached enthusiast for anything he took up, who had before the war worked in a family meat-processing firm of distinction, acquiring in the process expertise in butchery which was periodically most useful; and Neville Berry, whose father, Lord Kemsley, was a famous newspaper magnate. Neville himself had worked on the family papers in Glasgow and was passionately interested in all matters connected with the press. He knew all the itinerant war correspondents and they all knew him, and were frequent visitors to our Battalion in consequence. Their appraisals of the war situation were often interesting, in that their perspectives tended to be different from our own, but were generally superficial, I thought – with the exception of Chester Wilmot, who later wrote one of the best books about the campaign in north-west Europe.

Our council had no difficulty in setting our destination. Paris. We couldn't believe we'd get there – surely the Germans would still be fighting for it or in it? Nobody knew where the front was, or whether there was one. We decided to try to go via Chartres, last visited by me when we lived in Paris in 1939. At least, we thought, we'd see Chartres. There was a more direct road, through Dreux, but to Chartres we set out. Through Alençon.

The roads, of course, were completely packed with American columns, tanks, transport of every kind. Every town and crossing point was staffed by the ubiquitous American military police with their white helmets – 'Snowdrops'. Progress was laborious and needed a good deal of cajolery, bluff and a few downright lies. We had a small Union Jack in the car and it caused astonishment – but from the French universal enthusiasm. At one point, I remember, we had just passed an enormously long American column with great difficulty, and there seemed some near-empty road ahead for a while.

We then had a puncture. I have never changed a tyre quicker. As we worked we could hear the approaching roar of the column we'd just passed. We managed it, and at about four o'clock in the afternoon we drove into Chartres. We'd come about 130 miles; to us who had been inching from hedge to hedge in the bocage, or driving through the blinding dust of tank columns for a few painful miles as our only recent journeying, 130 miles seemed an extraordinary adventure.

The cathedral at Chartres was untouched. The superb glass had all been taken out. We found a crowded café open and had something to eat – I can't remember what – and then took the Versailles road, hardly able to believe our luck. We drove into Versailles, down the broad avenue which runs from the chateau, amidst hugely enthusiastic crowds, already making progress near-impossible. And at seven o'clock in the evening we drove into Paris, and reached the Etoile.

More vast crowds. Flags everywhere. The tanks of (as we learned) General Leclerc's Free French armoured division were parked under the trees of the Champs-Elysées. No sound or sight of battle except for a knocked-out German Panther tank in the Place de la Concorde, looking at the Crillon Hotel – which bore slight marks of damage. There were everywhere hosts of FFI – the 'freedom fighters' of the Resistance, with tricolour sashes, variegated small arms, and noticeable absence of discipline.

Within our little group, although the junior, I had a certain 'position' as it was known my family had lived in Paris before and at the start of the war. The others gathered round.

'Where do we go now?'

I remembered the geography of Paris reasonably well.

'The Ritz,' I suggested. I knew I could find the Place Vendôme. So to the Ritz we drove. We were travel-stained and we certainly had no easily negotiable funds, but Neville Berry was put in charge of that side of life and persuaded us (and, indeed, the Ritz) that any shortfall would be made good by Kemsley Newspapers.

And as far as I know it was. We were given a suite of rooms – most of the hotel had already been taken over by the Americans, and by American war correspondents. When we explored the long downstairs corridor and ordered Perrier-Jouet champagne I remember Ernest Hemingway materializing (I suppose inevitably), and, perched at bar stools, long rows of very chic Parisiennes who looked as if they'd been there every evening since the war began, and probably had. It was for us a surreal atmosphere, not made less so by the figure of Richard Powell coming through the door from the Place Vendôme clad in what looked like a suit of overalls, and with a rifle slung over his shoulder. Richard Powell, a tall and immensely elegant baronet in the Welsh Guards, had been taken prisoner somewhere in Normandy, had escaped, been looked after by the *Maquis*, and en route (I imagine) to report back to his Regiment had fetched up in Paris, walked into the Ritz and stumbled on us. August 1944 was like that. The world was dissolving, and not only were the contrasts unbelievable between all of this and the world of slit trenches, bivouacs and death we had left only hours before, but they were pretty striking between this and much of wartime England.

Tentatively, we moved into the Ritz dining room and found it possible to order dinner, although the headwaiter apologized, in perfect English, for the limitations of the menu. Peter Carrington complimented him.

'Did you speak English when the Germans were here?'

Face impassive, he simply said with a touch of reproof, 'I spoke German when the Germans were here.'

They had left the hotel only hours before. We met one aged Englishwoman who had spent the war there; she was very irritated at the recent disruptions to the Ritz's service. People came up in the half-light – there was an electricity failure, a sort of black-out, and the dining room was lit by candles – and introduced themselves. I remember a White Russian with a charming Chilean wife who invited us to some sort of party next day, and a Dutchman, de Beaufort, who was a cousin of our great friends the Van Boetzelaers.

Next morning we all went to the British Embassy in the Rue St Honoré. The figure of the old Embassy servant who slowly and cautiously opened the great door into the courtyard is indeed memorable.

He was like a man awakening from a four-year trance. We were the first British officers he had seen, and he stood, unbelieving. He told us the Embassy had remained undefiled.

'Goering wanted it! As if I'd have allowed that! The British Embassy!'

His name was Christie. He remembered, of course, my father and told me – which was to me a miracle – that all the furniture and pictures from our flat had been brought into the Embassy itself and were safe. Lord Malise Graham, my father's successor as military attaché, had had to leave everything hurriedly as the Germans swept through France in 1940.

'It's all here! It's all all right!'

My parents had long given up thought of any likelihood of seeing their possessions again, and at a time when others were homeless, all belongings destroyed, had never let the fact distress them. But this was remarkable news.

Then I went to our flat, in the Rue Cognacq-Jay. The same concièrge whom I remembered. Everything curiously normal in atmosphere; no sense of drama arising from the years of occupation, or their sudden conclusion. Life for a concièrge had simply continued. We had, for a while, been one family temporarily in residence. Then there had been others. That was all. Tenants came and went – that was life. I asked about our servants – our little butler, Lucien, had died two years previously. I can see, however, the very pale face of a dark-haired, rather plump young woman who was in the concièrge's office while we talked, while they asked about my mother ('*Madame est toujours souffrante?*' She had frequent migraines): this girl sat, listening, silent. Then she murmured something to me. She looked nervous. A whisper.

'*Vous êtes Juif?*'

'*Non.*' I hope I didn't sound curt, but the question had surprised me.

'*Je suis Juive!*'

There must have been a mighty pressure of relief, of escaping fears, behind that exchange. Next day, still dazed, we drove westward again, unsure whether our expedition would, when disclosed, land us in trouble: and uncaring. As we made our way towards Evreux we were surprised to see the familiar shield sign of the Guards Armoured

Division with its 'ever-open eye' on vehicles passing us in the opposite direction. Our absence had coincided with new orders to the British Second Army. The Normandy campaign was officially over. The pursuit was under way and we had better discover where it had reached, and quickly.

11

'To the Last Breath of Man
and Beast'

The pursuit was indeed under way. Much of it was exhilarating. Some of it was disagreeable. Scenes and sensations alternated and, of course, the exhilaration predominated. We had spent a good many years feeling that we were losers and now the enemy were on the run.

On 2nd September our Battalion spent the night on an airfield near Douai and crossed the Belgian frontier in the small hours of the following day. I have already recalled our entry into Brussels, and at every village along the way there was exultation, cheers, the waving of improvised Union Jacks and Belgian flags, the opening of bottles whenever a vehicle stopped; the intoxicating, sometimes distracting, atmosphere of liberation.

We had already experienced it in northern France, after crossing the Seine at Vernon during the same afternoon that we Paris adventurers rejoined our Battalion. Thereafter the Battalion had driven day and night through places with echoing names from the First World War – Beauvais, Amiens, Arras; places which had signified huge casualties; long, painful years of trench warfare and attrition in our fathers' time, the time, indeed, of our elders within the Guards Armoured Division – Allan Adair had won the Military Cross nearby in 1918. And then Douai airfield and the road to Brussels. Everywhere Germans were surrendering. It seemed impossible that they could ever again form a coherent front or for long check the onward march of the Allied columns.

Small pictures stick in the mind. I can see a cluster of French houses in a poplar-lined avenue, our Battalion or part of it halted along the roadside, an excited gaggle of civilians, a handful of surrendered German soldiers, probably until then billeted on those houses. One was a tall, strong-looking man, I think an *Unteroffizier* – robust, smart, confident. He was exchanging handshakes with the French civilians before departing to a prisoner-of-war cage. The display of friendship clearly embarrassed them, as there was the unmistakable feeling of a cordial relationship of some standing now somewhat regrettably interrupted.

But sometimes there was serious resistance, defensive shellfire, demolitions, casualties, blood. At Pont-à-Marq on the way to Brussels a determined German garrison held up the Grenadier Group and forced the King's Company and our No. 2 Squadron (now commanded by James Bowes-Lyon, who had taken over from Arthur Grant in Normandy) to fight as hard an action as the whole advance produced. The enemy had deployed anti-tank guns (including some 88s), mortars and plenty of their light machine guns in the houses of the village and in a factory on its outskirts. We, from the company-squadron group, lost twenty-two men killed and thirty-one wounded during the action. About fifty German casualties, including twenty-five wounded, were counted, and one hundred and twenty five prisoners walked back down our centre-line towards the prisoner-of-war cages. Meanwhile the rest of the Grenadier Group moved round on an alternative route and met little opposition. It was never possible to know whether the next bend of road would disclose Germans, and, if it did, whether they would be minded to fight or simply to surrender, grateful that for them the game was over. It probably depended a good deal on the internal discipline and motivation of the German unit in question, on whether the junior leadership saw anything of a chance. It also, depended, obviously, on whether the advancing troops were in sufficiently evident strength to mean business.

I remember vividly one unexpected scene that day – I was travelling in my scout car accompanied by a Free French officer who had been attached to me to provide (I suppose) some sort of local knowledge. As we approached the crest of a ridge on a minor but long, straight, tree-lined road (this was in Belgium) our driver jammed on the brakes and put the car in reverse. He – and we – could see at the start of the next village, about two hundred yards away, the unmistakable sight of a large number of figures in field-grey, perhaps thirty of them, apparently gathered round a horse-drawn cart on which some sort of map was hung. It looked as if they were deliberating. A council of war, or, rather, of escape.

I was attached to the Household Cavalry squadron advancing on the same route as ourselves, and my immediate task was to discover whether it was possible to get up a particular minor road network. I had a quick word with the French officer. We had a Bren gun externally mounted on the scout car although dust made its performance uncertain after movement until it could be cleaned. I had a Tommy gun and, of course, a revolver. We decided to advance at speed, firing, and not to stop. We were somewhat vulnerable if the Germans reckoned that this was a minor trick they might win; and they might so decide after we had passed or if we stopped. We were alone. But we needed to know about this road.

We therefore opened up with the Bren gun and raced forward. The Bren gun soon stopped, choked with dust. The group of Germans exploded into grey particles and dissolved into the ditches astride the road. There were a few shots. My Tommy gun magazine was soon exhausted. I could see one German, a sentry behind a Spandau, just before the first houses of the village and thrust the barrel of my Tommy gun towards him violently as we drew level; this had the desired effect as he dropped his hold on the Spandau and threw his hands in the air. A few of the enemy lay very still. When we stopped, a few hundred yards later, we looked back and the road seemed empty except for a few prone bodies. An episode without glory or achievement but we had continued on our road, as required, and we'd lost nothing. I radioed such information as I could and we pressed on. Whether the remaining Germans escaped I don't know. I hope so.

A visually bloodier memory from that day was Lessines. The small town of Lessines lies north of the main road Ath–Enghien–Brussels, on a subsidiary route which the Grenadier Group had been ordered to take through Pont-à-Marq and Tournai. Lessines had been pounded by artillery and possibly by air attack as a preliminary to our advance. It had been garrisoned, for how long I don't know, by considerable numbers of Germans, and their horses.

When I drove into the place there seemed to be no Germans, but the entire main street was packed with dead and dying horses. The wretched creatures, if not collapsed, were standing, often in their shafts, with blood pumping out of their wounds. The street was slippery with blood. The Belgian population were already cutting horse flesh, carving joints from the unfortunate beasts, whether dead or living. It was a dreadful sight and a dreadful place. Perhaps it is a peculiarly British trait – and mockable as lacking in proportion – to be so upset by the fate and pain of so many animals when men were dying nearby, but I certainly was. The feeling was strong in me that these, whatever the misdeeds of men, had had no choices. In earlier wars – and other theatres of this war – such sights would have been commonplace but nobody who has ever cared for horses can regret their disappearance from the battlefield, although mechanization may have meant a loss for romantic artists of warfare.

One other picture comes to my mind from that day. In it, again, is the French officer, François, who for an hour or two was my companion on my scout car. We found ourselves beside a group of German prisoners and he – a German speaker – took the role of instant interrogator as to the immediate whereabouts of German troops. Standing by our car, and addressed by François, was a grim-looking, grizzled, unshaven German soldier. He looked a veteran. He probably was a veteran: perhaps from the Russian front.

François was, of course, peremptory, stern, and I watched the German's face as he listened. On it was a sort of twisted, snarling grin; and a look of absolute contempt. It seemed to say – this is imagination, of course – that he, a prisoner, helpless, at our mercy, part of a defeated army, had seen more than we could ever suppose or envisage. More of battle. More of victory and defeat. More – perhaps – of the friendliness of François and his kind in the days of German ascendancy. You're cock-a-hoop now, that grin seemed to be saying. You've got the upper hand. But it wasn't always so. And perhaps one day it won't be again.

These were the days of instant *épuration*, of the cleansing by France of the stains of collaboration. It was not a pretty sight.

One could sense without much difficulty a mixture of motives and emotions. In the First World War France had lost over a tenth of her active male population – an average of one thousand Frenchmen a day had been killed. The Germans had occupied for four years much of northern France. The weary sense that this could not be allowed to recur had led many in 1940 to feel that an understanding with the apparently all-conquering invader was defensible; and in most cases the invader had behaved correctly. Human nature created periodic bonds of affection, not all founded on self-interest or lust. For some collaboration had signified a sense of tired acceptance, while for others it had been undoubtedly rooted in greed; but when people and their children are hungry greed is comprehensible. And until the end of 1942 it appeared highly likely that the Germans would win the war; or, at least, not lose it.

There were, of course, political and patriotic motives also at play. For some Frenchmen and Frenchwomen the 'Boches' were the unchanged, unchanging enemy. Traffic with them or feelings softer than hatred for them were alike intolerable. Such steel-true patriots certainly existed, and some, of course, had fled France.

Others found different political sympathies dominant. After June 1941, when the Germans invaded Russia, the Communist Party (strong in France before the war although subject to official hostility thereafter, and virtually underground after the debacle of 1940) was strong for resistance. Indeed, by the time our campaign took place, it had penetrated and sought with some success to dominate a good deal of the Resistance itself. Then there had been a significant number on the other side of politics, people who reckoned that Bolshevism was the greatest enemy of European civilization and that, perhaps regrettably, Bolshevism was being most effectively opposed by the German *Wehrmacht*, in whose ranks, in consequence, were a number of French volunteers. There was also a certain amount of resentment of the British (and, to a lesser extent, the Americans), particularly in the light of our bombing policy, which had led some to collaboration.

But the majority of the collaborators we saw humiliated and punished during our advance through France and the Low Countries were young women, and the nature of their offence was clear. They had, from greed, from fear, from desire, from genuine human feelings, sometimes love itself, consorted with German soldiers. The consequences were disgusting to observe. No doubt in some cases the punitive mob contained individuals with particular reason to hate the

German occupiers. No doubt in some cases the females concerned had flaunted or exploited the protection they had earned with their bodies to damage others. But, witnessing it all, it was painfully easy to imagine that some of those active in punishment might have themselves profited from the Germans when they could, and were clearing their own slates by zeal in persecution. It was also too easy to guess at the sexual jealousy behind some of it. Shakespeare has Lear say it memorably:

'Thou rascal beadle, hold thy bloody hand.
Why dost thou lash that whore? Strip thine own back.
Thou hotly lust'st to use her in that kind
For which thou whip'st her –'

It was, therefore, frequent to enter a place from which the Germans had recently withdrawn and to find one or two pitiful, whimpering women, clothes half torn from their backs, hair roughly and totally shaved so that they were disfigured and shamed, often bearing marks of beating and ill-treatment, surrounded by jeering groups of Frenchmen and Frenchwomen. We had not suffered as these bullies had probably suffered. We had not lived under German occupation. It did not lie with us to suppress this cruelty. It was not for us to pass judgement, so we drove on, through cheering crowds. I remember one particular place, a small town or village, where the gutter in the long main street was actually running with blood, although there had been no battle there. The blood was the blood of French girls, some of whom were crouched pathetically on doorsteps, hiding their faces and their shame, beaten up, pouring out their grief.

But this, of course, was only part of the story. Less evident to us was what some of the French had themselves suffered from the invader, background to the resentment and the hatred – the deportations, the arrests, the fear, the occasional notorious atrocities such as the massacre at Oradour. Such things emerged only here and there, not always authenticated, whereas what we saw was what we saw.

Prisoners flocked in, sometimes in ones and twos, sometimes in groups, formed bodies of men. On the whole they were treated, I think, correctly – roughly (and with personal possessions often illegally confiscated) but correctly. There was, of course, a vast prisoner-of-war organization on the lines of communication but our advance had been so sudden and so rapid that the organization was under strain. I can, however, see one picture which I greatly regret, and which was probably not unique. A few enemy soldiers, perhaps four, were lined up on a small plot of grass beside a minor road, parallel to the one on which I was travelling. They seemed to be under guard of perhaps two of our own men, who were obviously making them turn out their pockets, hand over desirables like watches. This, of course, was wholly illegal but it happened.

A few minutes later I happened to turn my binoculars back on this parallel road, by now some distance away. I saw what looked like four huddles of field grey, now on the ground, inert. I was on some mission or other. I did not immediately drive across, find the place, investigate. Sometimes a man of ours would (it was muttered) become 'trigger happy'. Sometimes he had, perhaps, lost a particular friend and hatred possessed him so that he turned on the defenceless. None of this is excusable and nor is my own non-investigation. For our record had blemishes and some of them were, by repute, ugly. One heard (not in our own Grenadier Group) of claims – boasts almost – that 'we didn't intend to take any prisoners', during a particular battle or phase of the campaign. Such brutality was not necessarily described accurately; some people feel more robust for the ability not to flinch from cruel conduct and brag accordingly; but there was here and there an undercurrent of inhumanity and it jarred. It jars still. I had looked the other way.

Several observations need making. First, the objects of war crimes allegations were, I think, often reputed to be the SS and there were stories – no doubt sometimes true stories – that atrocities against civilians had been discovered, attributable to SS units, and arousing strong desire for revenge. Towards the end of the campaign, of course, concentration camps were being uncovered and horrifying stories reported in the press of the murder and ill-treatment suffered by their wretched inmates. The SS were named as perpetrators and this seemed to justify counter-brutality without restraint.

In fact the Waffen SS, against whom we fought, were a completely separate part of the organization from the concentration camp guards, the Gestapo and the like. They were very well-disciplined, well-trained, well-led and outstanding soldiers; and they deserved to be treated as such by their enemies except in particular and rare cases.

I wrote home on 16th September 1944:

The SS are magnificent, a great thorn in our sides. We captured an SS officer the other day who talked long and seriously. '1940 was our hour,' he said, 'and there's no doubt 1944 is yours.' He gave it two months to total collapse but he was completely confident that in a few years they'd be back. He said they'd had to shoot a lot of Poles, Russians, French etc. because of the 'Terrorism' and perpetual attacks on German soldiers and supply columns and sabotage – 'when fighting for one's life one cannot tolerate such things – surely you as a soldier understand that?' He was indignant about the bombing – 'You began it. Cologne was the first city bombed.' He'd fought three campaigns in Russia: North Africa: Tunisia, Italy, France (1940) and France (1944). He'd been wounded five times (severely) and had a Typhoon splinter in the chest at the time of capture. But all he wanted was another go.

I wrote as a no doubt naive twenty-three-year-old, but such men merited the honour due to warriors, if anybody did. And most of our opponents were not, in any case, SS.

Second, the correct handling of prisoners depended not a little upon the circumstances of surrender. A British platoon might be fired upon by a German post and finally storm it. Fire – German fire – might be kept up against the attackers (bravely and effectively, causing casualties) until the last moment, and then the defenders would emerge, hands on high. In such circumstances it is rare that quarter will be given. Blood is up, and if it were not men would not assault. Comrades have fallen. Surrender could have been earlier. The rest is imaginable.

The fact is that 'war crimes' were committed by both sides (on the Eastern Front, of course, with every circumstance of barbarity). I do not like 'war crimes' procedures, least of all when long retrospective. They can be applied with legalistic zeal to the actions of men under pressures hard to imagine in the quiet of a courtroom; and, anyway as far as the Second World War is concerned, can be rigorously applied to the enemy while the eye turned on our own record tends to be blind. It makes it particularly disagreeable in later days to read of proceedings in England, made legal by a deplorable act of the British Parliament in the 1990s (the House of Lords, to their credit, opposing but overruled under the Parliament Act), under which an eighty-five-year-old Ukrainian was charged with killing three Jews in Byelorussia during the campaign on the Eastern front. There is a detestable inclination to double standards in these matters. Evil is evil and nothing can excuse the cruelty and savagery which marked in too many cases the regimes against which we fought in the Second World War; but condemnation must be even-handed or it loses all force. As an exercise by the victor alone it is repellent.

For another picture comes to me, in that connection, from the great advance – although somewhat later, when we had crossed the Belgian–Dutch border, which we did in September as part of another major operation. I recall it, however, because of an awful crime I, myself, fortunately avoided committing – one which, had I done it, albeit in good faith, and been in German rather than British uniform, would certainly have brought me to the gallows.

The Dutch welcomed us with as much enthusiasm as the French or Belgians. They had, in many parts of the country, had a particularly hard time and near-famine was rife. During this particular advance, near Eindhoven, the usual ecstatic crowds, sporting orange colours to show their patriotic enthusiasm for the House of Orange, were everywhere. Our main route was blocked by a series of blown bridges over the numerous small waterways, and I was sent, with an officer of the Royal Engineers riding in another scout car, to see whether there was a chance of getting the Grenadier Group up a particular chain of small roads. As in France there were Germans, mostly anxious to surrender, here and there. A considerable German army was still in Western Holland, west of the British north-running centre-line.

We, in our two scout cars, rounded a corner on a broad, well-surfaced road, and stopped. We both edged into the side and brought binoculars up.

A short distance ahead of us, running up a slight slope, at right angles to our road, was a thin hedge; half way up it was the unmistakable barrel of a machine gun.

Quick conference. I would advance along the road and spray the hedge with Bren gun fire as I approached it. My companion would cover it from our present position and give it all he had (another Bren gun mounted) if they opened up at me. Then, we hoped, the enemy party, likely to be small and fearful, would come down with their hands up, and we could continue our reconnaissance, which was urgent.

As I, in my scout car, approached the point where the hedge met our road, and nothing had happened, something, I don't know what, made me deviate from our plan and desist from opening fire. Instead I swivelled the Bren gun on its mounting so that as I passed the hedge I could fire up it and plaster those still, presumably, lying behind it.

As I passed, the gun still silent, I could see clearly up the hedge line. Figures, perhaps half a dozen, were lying or kneeling behind it. A happy group of small Dutch children, playing soldiers. A picture which still haunts me, heart in mouth, with gratitude.

After we had entered Brussels on 3rd September – and left it sharply next morning, driving towards Louvain, where our Battalion had taken up positions in the ill-fated May of 1940 – the character of the campaign changed. The previous fortnight had been extraordinary: pursuit, excitement, periodic battle, a sense that surely the end of the war could not be far away. Now, as we moved east and north-east from Brussels, there was a sense that the days of exhilaration might be behind us.

And so it was. There have been many reasons adduced why the pursuit of the German armies beaten in Normandy was allowed to become bogged – with winter literally bogged – and end in a painful and expensive winter campaign. Certainly to us the impetus seemed irresistible up to and beyond Brussels. So far it was a hunt – whips out and only the best line to find. I can see the road running into Louvain as we approached – a squadron of the Household Cavalry already there, and sporadic shooting sounding from the town. We had harboured in the gardens of the Royal Palace of Laeken the previous night, we had covered a hundred miles the previous day, nothing could stop us.

As we drove up to a road fork on the west side of Louvain we could almost picture the last German vehicle leaving the eastern bounds of the town. There was a small cheering group of Belgians standing beside the road, several of them priests or seminarists, and they seemed in a state of high excitement. One, huge, red-haired, and yelling his head off with enthusiasm, was pointing down the right hand of the road fork and managed, cassock flying, to get a foothold on the leading tank.

'Come on, boys, you're right up with him!' There was no doubt about it from voice and demeanour. This was an Irishman.

But very soon thereafter we came to a series of great water obstacles, the Albert Canal, the Escaut Canal. There were blown bridges, and bridging sites covered by German fire. There were even reports of German mobile columns on the march towards our flanks. We crossed in open order the heathland near the mining town of Bourg Leopold and lost our leading tanks to well-deployed anti-tank guns. We were told that SS troops were in position. There were large woods along the main roads from which ambush parties could operate only too effectively. The awful suspicion began to dawn that the party was over.

It was. Henceforth the campaign was going to be a matter of deploying and attacking small parties of the enemy holding, with skill and courage, key points on our route; or, laboriously, of our finding a way round. This was to set the pattern of the advance through northern Belgium, Holland and Western Germany. It is a form of warfare in which small bodies of troops, in defence, can inflict disproportionate casualties and impose disproportionate delay; and the terrain was well suited to it. Much of the ground astride the roads was soft polder in which tanks bogged. Roads were easily covered from woods and banks. Deployment for operations was laborious. Infantry were at a premium and the enormous mass of vehicles which constituted an armoured division and its logistic train often seemed to impede rather than exploit mobility.

We trundled on towards the Dutch frontier. We crossed the Albert Canal. By the night of 11th September, a week after leaving Brussels, we were approaching the Escaut Canal up a long, straight, tree-lined road. The Irish Guards were across the water and holding a shallow bridgehead on the far side, but it looked as if onward movement was liable to be astonishingly sticky. It seemed to us extraordinary. How had the Germans – surrendering in such huge numbers only a week or so earlier – recovered?

Montgomery has given his own reasoning in his memoirs. The Allies, he said, should have 'acted quickly in the middle of August, using the success gained in Normandy as a springboard for a hard blow which would finish off the Germans and at the same time give us all the ports we needed . . . To do these things we had to have a plan and concentration of effort. We had neither . . . had we adopted a proper operational plan in the middle of August and given it a sound administrative and logistic backing we should have secured bridge-heads over the Rhine and seized the Ruhr before winter set in.' This leads to the (by now familiar) complaint that Eisenhower dissipated Allied strength and that the objective could have been attained had Montgomery and his 21st Army Group been given sufficient strength. Instead, allegedly, there was an uncoordinated advance on several fronts from north to south, sufficiently strong nowhere.

I disagree. The advance in the northern part of the warfront, by Montgomery's Army Group, was not inhibited by absence of concentrated effort. That would imply lack of strength at the critical point, strength diverted to the Americans further south. There was no lack of strength, if by 'strength' is meant troops, equipment, firepower. There may have been, at the level and from the perspective of Army logistic planners, *impending* shortage of supplies, particularly petrol, but we certainly didn't suffer from it up to the point when our advance was checked, not by lack of fuel but by the Germans. Thereafter I accept that the Montgomery thesis is tenable – that the fuel situation (other supplies created negligible difficulties by that stage) might have forced a decision between north and centre if the ultimate advance was not to stall. That lay well in the future. In the autumn of 1944, had Montgomery been given what he asked – command of a 'thrust by forty divisions' north of the Ardennes – it is difficult to believe things would have moved noticeably better or faster.

Because the first truth is that by then the Allies had such a mass of vehicles, both tracked and wheeled, that rapid progress was absolutely dependent on a large number of parallel and interconnecting roads, and in the Low Countries these could not possibly carry the traffic involved. Lack of road space limited the force which could be deployed. Deployment off roads was difficult because of the terrain. The Armies were vehicle-bound. Infantry were absolutely necessary for the fighting, when it occurred, but nobody marched, although henceforth the distances were not great. A vehicle-bound army generates correspondingly greater demand for fuel – and more fuel-carrying vehicles. Internally and organizationally the Army, and every unit in it, was wastefully devised, and slow and laborious to move. This penalty was insufficiently offset by greater firepower and tactical mobility at the sharp end.

The second truth is that the Germans (Field Marshal von Rundstedt, with a cool, experienced strategic head, had been brought back in overall command in the West, having been sacked by Hitler during the Normandy campaign) had recovered something of their balance. The experienced, skilful staffs of the *Wehrmacht* had somehow assembled new troops, organized the disorganized, sorted out priorities, assigned tasks and ably distributed the very soarce resources. I can see that long, straight road running through woods towards the Escaut Canal on 11th September. Night was falling. A tank was burning beside the road. Other vehicles were on fire here and there. It was going to be necessary to move some forces through the woods, to get round the obstruction, the fires, covered as they were by German anti-tank and machine gun fire; and this was, in fact, done by the Irish Guards. But we were no longer facing a beaten army. We had, I think, relaxed somewhat, lost impetus. I suspect there may have been a few days at the end of August when a sufficiently vigorous thrust *somewhere*, taking risks, remorselessly driven, might – conceivably – have kept the Germans on the run. Patton, perhaps, might have done it – it needed a real thruster, backed from above. But I suspect that by the end of the first week of September the chance had gone.

The third truth about the situation, the slowing of the great post-Normandy pursuit and the failure to end the war in 1944, was, I consider, faulty planning. Nobody in my humble position could form any idea on such things at the time but I have had plenty of opportunity to think about them since. The bad planning was exemplified by our next operation, the operation which took us across the Escaut Canal and into Holland, the operation which was meant to see us over the Rhine and (according to Montgomery) to enable the Allies to encircle the Ruhr before winter. It was called MARKET GARDEN.

*

I can see our harbour area before the launch of MARKET GARDEN, immediately south of the Escaut, over which the Irish Guards had captured their bridgehead a few days previously – at once named 'Joe's Bridge' in honour of the unforgettable Joe Vandeleur. We – and they – had been at rest for a blessed interval, maintaining our tanks in pleasant meadows near the Army Corps and Divisional centre-line, which was to run from a place called Hechtel behind us (stubbornly defended by the SS against the Welsh Guards Group) over 'Joe's Bridge', and through Eindhoven to the lower Rhine at Nijmegen (called the Waal at that point); and then to the northern arm of the great river (the Neder Rijn) at Arnhem. Advance up this centre-line was to be as rapid as possible since it would be preceded by a great 'drop' of Allied airborne forces: the whole of the 1st Airborne Corps, led by our own General Frederick 'Boy' Browning, who had commanded our Battalion until 1939, and whose Corps now included the British 1st Airborne Division, the 82nd and 101st US Airborne Divisions and a Polish Airborne Brigade. We relaxed in glorious sunshine, enjoying a certain issue of German Army champagne captured from their special wine store in Brussels, relishing a few hours and days of comparative leisure and uncurtailed sleep.

And then, in the early afternoon of 17th September, we saw overhead the great fleet of aircraft – troop carriers, gliders, escorts. They had come from England and were heading towards Arnhem and Nijmegen – at both of which a substantial bridge spans the river, so that both needed capture if the Army was to meet Montgomery's aim of crossing the Rhine and launching an offensive to encircle the Ruhr. The aircraft, in impressively huge numbers, moved northward. This meant that at a certain hour, I cannot remember how long afterwards, we would be on the move ourselves. The Guards Armoured Division was the spearhead of General Horrocks's XXX Corps for Operation MARKET GARDEN, intended to link up with the airborne forces. Two other British Corps, VIII and XII, were to attack to widen the corridor driven northward by XXX Corps, on its east and west respectively.

The advance of our Division was preceded by a deafening artillery preparation – the Division's movement was supported by seventeen artillery regiments and heavy mortars from several other divisions.

Then there was a delay, of a very familiar kind – we were at immediate notice to move, but 'something' in front was holding things up. It was nearly dark by the time we moved across 'Joe's Bridge' and it was already clear that the race to Arnhem via Nijmegen would be liable to delays. A significant number of Irish Guards tanks – the Irish Guards Group had been nominated as leaders – were burning beside the road.

Progress, therefore, was slow. At frequent points the north-running road crossed a minor waterway and a well-placed demolition was enough to cause delay to an armoured column with its heavy vehicles. Our engineers were admirable but it took time to bring the armoured bridging equipment to the right point (and time to find that point, and reconnoitre the approaches to it) and there wasn't an infinite amount of bridging – or time. Nevertheless I remember the impressive silhouette of the long bridge across the Maas (Meuse) at Grave. This had been captured by the American airborne troops and took us across the first main water obstacle at about ten o'clock in the morning of 19th September. By then the operation had been running for over forty hours and was already well behind schedule. I didn't see him at that moment but friends told me that Boy Browning – immaculate as always – was standing on the bridge when our tanks arrived. The leading squadron commander was Alec Gregory-Hood. He dismounted and, covered in dust, unrecognizable, went up to the general and saluted.

'Who are you?'

'Sir, it's Alec!' Alec had been a subaltern in Boy Browning's Battalion.

'Good God!' was the characteristic response. 'I always said it would be cleaner to come by air!' And by then Boy Browning must have been fretting painfully about the timetable.

The next picture I have is of a Dutch café in the outskirts of Nijmegen, a few miles up the road north of Grave. There a quick conference was being held at midday on 19th September and orders were being given out. Beside our own people American uniforms were everywhere. Members of the Dutch Resistance were buzzing around us like bees, with information (we hoped) of where the Germans were. Our task and our hope was that an armoured column could smash their way through the town, using the main road to the Waal, and cross the enormous road bridge – Nijmegen lies entirely on the south bank. That would mean the southern arm of the Rhine in Allied hands, and a short drive – about thirteen miles, no more – up a broad, hard-surfaced, raised road to the northern arm of the river, the Neder Rijn, at Arnhem thereafter. Then the Allies would be across the Rhine.

The American 82nd Airborne Division, whose mission had included capture of the Nijmegen bridge, had been dropped some distance away to the south-east and west. They had then advanced into the town, on the south bank, and found it strongly defended. The Germans had prepared effective defences, had fired a large number of houses near the bridge and were in considerable force. The road approaches were covered by anti-tank gun and machine gun fire. The Americans had had a hard fight and suffered significant casualties. Like the British 1st Airborne Division at Arnhem they had been waiting for two days and nights for the relieving force of the British Second Army, led by ourselves. Meanwhile Nijmegen was in German hands.

A group from Alec Gregory-Hood's squadron and a company of the 1st Battalion, in their lightly armoured troop carriers, was composed and set off. Another group was directed on the railway bridge, which crosses the river a short way to the west of the road bridge and which was being used by the Germans for vehicle traffic, sleepers having been laid between the rails. Yet another small group – a troop of our tanks and two 1st Battalion platoons with some American infantrymen – was simultaneously sent to try to reach the main Nijmegen Post Office, where information (untrue) was that the Germans controlled remote firing mechanisms which could demolish the bridge; and the bridge was what mattered. Street maps of Nijmegen were distributed. We soon heard that the first group, aiming at the road bridge, was held up, that our troop leader, John Moller, had been killed and that the town south of the bridge was stiff with Germans. Similar reports came through from the party moving towards the railway bridge, who were eventually halted, not far from the southern bank, and surrounded by Germans; they spent uncomfortable hours isolated from the rest of us. The group directed on the Post Office actually got there. Communications were near-impossible in the built-up areas with the radio sets of those days. To discover where people were and what had happened generally needed physical contact and a visit.

By nightfall on that first Nijmegen evening, with our groups at various points in a town strongly held by the Germans, it was evident that Nijmegen would have to be cleared methodically, and that that would take time. This was grim news – the operation had now been running about fifty-five hours. Our hopes of rushing a bridge across the enormous Waal had been frustrated. The bridge itself had not been blown, but to cross the river would need a battle.

And so it proved. More recently I have seen many films and television programmes dealing with MARKET GARDEN, in some of which it was suggested – sometimes by distinguished commentators – that the delay in reaching the bridge at Arnhem (being defended by 1st Airborne Division with great gallantry) was caused by sluggardly conduct or procedural niceties. I have even heard that 'there was nothing to stop them [our Division] – nothing there' (between Nijmegen and Arnhem). Such comments are fantasy. Nijmegen was full of German troops, street-fighting is a slow, laborious business, and before it was sufficiently advanced there could be no further attempt on the bridge. The attempt by John Moller's troop on our first afternoon had been frustrated.

The fighting in the streets, therefore, was likely to go on throughout the next day, 20th September. I was sent by Eddie Goulburn to see our Brigade Commander, Norman Gwatkin, and to give him details of the plan to clear Nijmegen. I arrived at Brigade Headquarters, just outside Nijmegen, at about four in the morning. Norman Gwatkin was a man of enormous character. A Coldstreamer, with a high colour, a choleric expression, a loud and infectious laugh, he was loved by our Grenadiers and known as were few senior officers. 'There's the Brigadier!' they would say, chuckling, and I remember one Sergeant adding, 'and he's an inspiration to the men!' – a rare, articulate observation. He cheered all men, wherever they were and whatever the circumstances: and when an advance was held up by German defensive posts and the situation was obscure the column would generally be passed by the Brigadier, driving himself in a jeep, small pennant flying, pipe in mouth, heading for the front, for the tip of the spear, to see what was up.

On this occasion I stumbled in the darkness round the vehicles of Brigade Headquarters and was told the Brigadier was asleep in his caravan. 'So you'd better go and wake him up!' said the Brigade Major,

Miles Fitzalan-Howard, with an unsympathetic smile. I found the caravan steps, climbed, knocked and entered. Norman Gwatkin turned on a light and opened an eye. I explained I had brought Colonel Goulburn's plan for the battle of Nijmegen and the capture of the bridge, if not blown.

'Shall I show it to you, Sir?' I had marked a town map.

'No, thank you,' he said, very kindly. 'I'm sure if Colonel Eddie is satisfied with it, it's an excellent plan. Please thank him. Goodnight.' He turned out his light and was no doubt asleep again by the time I was down the caravan steps. Another good lesson of its kind.

Earlier in the evening I had been sent to try to make contact with our group which had aimed at the Post Office. Communications had failed utterly and nobody knew where they were or if anything had happened. I eventually discovered the Post Office, without harassment by Germans, and found our Troop commander's tank outside it. The Troop commander was Jim Scott, later to be a neighbour and dear friend in Hampshire.

Jim, who had been trying to make contact with Battalion or squadron headquarters as indomitably as we had been trying to get through to him, was curled up with his radio headset on the turret floor of his Sherman, as far down as it was possible to get, hoarse with shouting. He had found, he said, that the intolerable radio interference in his earphones was marginally better in that position and he had adopted it. Now, after a taxing hour yelling into the ether in this exceptionally uncomfortable position, he looked up and saw me at the turret hatch.

He told me long afterwards that it was a great disappointment. He was sure – or almost sure – that he had managed to make some sort of contact, and now I'd spoiled it by turning up in person. He was our best Troop commander and a man, throughout life, trusted and loved by all who had dealings with him. Now he explained that, as far as anybody could discover, there was no detonation plunger mechanism in the Nijmegen Post Office. No importance at all in the Post Office, in fact.

Throughout the next day, 20th September, fighting continued and the clearance of Nijmegen proceeded. Towards the end of the afternoon the Valkof was attacked by the King's Company, supported by the tanks of James Bowes-Lyon's squadron. The Valkof was a high wooded mound, an ornamental public park with mock fortifications and many tunnels. It commanded the final approaches to the main road bridge and the Grenadiers of the King's Company climbed the very steep slopes to its summit while our Sherman tanks poured in fire from between houses on the other side of the moat. Vicary Gibbs, the King's Company acting commander, and several more were killed but eventually the approaches to the Waal seemed clear.

At seven o'clock on that evening of 20th September a column of our tanks, commanded by Peter Carrington, rushed the bridge. It was an exciting moment, with, at any moment, the possibility of a mighty explosion, the bridge sundered and the adventure over. Then we heard, listening to our radio sets, that there had been no explosion. We were across the Waal.

Next morning, 21st September, I accompanied our Commanding Officer, Rodney Moore, to the far side. The huge structure was in our hands. Without the bridge at Arnhem it was of little operational significance, but we didn't know what was happening at Arnhem and to us it seemed that we, the Grenadiers, were over the Rhine. A few destroyed vehicles, a few corpses in field grey lying by the bridge approach, and then the mighty river. On the north bank Peter Carrington was in control, brisk and assured as usual, but annoyed by a German high-velocity gun, I expect an 88, which was firing shells at our little bridgehead.

Further west our group aiming at the railway bridge reached it at 9 o'clock that morning. Rodney Moore sent me to make contact with the group commander. This was Johnnie Neville, Alec Gregory-Hood's squadron second-in-command. He was a delightful man, tall, saturnine, an exceptional soldier (a businessman in civilian life), with a sardonic sense of humour and a kindness of heart he ineffectually tried to conceal. Affecting a good deal of admiration for most things American (which experience of business had to some extent inculcated in him) he was only slightly older than me and my contemporaries, but in sophistication he seemed a whole generation senior and we held him in awe. He was downright, brave, witty and competent.

He was standing on the south end of the railway bridge, having spent by now two nights and a day surrounded by elements of the

Wehrmacht, and wore his usual rather mocking grin as he told me what had happened. What had happened, as he explained with his usual economy of language, was that after a considerable fire fight the Germans had decided to pack it in. They'd moved – fast. He hadn't lost a man; about 150 enemy dead were counted. I remember it as an occasion – there were many and they always struck me with surprise – when the entire German defensive position on the bridge and by the southern ramp up to it was covered by a vast mass of *paper* – army forms of one sort and another, returns, indenting forms, report forms. They were blowing in all directions. Paper is, or was, a considerable element in the detritus of war.

On that morning of 21st September the Irish Guards Group took up the lead, and tried to get up the road to Arnhem. They couldn't get far, losing tanks to enemy fire almost immediately. The road runs on raised dykes, deployment for armour off it is impossible and it resembles an attempt to drive in the face of the enemy through a tunnel on a one-vehicle front. By this time troops of the American 82nd Division, crossing the wide river further downstream in borrowed and unfamiliar British flat-bottomed assault boats with canvas sides – and crossing it under fire, an outstandingly brave performance – had joined up with us on the north bank. An infantry division was brought up and later reached the south bank of the Neder Rijn, but by then our Airborne troops at Arnhem had been worsted. It was all over – had been over since early morning that day when the gallant remnants of the British parachute battalion holding the north end of the Arnhem bridge were overwhelmed.

The tactical flaws in MARKET GARDEN have been discussed frequently and I can add little. The command and communications set-up was peculiar. Boy Browning had command of his 1st Airborne Corps divisions after they dropped or landed, yet the land battle would inevitably lie with XXX Corps (General Horrocks), under which were the advancing divisions, including our own. When artillery is required to support another formation (and the main weight of artillery would inevitably be with XXX Corps) such things matter.

Clearly there can be dispute until the end of time about the dropping zones for the airborne divisions, and their distance from the key objectives, the Arnhem and Nijmegen bridges; such disputes generally turn on factors of time, space, security and likely enemy reactions, and no doubt some judgements, with hindsight, could have been better made. There has also been plenty of argument about whether more could have been made of the comparative effectiveness of glider-borne troops (which land united rather than scattered and are thus more quickly and effectively deployed) over parachutists for the key objectives where time was of the essence. Also discussed incessantly has been the intelligence available to the airborne commanders and their deductions from it. It has been suggested that the presence in the Arnhem area of 9th and 10th SS Panzer Divisions – resting from the Eastern front, depleted in numbers but being refitted and always formidable – was or could have been known. 1st Airborne Division was dropped into something of a hornets' nest.

It also seems curious that no airborne forces were dropped south of the Arnhem bridge – between the two bridges – until 21st September, when the battle for Arnhem was already lost. This was attributed to weather but it was surely crucial to the concept. The ground between Arnhem and Nijmegen was wholly unsuitable for rapid advance by armoured forces unless an intermediate force could be got into position.

Overlaying all these points was the timetable for the ground forces' advance, in relationship to the amount of time the airborne forces would need to hold their objectives. This timetable was impossibly optimistic and implied a bad appreciation of terrain by planners. Furthermore the Nijmegen bridge – key to *any* attempt to drive to Arnhem – was perhaps not given a sufficiently decisive priority as an airborne forces objective. The British XXX Corps, the relieving force, therefore found two major rivers ahead of them after crossing the Maas, with bridges over both all or partly in German hands and with the town of Nijmegen thick with German troops. Not a situation lending itself to rapid solution.

Then there is the question of why the operation was aimed at Nijmegen and Arnhem – at two rivers – in the first place. To aim – if there was to be such an attempt at all – further upstream, at somewhere like Wesel, or Rees, where the Rhine was ultimately crossed, would have meant concentration on only one crossing. It has been said that this would have exposed the airborne invasion to dangerously heavy flak from the air defences of the Ruhr – it would have taken place some thirty miles nearer the latter. Thirty miles? I find the argument unconvincing. And our airforces had plenty of experience, by then, at blanketing off anti-aircraft fire with the weight of their preliminary bombardment if that was the need.

But, in my opinion, more fundamental than any of these operational questions was the concept, the object, the overall purpose. This was defined by Montgomery – and Eisenhower supported the operation, and had assumed authority after Normandy as land forces commander – as to debouch from the Rhine, encircle the enemy forces in the Ruhr, isolate it, and thus make it improbable that Germany could continue the war into the winter. It must be self-evident that for this enormous advance by a most circuitous route the supply line of communication would have to be adequate. Huge tonnages would need to be shipped into the theatre and transported forwards. This placed an absolute premium not only on transport vehicles but on port and road capacity. Yet in the autumn of 1944 much of the Allies' supplies were still coming from Normandy. The critical port was Antwerp, with huge capacity and suitably placed for an advance to or round the Ruhr; and Antwerp was not yet usable because the Germans had left strong forces on the bank of the Scheldt between Antwerp and the sea and they were still active.

Without Antwerp MARKET GARDEN might have succeeded operationally had every factor or decision which turned out wrong gone the other way; but without Antwerp, I do not believe that MARKET GARDEN could possibly have been exploited for the (only) purpose for which it was devised. Some might rejoin that the existing line of communication might have still done the job (that is, enabled Montgomery's 21st Army Group to advance deep into Germany from Arnhem) had the American Armies further south been reined in. I doubt it – and doubt even more the strategic and political practicability of reining in General Patton, whose Third Army was racing towards the Southern Rhineland. As it was, the alleged reluctance of Eisenhower to give priority to Montgomery's thrust had no effect whatsoever on the way things went. Operation MARKET GARDEN was, in an exact sense, futile. It was a thoroughly bad idea, badly planned and only –

tragically – redeemed by the outstanding courage of those who executed it.

One figure remains very strongly in my mind from those September days in Nijmegen when the operation as earlier conceived was obviously over. After it was clear that there was unlikely to be dramatic further advance but, instead, that there would be scrappy fighting, with no self-evident object, on the 'island' between the two rivers, I was told to report for a day or two to the headquarters of the American 82nd Airborne Division. Certain measures, and especially artillery fire, should be coordinated. 82nd Division were on the eastern outskirts of the town.

The Divisional commander was General Gavin, Jim Gavin. He later achieved the highest positions in the United States Army. He was a man of deeply impressive character and appearance – tall, handsome, immaculate, youthful-looking, and rather quiet. He was, I thought and remember, so courteous in his general demeanour (while clearly possessing absolute and unquestioned authority) that he brought to mind a favourite maxim of my Uncle Alistair, that manners and morals are at a certain level the same thing. Jim Gavin's distinction and courtesy had moral force. And he commanded a superb division.

Another picture comes to me from those days immediately after the battle. I knew that Oosterhout, the home of my parents' friends Pim and Ethel Boetzelaer, where I had stayed as a boy, was very near. One day I found myself on the north bank of the Waal and drove there.

The house of Oosterhout had been occupied by the Germans, and then by us as a medical dressing station, and by the Irish Guards. It was always curious to explore in the midst of war a scene only familiar in utterly different circumstances – rather like my visit to our Paris flat from Normandy. I wrote home (and sent a letter, also, to Baron van Boetzalaer, who was now Dutch Ambassador in Washington):

The twin grandfather clocks are all right, and some of their nicest things have been locked up in an upper room. The piano is all right.

I opened one drawer and found a lot of cards which Ethel must have used to mark people's places at dinner, among them General Mason Macfarlane and the American and Italian Ambassadors, which might amuse her . . .

Such bizarre contrasts (a mortar bomb had exploded by the front door) served as a reminder – hardly credible at the time – that there was a world of pianos and families and dinner party place-cards which was once reality and might become so one day again; that war is an aberration.

12

Farewell to Armour

The house I had selected as our Battalion Headquarters Officers' Mess was square, white, agreeable. It was in a side street off the main road running eastward through a Belgian village towards Tirlemont from Louvain. I was on a billeting advance party, and we had been sent westward that morning to find quarters for the battalion, suitable for a few days' break over Christmas.

The whole Guards Armoured Division had been withdrawn from the positions we had occupied for six weeks after the MARKET GARDEN adventure – positions in the 'Maastricht Appendix' of southern Holland, on and in one case just over the Dutch–German border. These positions were in a mining country and the troops had sometimes been able to use the miners' showers, which was a blessing; but it had been a dull, static life. Defensive positions had been manned, but the enemy was some distance away, although there was periodic shelling. Some miles to the south-east we heard of slow, slogging American successes in and round Aachen. We had moved from the flooded fields of northern Holland with relief but the winter of 1944 was damp and tedious. Then had come the splendid news that we were to travel to Belgium for a Christmas break.

The immediate aftermath of MARKET GARDEN had seen us withdrawn south from Nijmegen to take part in a number of rather desultory encounters against the Germans west of our centre-line, Germans who were from time to time, and sometimes in considerable strength, seeking to cut our south–north line of communication or themselves to escape eastward towards the Reich, depending on how one looked at it. These encounters included one fairly full-scale attack at a place called Heesch, where we suffered some casualties (including my sometime Troop sergeant killed, a wonderful man); and some moments which contained a good deal of comedy, as when we contacted the American 101st Airborne Division at Veghel, on the centre-line, to find them convinced that a major German operation was threatening them. It wasn't. The 'threat' was us.

Eventually we had moved in early November to the Maastricht Appendix. And now the prospect of Christmas in Belgium, which seemed like the Promised Land.

The Belgian family who owned the house on which I had my eye were hospitable and cooperative. Of course, by all means, they would be delighted to accommodate our small Mess. They showed me rooms which could easily be made available. I explained that this invasion would be some hours away – our tanks, the whole Division, were trundling westward along the *pavé* on their tracks and would be unlikely to arrive much before ten o'clock, perhaps even midnight. Very well – and would I not in the meantime dine with the family? One always felt a possible embarrassment at this sort of hospitable gesture because one didn't know what their housekeeping situation might be; it differed, household by household. I needn't have worried. At eight o'clock I was sitting down *en famille* to some excellent cutlets and a most drinkable Burgundy. It looked as if our Christmas break was starting well. It was 20th December.

Suddenly the dining room curtains parted and into the room through a french window stepped the figure of Jock Askew. Jock Askew, of Lady-kirk in Berwickshire, had served as a Regular subaltern in the Regiment in peacetime, resigned his commission for a brief while and returned at the outbreak of war. He was a quiet, rather retiring person with considerable public spirit; one who tended to see things rather darkly but who invariably put the interests and happiness of his soldiers well above everything else. Commander of our Headquarters squadron, he was now leading our advance party, and had just been overseeing other tasks. He irrupted into the dining room where I was eating and drinking happily. He looked as if there was something on his mind. I got up from the table. At the least I supposed some attempt at an introduction to my host and hostess was in order, but it didn't look as if it was going to be that sort of evening. With a muttered word of apology, Jock beckoned to me. We had a murmured colloquy in a corner of the Belgians' dining room.

'You'll have to come along.'

'Right. What's up?'

'They may be here by morning.'

'The Battalion? I thought they'd be here by –'

'Not the Battalion. The Germans.'

'THE GERMANS?!'

'The Germans. They've attacked in the Ardennes. They're moving fast. They're approaching Namur.'

'NAMUR!'

'And Liège.'

'LIEGE!'

LIEGE! It was unbelievable (and, as it happened, untrue). For several days there had been word of some sort of German initiative, and two days previously we had heard sounds of tank engines and movement to the north of us, near Sittard in the Maastricht Appendix. It was generally reckoned that these were little more than demonstrations – and they later proved to have been recordings and part of a German deception plan. But the demonstrations had had a purpose. Far to the south of where we had been, directed on the Meuse and thereafter on Brussels and Antwerp, three German Armies with twenty divisions, including twelve Panzer divisions, were marching westward through the Ardennes. They had been marching for four days when Jock told me the news.

As it appeared at first, the German offensive – whose scale and scope were entirely unexpected and for some time unrealized – had been launched at a sector held by the Americans and would not directly affect the British; and the Guards Armoured Division had been told to go ahead with its plans, which included our Christmas break near Louvain. But suddenly the German tide seemed to be lapping near us, Christmas break or no Christmas break. By the time I sat down to cutlets and Burgundy with my kind Belgian host and hostess on the 20th December, General von Manteuffel's Fifth Panzer Army had reached Hotton, only twenty miles from the Meuse.

And on our side considerable rethinking had taken place. The German attack had made a deep penetration in the American front – General Bradley's 12th Army Group – and now all American troops north of the penetration (two armies) were placed under Montgomery, who was also requested to help with part of his own 21st Army Group. Montgomery, therefore, had decided to place a British Corps (XXX) with four divisions behind the Meuse, to deploy strong detachments on the Meuse bridges and to be ready to counter-attack. This involved major redeployments and as part of them our brigade, 5th Guards Brigade, received orders to change direction while actually moving back to our Christmas break area near Louvain. We were bound now for a different area, near St Trond, and were to be ready for anything.

Our advance parties were collected and set on the road for quite different destinations. I never saw my Belgian hosts again, and we did not have to impose ourselves on them. Meanwhile word was running free among the Belgian population. Exaggerated as usual, it was causing considerable agitation. 'Liège! Namur!' I heard one elderly lady moan as we were assembling our jeeps and scout cars for the new move – '*Ils connaissent cette route-là! Ils connaissent cette route-là!*' Disquiet was understandable. We learned that a good many German soldiers had said, probably not very pleasantly, 'We'll be back one day!' as they had moved eastward out of Belgium only three months before. To a Belgian of that lady's age this looked like being the third German invasion.

As things turned out the Germans never got nearer to the Meuse than five miles. We spent, near St Trond, the coldest Christmas I remember and the troops of XXX Corps were never committed to counter-attack. The Grenadiers of Battalion Headquarters ate their Christmas dinners in a magnificent red-brick convent – as I wrote home on 26th December:

... by the kindness of the Mother Superior. This lady is a wonder. She is red-faced, volatile, witty, energetic, capable and charming, looks as if she could drink a bottle of port and walk 20 miles every day, is an absolute fund of kindness and generosity, and controls the activities of several hundred orphans in an inimitable way!

I can see her now, a face 'slightly Chaucerian', I wrote, 'and [with a mixture of similes] looks like a Holbein'. The Americans recovered after the intense shocks of the first days. Essential road centres, notably

Bastogne, held out in spite of encirclement. General Patton's Third Army moved with heroic energy to reinforce from the south. And on 30th December the Allied counter-attacks began – Bradley's from the south, followed by Montgomery's from the north and north-west four days later. By 23rd January the British and Americans had joined hands, the Americans had taken St Vith, and the Battle of the Ardennes – a brainchild of Hitler – was over. No significant pictures from it are etched on my mind since our Division played no active part. Our next move was to be north again, to take part in another major operation; one to clear the country between the Rhine and the Meuse, through which ran the German 'Westwall', the Siegfried Line. Operation VERITABLE. Slow. Immensely wet. Immensely muddy. Beastly in every way.

When Operation VERITABLE finished, the west bank of the Rhine as far south as the junction with the Moselle at Koblenz would be in Allied hands. The Operation involved movement through the (rather beautiful) great woods lying on the Rhine's west bank, through or near places with historic names, the Reichwald, Goch, Cleve. We were now in Germany, and there was a sense (and a policy) that there should be no restraints laid on destruction. If a building might house German troops we tended to knock it down or set it on fire. Just to be sure.

These places were in ruins, surrounded by flood water, desolate – although it was nothing to the awfulness of destruction we were to see in the Ruhr. It was a time of momentous events in the political world. Churchill, Roosevelt and Stalin had met at Yalta in early February and there was a good deal of press coverage, most but not all of it triumphalist in tone. I can see a farm kitchen, taken over by us near a place called Bonninghardt, just as our own part in VERITABLE ended. There was lively argument, and my own views tended to find little favour at that time. Argument was accompanied by the deafening noise of our artillery bombardment, which went on, and on and on. We were more or less in the gun line. I could let off personal steam in letters home. I wrote home on 25th February.

What do you think, of the Crimea conference? It fills me with utter gloom . . . Poland has been sold, which one knew would happen but is none the less disgusting and humiliating when it occurs ... one can understand why the most active Polish patriots have been the first to suffer. A man who resisted the Germans will resent slavery, and unless politically 'sound' is therefore dangerous.

And I could not be other than repelled by a decision announced that the damaged towns of the Soviet Union would be reconstructed by German labour, fair though that sounded. It was only too easy to forecast a world of brutal slavery wherever the Red Army's writ ran, and I said so. In the same letter –

All this has been ratified, and yet are the very things against which, in one manifestation, we went to war. I cannot see that this war has or will have accomplished anything except a military decision as unimportant as a victory in one of the dynastic wars. The root of evil still flourishes, and everybody knows and daren't say. Wretched Europe!

I undoubtedly felt miserable about what looked like being the forced Bolshevization of a large part of central and Eastern Europe, amidst every circumstance of atrocity. Every report from those parts made this clear, whatever the euphemisms adopted.

But almost the worst thing, and the hardest to bear, was the sense that we – our own people, my own friends very often – were refusing to admit this; were frightened to face its implications; and were taking refuge, instead, in a blanket condemnation of all Germans which thus seemed to excuse all other crimes. I could understand, although I could not admire, the instinct of my companions, or many of them, which led them simply to look forward to getting the whole bloody business over, without too much scruple or reflection, so that the British could return to better lives; but such indifference (for that is how it struck me) to the fate of millions of fellow-Europeans repelled me. It had been perfectly clear, to give an earlier example, that the Polish officers whose grave was found in the Katyn forest had been murdered by the Russians in 1940. To most this possibility, let alone likelihood, was often regarded as near-disloyal to the Allied cause if mentioned. I had some bitter arguments with friends, who were not stupid but were determined to believe only good of those who were fighting the same enemy. I was often a difficult companion in those days. Naive, I remembered the idealism which had led me and Tom Miller and a few others to shout out, with equal unpopularity, against appeasement of Hitler. Those ideals, and most others, now seemed betrayed.

And this general malaise of the spirit was, of course, increased by periodic loss of friends, for there was a drip-drip of casualties. 'I'm always delighted,' I wrote home in the same letter, 'when my friends are wounded.' It meant they would probably live. The Rhineland in the winter of 1944/45 was an awful place and every circumstance, climatic, physical and political, seemed to combine to depress. I wrote on 15th March:

I do loathe all this destruction and suffering. I haven't got at all the right temperament for war. I loathe the sufferings of the old and the children, of whatever nationality. It is only possible to hate from a distance. You know how people chuckle and say '1000 more bombers over somewhere last night' with glee, but when one sees the results one feels nothing but pain. Please don't misunderstand me – I know very well that the Germans started it and exulted over the indiscriminate bombing of England, Holland etc. They deserve it back and it's probably no bad thing that they've had it – but it's still impossible to relish the sufferings of civilians etc and if you were here you would feel exactly the same.

All this, perhaps somewhat obvious as well as sanctimonious, was exacerbated when we saw the incredible destruction in the great industrial cities of Germany and learned of the extent of the civilian casualties.

Our bombing policy has been endlessly discussed. Whatever its wisdom, morality and strategic effectiveness it was carried out by particularly brave men, whose sacrifice was great and has often, I think, been insufficiently recognized and memorialized. Material damage to German war production may have been less than claimed, but there could be little doubt of the terrorizing effect of such raids as those on Cologne (the first thousand bomber raid); or on Hamburg, with its firestorm (forty thousand civilian deaths, many of them inevitably women and children); or on Dresden, still to come and largely afflicting the mass of terrified civilian refugees from the advancing Red Army; or on Berlin, again and again and again. These actions derived from our officially endorsed policy, of 'destroying amenities and wherewithal to live in the industrial areas' of Germany. When one saw the consequences, it was impossible to think that any coherent society could have survived much longer that level of death and destruction. All operations of war, after all, are about affecting the enemy's mind. This sort of attrition, taken to ever further pitches, must ultimately destroy that mind. There have been more recent bombing operations in minor wars, but nothing has approached, or – I hope – could approach the awful devastation of the Second World War.

I hold particularly a picture in memory of the great city of Cologne. From miles away the only evidence of a distant city were the two spires of the noble cathedral, piercing the sky, damaged but standing, inexpressibly moving. Round the cathedral, throughout the centre of the place, there was nothing but rubble. I had seen the results of German attacks on London and elsewhere in England and experienced the whistle and crash of bombs, the roar of fires; the agony of Germany had been, it was clear, on a completely different scale, and had gone on at an intensive rate for much longer. The casualties in Hamburg, on one night alone, were more than the total from German air attacks on the whole of England throughout the war.

From the rubble in Cologne I can see a limping man and a shrivelled old woman emerge, on the edge of what had been a street. They walked very, very slowly, having come, I suppose, from some surviving underground cellar or refuge. Their reactions were minimal – traffic accidents where our military vehicles struck bemused and sluggish civilians 'devoid of road sense' were frequent. Their faces were pale yellow from hunger. I leave it to theologians and moral philosophers to debate the ethics of such ways of waging war; and I do not believe it possible in modern times to draw a tidy line between soldier and civilian. Nor do I – and nor did any of us – underrate the absolutely fundamental part played in our victory by Allied control of the air. It was the crucial ingredient. I did, however, find distasteful the relish with which our strategic bombing was described, a relish explained but not excused by the fact that we had, earlier, ourselves been shocked and frightened by the course of the war: fear, when it passes, begets cruelty. I do not regret the way I wrote at the time, simplistic and superficial though it may have been.

The war was moving towards what must be a final phase. We had soon cleared the west bank of the Rhine. The winter was almost over. Ahead lay the heart of Germany. The approach to the Rhine in our sector was through extensive woods and I remember a disagreeable morning when the Irish Guards Group – advancing immediately to our south – were held up and pinned to the ground by some well-sited German anti-tank guns. I was sent to make contact with their Commanding Officer and found myself, in my small scout car, at the receiving end of one of these guns firing at shortish range at anything which moved. They exploded a round or two in the trees above my head and my skull was lightly peppered but no more. I was always lucky. On the 30th March I remember the night sky lit by multiple searchlights – 'artificial moonlight' – as we moved down to the Rhine crossings.

The forcing of the great river had been preceded by another enormous airborne operation, and was undertaken in our XXX Corps sector by troops of 51st Highland Division. It had all gone well and our job was now to take up the running on the east bank. For the next five weeks we advanced through northern Germany, all knowing that the war would – must – end very, very soon. Meanwhile our progress was uneven. Many of the farms and villages were undamaged, even prosperous. The towns, on the other hand, were in many cases shattered. Not since the liberation of places pulverized by Allied bombing which we had seen in Normandy had we found anything to compare with the towns on the outer fringe of the Ruhr.

We, however, were primarily concerned with the skill (and courage) with which the enemy, beaten as he must know himself to be, was opposing and delaying our advance with well-planned minefields, well-sited anti-tank guns, well-deployed tanks or self-propelled anti-tank guns – few in number but so handled as to multiply the effect of each weapon many times.

It was during this phase of the campaign that I was able to visit Sergeant Major Lord in his liberated prison camp at Fallingbostel, as already described. This was on 19th April. We were by then south of Hamburg, and it was clear that this was the culmination of the German war, a few flickers from the waning fire, casualties for the unwary perhaps, a sense of a too-drawn-out final scene, with cast and audience both bored. I think the end in 1918 had been rather similar – a drama petering out rather than ending with a sound of trumpets. There was, however, one extraordinary happening still before us.

The Grenadier Group had attacked a place called Zeven, where a number of roads meet, south of Bremervorde. Zeven and two small places east of it were defended by the Germans with surprising energy: several of our tanks were knocked out, there were a good many mines and a lot of shelling. Miles Marriott was hit by a mortar shell and evacuated. It was unclear how seriously he had been wounded and I wrote home optimistically a few days later, but he died in a Brussels hospital as peace came.

Zeven – which held a considerable force of German armour, infrequently encountered at that stage of the war – was ultimately taken on 24th April. North of Zeven, beyond the west bank of the small river Oste, was an enormous concentration camp, by name Sandbostel, of which we had never heard. And from Sandbostel camp a written message had been carried – I cannot remember how – which reached our Battalion Headquarters after Zeven fell.

I saw this message. It was from a French officer who was among the inmates. I cannot exactly recall the text (it was written in English) but I remember the opening words, on the lines of 'a very tragic situation exists in the camp at Sandbostel', and it went on to refer to the starvation, the typhus, the total breakdown in administration and order, the cannibalism (I think he mentioned it: it certainly existed). The letter continued to the effect that the German officer in command (from whom a note was enclosed) wished to give every assistance to the relief which he hoped the Allies could provide on humanitarian grounds. Food and medical supplies on a large scale were the urgent requirements. Soon – I cannot remember how this was arranged – a German officer, blindfolded so that he saw nothing of our deployment, was leading some sort of improvised column towards the place under a white flag and we were assured that headquarters were organizing a Red Cross party with aid.

Unfortunately the camp – which had been more or less evacuated by the German guards – had been reoccupied thereafter by troops of the Waffen SS, who had decided to defend it in the orthodox manner, helped by the existence of the river Oste and by the enormous extent of the perimeter wire. Sandbostel had been a prisoner-of-war camp, originally for French prisoners, and there were about eight thousand of these, one of whom had taken the initiative described. When the great Russian advances began in the east, however, the inmates of other concentration camps were marched westward; and about fifteen thousand of them had reached Sandbostel, which was, of course, wholly ill-equipped to deal with the situation. The result was breakdown, starvation and mayhem – we were told that 2,500 deaths had taken place in the previous three weeks. Eventually the place was taken by the King's Company and our No. 2 Squadron (now commanded by Neville Wigram, James Bowes-Lyon having returned to England, ill and temporarily unfit for duty). I had rejoined this squadron, my earlier home in the 2nd Battlion. I can see too, vividly, the inmates of Sandbostel, who were soon in some cases outside the wire and roaming the countryside in their obscene, pyjama-like uniforms, their limbs shrunken to skeletal proportions, their skin yellow and parchment-like, their voices incomprehensible and, in the case of too many of these wretched creatures, their minds obviously gone. Scenes from the Inferno. Such was, for us, the end of the war in Europe, for within a few days we were told that all hostilities were to cease next morning, 5th May.

Two days later, I was given orders to drive to a small village a little way to the north and near the estuary of the Elbe. I was to go with the squadron second-in-command, Ian Farquhar, and was to help prepare the village for occupation by our men. Suitable accommodation was to be cleared of German inhabitants, who were to be given two hours to get out. No houses were to be shared with Germans. There was to be absolutely no fraternization or ordinary cordiality between the Germans and our men. Harshness and implacability were to be our watchwords. We were also to take the surrender of a German unit at present said to be in the village, whose commander would be warned of our imminent arrival, and to give instructions for their movement (all German troops, hundreds of thousands of them, were to march to various collecting points, whence they would be transported to improvised camps for 'screening', onward movement and incarceration).

The village was charming in appearance, with red-brick houses, some of substantial size. Most, in the north German way, had large byres attached. All were set well back from the road, with broad grass rides in front. The place was untouched by the destruction of war. In the middle was an attractive church, probably Lutheran. Behind the church was a village green. On the green was drawn up a company – about a hundred – of German soldiers. We were expected, and as we dismounted from our scout cars the German officer in command emerged from the church to meet us. He saluted. We saluted.

He was immaculate. This was a medical company, and his second-in-command was, I think, an *Unteroffizier*. There were no other commissioned officers. The Company commander's black field boots were brilliantly polished, his cap set jauntily at a slight angle. We gave him various instructions. He nodded, and said he only had one request. There were two civilian nurses, two women, with the unit. He asked that they should be dealt with correctly. We gave assurances.

The soldiers, towards whom we now moved with some curiosity, were also immaculate. Trouble with turnout had clearly been taken – these were men determined not to let themselves or the *Wehrmacht* down in the eyes of their enemies. Morale among soldiers manifests itself by small signs, and here it seemed pretty good – evidenced by the *Unteroffizier*, who, having received word from his superior, now approached them, called them to attention and gave out a few details. Drill was impeccable. He obviously cracked a joke and there was an answering roar of laughter – we were at some distance and it may well have been at our expense. These men were in good shape. They came from 7th Parachute Division, whose uniforms (the Parachute troops had been formed from the Luftwaffe) were a slightly different shade from the ordinary cloth of the Army. Their discipline and spirits were manifestly high. We had met these Parachute troops many times and always with respect. Like the Waffen SS, they constituted something of an elite.

We then went round the village, earmarking premises for our occupation and giving orders to the unhappy inhabitants. These were country folk, and clearly in many cases had lived in their houses all their lives. Often there were elderly relatives sharing. All – and such possessions as they could take on whatever carts they could assemble (unless marked by ourselves as required to stay) – had to be clear by the appointed hour. When our squadron drove in with its Sherman tanks we wanted all accommodation ready, empty, chalked for particular troops, for messes, for stores. We acted peremptorily and with relish.

After a while it was perfectly clear that the inhabitants, in understandably mutinous mood, were going to be behind schedule in clearing their possessions from their houses (where they were to go was a matter for them). The operation was being accompanied by a lot of loud, grumbling expostulation. There were insufficient signs of urgency. We made one or two threatening observations and gestures, pointing at our watches. These were greeted with shrugs and had little effect.

I found the Company commander and told him that the inhabitants – civilians all – were being dilatory in obeying our clear orders. Time was running out.

He nodded, and strode into the main street. It was full of carts, resentful civilians manhandling furniture and luggage, disorder. I can see him now as he stood, legs astride, hands on hips, in that village street. Then, suddenly, he raised his voice, with an earsplitting yell of command – a scream, conveying violence and menace.

The effect was astonishing. It was like an old film shown at accelerated speed, or a modern television sequence put at 'Fast Forward'. The Germans moving in and out of houses, loading carts, manhandling possessions, suddenly moved at three times the speed and with unbelievable energy. They were galvanized. They were also terrified. He could do nothing to make life unpleasant for them, to coerce, to punish. We could do much. But such, among Germans, was the authority of the representative of a beaten army, if he wore the uniform of an officer of the *Wehrmacht*.

For the Allies 1945 was the year of victory. It was also a year of horror. Nothing like it had been experienced in Europe since the Thirty Years' War. We were near the estuary of the Elbe and from the east bank, further south, great numbers of terrified refugees had fled into territory occupied by ourselves, risking anything to get away from the Russians.

Often refugees would appear in our areas. Individuals would turn up, requiring some administrative decision. We became aware of the appalling atrocities the Red Army were inflicting upon the civil populations not only of Germany but of all places it occupied. Indiscriminate massacre was commonplace. Women, and children of both sexes, were raped ceaselessly, and frequently murdered after rape. It seemed that a horde of wild beasts were trampling over a part of Europe. A little later we learned more of the expulsions of the huge German minorities in Poland and Czechoslovakia; the cruelties inflicted on these people were appalling, but seemed to stir Allied consciences very little. The German people, through their iniquities, had seemingly forfeited claims on the mercies of mankind.

I can see a tall, impressive-looking man with a somewhat nautical appearance brought before me in that same village by the Company Sergeant Major. He was, he said, a ship's officer. He was a Lithuanian and had found a post on a German merchantman.

'You were serving the Germans.'

'Yes, Sir. I had to escape from Lithuania.'

'Why?'

'To escape the Bolsheviks, Sir.'

It was clear that he found it incredible that this needed explaining to any civilized man. And certainly the British people were surprised and shocked at that time to discover that many European peoples regarded the Soviet regime and the Red Army with a horror and alarm greater than that previously aroused by Nazi Germany. With reason. This, however, was still the time of alliance with Russia, and in England the idea had been peddled for most of the war that anybody in Europe who feared Russian domination was a reactionary traitor, deserving neither mercy nor audience. Any sympathy with the victims of the Bolsheviks, therefore, smacked of incipient leniency to the Germans.

And there was plenty of reason to be wary of this. In those days we, and the world, began to learn the horrifying secrets of the concentration and extermination camps, as these were overrun by the advancing Russians and in a few cases by Americans or British. Not far from our own march Belsen had been liberated, and the ghastly photographs of mass open graves with their starved, shrunken occupants were published in every paper and magazine. We had seen enough at Sand-bostel to realize that many of the deaths had arisen from disease and malnutrition rather than murder; and that disease and malnutrition had largely been caused by breakdown in administration and transportation. But while this may also have been so to some degree at other places, like Belsen, details were now also being published of the enormous scale of deliberate mass-murder with every circumstance of atrocity. It was clear that the German Government, or that part of it represented by Heinrich Himmler and his SS empire, had deliberately instituted a policy of genocide – of the planned mass-murder of an entire race, the Jews. Not only Jews, of course, had been the victims but it appeared that Jews composed the majority, and that their offence had simply been to be Jews. Now stories of torture, brutality, methods of execution and details of humiliation appeared daily. Some were exaggerated, many were not. The numbers of the victims – soon to be described in millions – numbed our imaginations.

It may be thought that this can hardly have been surprising to us, that Nazi racial policy had never been much disguised. There were, however, degrees of disclosure. That Jews were suffering hostility, discrimination and bullying had certainly been clear from before the war – I had myself witnessed it in 1937. Then, throughout the war, there had been periodic reports published from occupied Europe which disclosed various stages of persecution. Perhaps inevitably in the atmosphere of wartime, these tended to be taken with a pinch of salt. Propaganda, we often thought, must paint the enemy thoroughly black – nothing wrong with that; but perhaps one should be careful of taking it all as indubitable truth. The Allies had made formal statements accusing the Germans of 'bestial crimes' (as early as 1942) but details had only come gradually, and for some time lacked authentication. Although the pictures (from a few who escaped) had started to become clearer to Western governments from the preceding summer, 1944, the awful details were only unfolded in the last months of the war and in its immediate aftermath; and they were, of course, to an extent submerged by the great tide of the war itself.

And the scale of the horror and the crime was difficult even then to take in. The attempted murder of a whole race simply defeated comprehension. It had, of course, been incomplete – I thought of the

Jewish girl in the concièrge's room at the Rue Cognacq-Jay. But the policy had clearly been applied with as much energy and as widely as German resources had permitted. It was difficult – but, I think, important – to translate these frightful statistics, now being assessed and disclosed, into actual human sufferings on a scale which the mind could grasp. I learned in letters from home that the Wieners had been murdered in a concentration camp, and this, to me, symbolized the holocaust, although the Wieners were but one couple among however many millions it turned out to be. I could so easily see Monsieur Wiener. And Madame Wiener.

The Wieners were friends of my parents in Brussels days, 1933–34. They were Jews. At that time I had never met a Jew and was curious. I was told that Madame Wiener was a most skilful artist. She specialized in silhouettes (and did one of me for my mother). A talented draughtswoman, she drew heads beautifully and told me various facts about profiles and what distinguishes them, talking clearly, kindly, interestingly and without patronage. She was a small, dark, handsome lady whom I remembered with affection. She had liveliness and charm.

With equal affection I recalled Monsieur Wiener. He was a tall, elegant, grey-moustached man, with a lined, kindly face. He loved horses, was a keen racing man and took my sister Gloria and me to a race meeting (I think at Boitsfort) one Sunday afternoon. I remember one particular horse. It was called 'Sire d'Halouwin' and I think M. Wiener had an interest in it. At any rate he said to me, with absolute conviction (only equalled in my memory on one occasion by Uncle Reggie Marriott), 'That horse, David, will win!'

'Really?'

'Yes. Really. Watch its stride. None of the others will compare. I will lend you some francs, David, and you can bet on it on the Tote and pay me back from your winnings!' I did. The horse won. I repaid a smiling M. Wiener. And now I learned that the charming, elegant Wieners had ended as corpses stuffed into some oven in Poland.

The world has had its fill of these terrible happenings, crimes originated by the comparatively few which nevertheless contaminated a whole nation. It was, I think, regrettable that awareness of these horrors first became widespread at a time when the German people were, because of defeat in war, at the mercy of the victors. It aroused such revulsion that there was a widespread feeling that nothing was too bad for those who shared nationality with the perpetrators. Justice is the first victim of indignation; and this weakened the restraints which are particularly incumbent on those who have power over others. Conquerors, and administrators of a conquered people, should not be additionally given a sense that those at their mercy are morally beyond the pale. It was no doubt natural that among peoples recently subject to German domination – Poles, Czechs and others – desire for revenge drove out all decent human feelings in too many cases: we heard, in such a way as to believe them, ghastly stories of the atrocities being inflicted on the German populations now themselves at the mercy of others. 'I suppose it's understandable,' friends sometimes said, but they said it with unease.

And in fact the defeated could on occasion shame the victors. I remember the railway station in Hanover – shattered, evil-smelling, full of wretched would-be travellers from one scene of destruction to another. There was one fast, well-equipped train which ran to Paris, of course reserved for Allied passengers. This was a year after the end of the war and I needed to get to Paris, where my mother was ill in hospital. There were a few sleeping coaches. It is a long journey and to get one of these (which I had been told was impossible unless one were of exalted rank or on important business) would make a great difference.

I found the German stationmaster and asked if he could help. He was a tall, gaunt man, smart in the dark blue uniform and red cap of German railway staff. All Germans of his generation wore uniform well. He looked doubtful but said he would try. Soon I was in a first-class *wagon-lit*.

In those days I smoked a good deal. I produced a box – I suppose 50 – State Express cigarettes. Cigarettes were the currency of barter in starving Germany. I was offering him, illegally, what probably amounted to several weeks' food for a family; and this at a time when Germans were said to be offering everything they owned – their talents, their bodies – for cigarettes. He drew himself up and bowed, courteously. His English was good. 'Thank you Sir, I am a German official and it is my duty to help you. But I do not want your cigarettes.'

*

The end of a great war inevitably induces reflections, stock-taking, comparisons. How had our experiences compared with other generations in the British Army – and how had the experiences of different parts of the Army compared with each other? The first, and most frequently employed comparison, was between the two World Wars, and the most used statistic was the disparity of casualties suffered as between the war my father experienced and the one now just concluded. It was true that more British soldiers fell in the First World War than in the Second, but this was not because the fighting was more intense, although in some cases it was. Nevertheless the First War (as far as the British Army was concerned) was shorter – of overall longer duration but shorter in the sum of campaigns the British fought.

The Army itself had been larger in the First World War, particularly when the main combat arms were counted. To take the sort of domestic illustration with which we were most familiar, our Regiment, the Grenadiers, had fought between 1914 and 1918 for four years on the Western Front, fielding four battalions for much of the time; in the more recent struggle battle intensity had been more varied – with, for several years, a desperate struggle in Italy (three Grenadier battalions) following another in North Africa, and culminating in the eleven-months north-west European campaign, which also involved three Grenadier battalions. The conversion into armour of some of our battalions (and the long period of inactivity for them between Dunkirk and D-Day) also much affected the experience – and the losses. On the whole we survivors reckoned we'd had it easier in the armoured parts of the Regiment – anyway for most of the time.

These things were talking points, little more. Most comparisons mislead. The war was, with luck, over. As far as our own Battalion was concerned the news soon came through that we were to lose our tanks and revert to the infantry role. The Guards Armoured Division was to pass into history although, for a while, the Battalions of the Brigade of Guards forming part of the Rhine Army in occupied Germany would constitute a Guards Division. Nobody yet knew what demands, if any, the continuing war against Japan would make on any of us. The great immediate relief was that the war against Germany was over, and for a while there would be no more bereavement, no more losses of friends beyond those – some very recent – already incurred.

A great parade was held on 9th June to mark the end of the era. It took place on Rotenburg airfield, some miles east of Bremen. The parade was named 'Farewell to Armour' and was well conceived. The Commander-in-Chief, Field Marshal Sir Bernard Montgomery, took the salute. All the tanks – freshly painted and impeccable, from the white-painted insides of turret hatches to the gleaming tow ropes – were assembled on the enormous airfield, the four armoured battalions facing inwards on the outer rim of a great oval shaped arena. Completing the oval, and facing a saluting base constructed by the Divisional engineers, were the Household Cavalry armoured cars and the guns of our artillery, of all types. In front of these, flown from England for the occasion, were the massed bands of the Brigade of Guards. Behind a low ridge to the rear of the artillery, initially invisible from the saluting base, were drawn up a further thousand men representing all Regiments of the Foot Guards. When the armour had been given the command to start up, and 250 tanks had driven off and past the Commander-in-Chief – crossing each other to the music of the bands in a complex, unrehearsed and perfectly executed balletic movement – the marching infantry moved forward, halted in front of the saluting base and presented arms.

Montgomery then spoke. He congratulated us on our achievements. He endorsed the decision that we should revert to the infantry role with wise and well-chosen words. And, which was much appreciated, he paid a handsome tribute to Allan Adair in the presence of us all. That afternoon the first post-war Derby was to be run in England and beside the enormous luncheon marquees a Totalizator and race list had been set up. I think the Field Marshal left before the race. It is extraordinary in modern times to think of the speed with which all those arrangements were made. The war in Europe had ended on 8th May. Nobody knew for certain what would happen immediately thereafter. Yet four and a half weeks later there had been organized a vast parade involving thousands upon thousands of men; hundreds of vehicles; the flying from England of great numbers; the construction of stands and a saluting base; the printing of programmes; the instructions for the troops; the administrative arrangements. All this in time of peace would be regarded as intolerably rushed if it were proposed for a full year away. It happened at that time as the most natural thing in the world. It was still wartime. Things had naturally to be organized fast. Plans were made. Orders were issued. That was that.

To make up the right numbers for the various parts of the parade it had been necessary to divide men in every squadron into different categories. I was told by Neville Wigram to keep an eye on this selection process. Each tank crew, for instance, was naturally to include a driver and commander but only to consist of three rather than the five men of the tank's complement, the balance joining the marching party. Furthermore, some tanks were by now less mechanically reliable than others, which had to be taken into account. Nobody wanted a break-down at the critical moment of drive-past and drive-off, and nobody wanted an unresponsive engine on the command 'start up' (nor were there any). Some men, too, were by build and nature smarter than others and would give a more distinguished impression on the march.

I made a mistake in carrying out this task. Because there had to be fairly arbitrary choices made if the right numbers were to be achieved, in each tank, in the marching party, men's own wishes were necessarily ignored. This was normal military procedure, of course – a man paraded where he was told. Nevertheless there were susceptibilities greater than I had supposed and I regret my insensitivity. These men – the tank crews – had seen a great deal in these armour-plated, tracked monsters. They had shared fear, privation, bereavement with a handful of others. The tank had been their home, had housed them, protected them, witnessed their emotions. Now some – two out of every tank crew – were told that they could not stay with the machine on its last day.

We owed everything to these men, our Guardsmen – to their patience, their sense of humour, their endurance. I remember one tall, reddish-haired man I knew well – a good soldier, a radio-operator, he had served a long time in one particular tank – and the tank had survived. He was now detailed for the marching party. I happened to pass down the line of tanks in our last harbour before the parade, and saw him. I realized – and cursed myself for the lateness of the realization – that he was deeply distressed. He had just been given his orders. Dismounted, he would march on his feet. I had underestimated the deep feelings which inanimate, mechanical objects can generate. Traditionally this has been comprehensible with ships. I was now seeing it among the tanks.

It is curious how often the enemy, with a sentiment or a song, gave expression to emotions of our own. Many years afterwards I came on a song composed in the German High Seas Fleet as a mournful tribute to their ships and their comrades after they scuttled themselves in Scapa Flow in 1919. The tune – an excellent tune – was that later made infamous, with very different words, as the *Horst Wessel Lied*. I recall

> *Wir hatten uns so schön so schön zusammen gefunden,*
> *Es war für uns*
> *Die alleschönster Ort –* *

Not exactly our sentiments, perhaps, as our Shermans rumbled over the skyline and we ourselves bade 'Farewell to Armour': but with an echo every one of us could recognize. Henceforth the landscape would be different, but the music would take a long time to die away.

---

* We were so happy there together,
  It was for us
  The fairest place on earth –

THREE

13

No War, No Peace

The war in Europe was over. I have often been asked whether the end of the war and the demise – final and irreversible demise – of Nazism and its evils did not bring a lightening of spirit, a general relief that so foul a shadow had been lifted from the world. Of course this was so. The Nazi regime had bred and supported monstrous evils by the infliction of pain and suffering, whether for the gratification of the inflictor or through callous indifference. There had been plenty of that.

The reservations felt in our relief, however, were real and derived from awareness of how much these evils persisted, often now cloaked in righteous outrage at what had gone before. Wholehearted gladness at the triumph of right was often embittered by the sense of humbug, of sanctimoniousness. There was still too much vile cruelty in the world for us to be able to say with true satisfaction, 'Good is victorious.'

Nevertheless we made ourselves as comfortable as we could in houses and buildings in Germany; there was, at the start, little formality about requisition of houses, furniture, anything we wanted. Houses were easily obtainable. We were the conquerors. All was available for us. Such power is corrupting, albeit enjoyable. We enjoyed and were corrupted. Until recently we had been used to smashing a building to pieces if it might house the enemy – and such habits take a regrettable time to die. We had cultivated too lightly the habits of easy destruction if the fancy took us: I myself fell too often into this habit.

The immediate military tasks were tedious. After the great farewell parade our Battalion was moved from the north (where we had witnessed the last spasms of the campaign in Europe, with the enemy fighting a skilled withdrawal up to the very end) to the Rhineland, and set about the re-establishment of 'peacetime' routine and the recovery of 'peacetime' standards. This did not come quickly or painlessly. In our Battalion the losses among senior NCOs had been high, and demobilization began very soon after the end of hostilities – and the reimposition of routine demands much from senior NCOs. Furthermore, knowledge of peacetime routine was confined to comparatively few. How were things previously done? And should that system be automatically restored? To what extent was it desirable to examine our former habits and procedures with open minds? Every Regiment was confronting these problems and finding, in many cases, different answers. And, of course, a generation of soldiers recently engaged in warfare often had little stomach for the minutiae of peacetime soldiering. Meanwhile there was a protracted exodus of key men and promotion rolls became ragged and unpredictable. I was by now Adjutant of the Battalion (in effect, its Chief Executive, and largely responsible for its discipline) and often felt I was standing on shifting sands.

Our military duties were for a while concerned largely with handling the huge number of displaced persons, the flotsam and jetsam of war, drifting around Germany, uprooted by campaigns, bombing, invasions. In overall charge of these problems the Allied Governments had established a Control Commission, and appointed – or nominated national Governments to appoint – Military Government officers with authority not unlike that of District Officers in colonial days and with a hierarchy of authority and responsibility. Of course such a system can lead to corruption – and disgraceful stories about the Control Commission were rife. Nevertheless I think the victorious allies (the Western Allies) on the whole did a good job. When I, a little later, had dealings with a fairly senior British commissioner (ex-Indian Army) I was impressed with his fairness, kindness and good sense. He very obviously had the complete trust of the medium-level German civil servants with whom he had to deal and the spirit he was inculcating was principled and respected. It made me proud and helped counterbalance the tales of low- (and not so low-) level greed and immorality. I don't believe we did badly at the end of the Second World War in Germany, and it must be remembered that the Nazi regime had produced its own sort of immorality – and an entire level of local administrators who had to be replaced for political reasons, leaving a void of practical experience.

In the east, of course, matters were different. East of the Occupation zone allotted by the victors to the British, Americans and French, a brutal and dictatorial system was being imposed by the Soviet Union. But it was not easy to find out what was going on in the Soviet zone: there were for a long time rules against fraternization with the German population, rules which were understandable but which the troops, on the whole, found unnatural and absurd – and which they therefore ignored. It was thus rare in those days that an opportunity arose for an officer to discuss these things with an intelligent German, but on one occasion early in 1946 I did so. He was a member of a once-prosperous industrialist family and had, I think, been 'de-Nazified' – certified clean. He talked about what was happening in Saxony, which he knew well. Saxony was all in the Russian Zone. He looked at me dourly.

'All the people being installed in power there are the same as before. Some were shot but otherwise they have taken off their brown shirts, that is all. Nazis. Same old people.'

'Although surely fundamentally hostile to the Communists?'

He smiled at me pityingly.

'These people understand power and how to make themselves feared. That is all.'

A little later he said, with passion, 'You must never trust us! Never, never, never! We are mad!'

I was disturbed but have not forgotten; I recorded the conversation in a letter home.

War crimes, and war crimes trials, impinged a lot on our existence. A friend of mine in the Battalion was Philip Byam-Cook, who was on the edge of a highly successful career in the law and who was, therefore, much in demand in the world of war crimes investigations, on one side or another. One evening he appeared in our Battalion Headquarters Officers' Mess. There were only two or three of us there and Philip approached me.

'David, I'm looking after a very senior officer in the RAF. Do you think we could put him up? He's over here as a witness in a war crimes trial.'

Of course we were delighted (the visit lasted more than a week), and the more delighted because he proved to be a particularly charming person, an Air Marshal, Ivelaw Chapman. Sir Ronald Ivelaw Chapman, as he became, had been shot down on a raid over Germany, had escaped, been recaptured, tortured in order to extract the names of those in the Resistance who had helped his escape, and was now our guest.

I had many long talks with him. I seldom remember a more impressive man. He told me, under my no doubt impertinent and immature probing, exactly what had happened to him – how he had a gravely injured shoulder from the crash, how the Gestapo interrogators had beaten him on this shoulder, on and on and on. How he admired some of the Resistance chain who had helped his escape – 'wonderful people!'

I never met a person with less bitterness. He spoke of his tormentors at that time with something like pity.

'I could see they didn't like what they were doing. They were quite young – I was sorry for them. I knew their feelings would give them hell one day.'

Such encounters – few in life – show what grandeur the human spirit can attain. The former German commandant of his prisoner-of-war camp (a decent man, he said) was being arraigned and 'I felt I had to do, say, something for the fellow if I could. That's why I'm here.'

Philip Byam-Cook had found him as a witness for the defence. He became an Air Chief Marshal and Vice Chief of the Air Staff. He did me – an unimportant young Grenadier officer – a lot of good.

There were, of course, massive 'repatriations' of people, notably ex-prisoners of war, who were due to be returned to their own countries – or what the victorious authorities deemed were their own countries. This made a good deal of trouble because such was the internal condition of most of the countries of eastern Europe that those to be returned feared the prospect intensely. Not only did this apply to the nationals of such countries as Yugoslavia, where the Communists, led by Tito, were in power (and creating mayhem among the anti-Communists, whose leader, the ex-Royalist officer Mihailovic, was condemned to death and shot in July 1946), but it also applied among the wretched millions of Soviet prisoners of war, who were under no illusions about the fate of any ex-Red Army soldier who had 'allowed' himself to be taken prisoner. They were, we understood, shot in huge numbers as politically unreliable. A friend of mine (a Russian speaker) had to accompany a ship bound for Odessa with a large consignment of such men on board. They were marched to a vast shed on the dockside, whence those on board could plainly hear the machine guns open up.

For the months immediately following the end of the war until December 1945, we of 2nd Grenadiers Battalion Headquarters occupied a large, hideous and comfortable *schloss* near Siegburg in the Rhineland. The officers' quarters were there, and it was there one autumn morning that I was called by my orderly, Guardsman Wright, at the usual time.

'Good morning, Sir.'

'Good morning.'

'What do you think of the atom bomb, Sir?'

There had just been the news of Hiroshima. The impact of nuclear weapons, soon to provide a new and terrible dimension to the world balance of power, took a little time to sink in. At first our reaction was that the destruction, huge though it was, made the weapon different in degree but not in kind from the devastation we had by now seen in the Ruhr (and would shortly see in Berlin, where our Battalion was moved in 1946). This reaction was not necessarily mistaken, but a certain awe accompanied the realization that perhaps war, as we had known it, was a thing of the past. Perhaps – because at the same time we were unavoidably aware that just beyond the interzonal boundary was a huge Russian Army, millions upon millions of men and guns, nominally still Allies of ours but, as even the dullest-witted could not avoid knowing, really a possible future enemy. But the dropping of the first nuclear bombs also seemed to make sure of the imminence of the war's final end. Nobody yet knew what troops might be required in the Far East for the next stages of the war against Japan, but they might include us. Nobody looked forward to the prospect. It seemed that Hiroshima and Nagasaki had eliminated that chance. We weren't sorry.

When we moved to Berlin in 1946 – a skeleton of a city, yet with a sort of life and music already beginning to revive, movingly, hauntingly

– we were of course in occupation of the 'British Zone' of the city (the least destroyed quarter) – and could actually see and move among the troops of other occupying powers. The Russians were everywhere, although the savage excesses of murder, rape and robbery which had marked the early days were now abated. I was lucky in getting permission one day to attend a meeting of the Four-Power Commission which governed 'undivided' Germany from Berlin. It was interesting as a spectacle, a ritual, of determined 'immobilism'. The representatives of the four Powers (who were in fact the Commanders-in-Chief of their respective national forces) had their instructions, had no possible discretion in their interpretation, and that was that. Nobody could suppose that the Russian Marshal Sokolovsky, for instance, would suddenly decide to be impressed by the arguments of Field Marshal Montgomery or his American colleague and would deviate from an order underwritten by Stalin. It was, nevertheless, fascinating to observe. When, many decades later, I had the task of representing Britain in the councils of NATO things were not entirely dissimilar.

We were visited often by very senior officers, who found Berlin an instructive, if terrible, study. The Adjutant-General, Sir Richard O'Connor, came. I knew my father greatly liked and admired him and was delighted to find that his ADC was my very old and dear friend Simon Phipps, of the Coldstream Guards. I knew that Simon was O'Connor's nephew by marriage and we arranged to have dinner together on my next leave in England, due shortly.

This happened – in Claridges. Simon asked what my plans were and I told him. Everyone's life was in turmoil, but I was already determined to remain in the Army.

'And what about you, Simon?'

'I hope to go into the Church,' Simon said, with a deprecatory smile about how this appeared in Claridges, where we were having as good a dinner as the rations of those days permitted. I was completely surprised – yet unsurprised when he did exactly what he had proposed, and attained great distinction as a churchman and bishop, charming, wise, witty and kindly.

But my own plans were not smiled upon by my father. He had made very clear that he would wish me to find – and train for – some other profession. He was too generous-hearted to make difficulties but he made it clear that in his opinion the Army was a disappointing sort of profession, tolerating too many indifferent performers, rewarding people poorly, and unchallenging to the intellect. He reckoned I could do better. The trouble, as I made clear to him in letters and at our occasional meetings, was that I loved it. I felt totally involved in my Regimental duties and, more and more as I read more and talked more with friends of wider experience, I felt absolutely committed to the 'profession of arms'. When one feels like that one must obey one's heart, and my heart was committed. I thought, too, that my father's opposition was probably caused to some extent by the disappointing course his own career had run – pretty well discarded at the age of 53 during a major war, having served with outstanding distinction as a young man in the First World War.

This feeling of mine was strengthened by personal contacts. Most of my surviving friends in the 2nd Battalion had either left the Army, having never intended a long-term future as Regular soldiers, or were now intending to leave for more enticing pastures or in pursuit of interests or responsibilities near to their hearts. At the beginning of 1947, however, a new Commanding Officer arrived to take over our Battalion. I was still Adjutant – by now quite an old hand in the job and knowing the Battalion better than most people.

Our new Commanding Officer had a great reputation. His name was Geordie Gordon Lennox and he had commanded our 5th Battalion with immense distinction in North Africa and Italy in some of the hardest fighting our Regiment experienced in the war. I knew him slightly because he had been my father's Brigade Major in 24th Guards Brigade after the ill-fated expedition to Narvik, and he was a close family friend of both my father and mother. He was a dedicated Grenadier – his father, Lord Bernard Gordon Lennox, had been killed in the Regiment at First Ypres; and he was, above all, a brilliant tactician and a leader of inspirational qualities. He knew more than anybody I had so far met about what does and does not work on the battlefield. He was, furthermore, a man of outstanding character and charm – elegant, immaculate, a formidable disciplinarian, quick-witted and professional to the tips of his fingers. I rate it as one of the most fortunate circumstances of my life that I was his adjutant at that time – and, even more, that I became his Brigade Major (chief staff officer) for some years when fortune later took me to Egypt. I learned a great deal from him, gratefully and happily.

On a personal level, of course, there was much to learn because life and experience in an armoured battalion (anyway now receding in time) had been very different from the business of being again an infantryman. In this matter of learning, the professional experience of friends who had been in the infantry battalions of the Regiment was of great benefit. Nevertheless I felt a certain lack of expertise when told that on giving up the adjutancy I was to command the Grenadier Company in the Guards Training Battalion at Pirbright, to which recruits went after 'passing out' from the Guards Depot at Caterham. Pirbright had the task of turning recruits (with basic skills, comparable to those with which I had once left the Depot for Windsor) into trained Guardsmen. The Training Battalion course was for ten or twelve weeks and it was clear that the company commander could and should learn plenty on his own account.

This was made both possible and agreeable because of the people I joined at Pirbright. There was in the Training Battalion a Regimental Company from each of the Foot Guards Regiments, all commanded by Roddy Hill of the Coldstream, a small, neat and very 'Regimental' officer with a great reputation as a fighting soldier, devoted to the Brigade of Guards and very knowledgeable about its customs and *esprit*. And of the other officers in this composite Battalion there were the Scots Guards Company Commander, Charles Graham of Netherby, who became one of my dearest friends – kind, generous, amusing – and remained so until death took him from us in 1998; and the Coldstream Commander, Edward Imbert-Terry, who had been a near contemporary at Upcott's, then wounded and taken prisoner by the Germans during the attempted commando raid on Sardinia in 1943. I could also learn from my own subordinates, which one should always welcome – among these were Gilbert Lamb, a splendid, loyal friend who had served in the 5th Battalion, and Harry Mildmay, an outstanding subaltern and young man of great charm and personality who sadly died in 1949.

Pirbright, therefore, was an instructive and useful chapter in life, made additionally memorable by the fact that in the summer of 1948 the Brigade of Guards resumed full dress clothing for ceremonial duties, which was thought by the Government to be something of a tonic for dreary, monochrome post-war England. My company of trainees found one guard for the Birthday Parade and I was proud of them (the parade was, to our great disappointment, cancelled because of rain).

In the summer of 1948, however, I was summoned to London by the Regimental Adjutant, Eric Penn. My three senior squads, who had completed most training (albeit for only a few weeks after the Guards Depot), were to be sent immediately to our 3rd Battalion, to form a new company. Thereafter the 3rd Battalion, and two other Guards Battalions – Coldstream and Scots Guards – were to move to Malaya, where there was a worsening emergency and reinforcements were apparently urgently required. A new Guards Brigade (2nd) was to form.

Ahead of the brigade advance parties three nominated company commanders, one from each of the battalions, were to fly out to receive a crash course of jungle training. We were told that morale among the local population, and particularly the European population, was fragile at best.

This was a dramatic change of circumstances. I was the nominated Grenadier company commander – my colleagues were Edward Imbert-Terry of the Coldstream and Peter Fane-Gladwin of the Scots Guards, a tall, slender officer, very 'Regimental', like Roddy Hill, whose experience 'East of Suez' had been so far with a Battalion of his Regiment in pre-war Egypt. The rest of us, however, had none at all. We were accompanied by three sergeants, one from each Guards Battalion. The atmosphere in England had been 'let's get back to peacetime,' and as quickly as possible. A campaign in the jungle had not in the least featured in the expectations – or hopes – of most of us.

A long flight of the sort we now undertook was in those days a novel experience. We crossed to Amsterdam during one night and then boarded a Constellation aircraft – KLM, and very comfortable. Most of our baggage was due to follow by sea with the advance parties of the brigade. We were almost wholly unprepared as regards clothing but were told that it would be easy to remedy this in Singapore (and it was). We flew, I remember, via Rome (a refuelling stop), Cairo (a night stop), Basra, Karachi, Calcutta and Bangkok. A long journey which took, I think, four days. The heat hit us first in Cairo and I remember boarding the aircraft to leave Cairo in the still cool morning. By the ladder was standing a splendid-looking Sudanese, jet black face, immaculate uniform, flashing white teeth.

'Next stop Basra!' He smiled at us. Then he added, quietly, 'Very hot, Basra!' It was.

Eventually we flew into Singapore airport to find quite a reception committee. Much had been made by the authorities of this reinforcement by a complete Guards Brigade. We were told before we left our Constellation that a few words to the press would be expected. Edward and I, acting in total unison, pointed to Peter Fane-Gladwin.

'Major Fane-Gladwin is the senior of us. You should speak to him.'

Peter did not like this sort of task and looked irritated. A Staff Officer (no doubt Public Relations) approached him.

'Excuse me, Sir,. I think the press would like to hear something from you.'

'Well?'

'First, Sir, does the arrival of the Guards [Peter bridled at this usage] indicate that people at home are at long last taking the situation in Malaya seriously?'

'Good Heavens, no,' said Peter. 'Most of them don't know where the place is!'

People were kind to us, took us in hand, showed us the ropes; and within a very few days we were kitted out with hot-weather uniform and given a lot of indoctrination, including a session with the Commander-in-Chief, General Ritchie. We were slightly surprised to find that according to our hosts our necessities included such items as white sharkskin dinner jackets and other things which seemed to indicate a more gracious future than jungle warfare.

There was nothing to criticize in this: the truth was that the European population of Malaya, including the military garrison, was in the process of recovering from the shock of defeat by the Japanese, and the highest good they could envisage was a Far Eastern version of 'Back to peacetime'. This was in some ways easier to achieve than in Europe.

There appeared to be no shortages. European clubs were running happily. Restaurants were admirable. Golf and polo had restarted. In the background, however, was 'the security situation', casting its shadow; and, inevitably, blame for this shadow was put on the British authorities. I remember meeting a woman watching a game of polo in Singapore, to which we'd been taken on our second day there. She was an 'old Malaya hand' and had suffered Japanese incarceration, although in her case, I understood, mercifully brief. She fixed me with an angry eye.

'Well, are the British Government going to deal as they should with things here?'

'Let's hope so.'

'I doubt it,' she said, 'there's no understanding at home of what's needed in places like this. We're weak, weak, weak!' I reminded her I'd only just arrived. She continued, 'There's not a strong man here. Not among the lot of 'em!' I made appropriate noises. It was easy to guess that her programme for the restoration of order in Malaya would, in W. S. Gilbert's words, probably have included something with boiling oil in it.

Such attitudes among the local British population were not universal but they existed and were understandable. The war against Japan – a brutally unsuccessful war in its early stages, often shamingly so – had extinguished much confidence. The present 'security situation' – and some very bad things were being done on the isolated rubber plantations – held unpleasant echoes. People were alarmed and needed to feel that they were supported by strength. The 'enemy' was no longer Imperial Japan, but was in some ways a more difficult opponent with which to grapple: a subversive and often cleverly organized system of Communist cells, supported by a network mostly based on the 'Malaya People's anti-Japanese Army', a guerrilla force spawned by ourselves during the war – commendably so. They had once done much against the common Japanese enemy. Now they wanted the British out – and the European planters, miners and investors out. The method, of course, was terror – to rule by murder and intimidation the local population on whom we depended for supplies and communications and for the prosperity of the country.

Such situations demand very intelligent handling. To separate the terrorists – and the term is not unfair – from their supplies while giving some hope to those who cooperated with ourselves was important. It did not simply demand 'a strong man', although strength was necessary. It also demanded giving all races a hope for political and economic progress. Ultimately – to move in time well beyond my own story – the Malayan problem was brilliantly gripped by Sir Gerald Templer, with a combination of military, political and covert measures which finally brought peace to that beautiful country. As we became somewhat acclimatized (our Battalion arrived from England, by sea, in October) it was fairly clear that the British had brought a good deal of the trouble on their own heads. Malaya was a country divided by race – Malays and Chinese, at that time, about balanced each other numerically, and there was a sizeable Indian population. British policy had been (we were told) to support Malay supremacy, threatened by the Chinese birthrate. The Malays, it was explained to us, were fundamentally pro-British.

Whatever the truth of this it was very clear that the Chinese were a great deal sharper. They had, unsurprisingly, got most of the influential jobs in the administration except where specifically excluded. Nevertheless, the insurrection we were meant to be dealing with was, in essence, a Chinese insurrection, although led by the 'Malayan' Communist Party.

Our Battalion were ordered to be ready for operations some three weeks after their arrival at Singapore, having moved up country by rail, and my company was to be the first committed. Before this we three company commanders who had flown out underwent our planned jungle warfare course in Johore, a very arduous experience involving learning how to move, heavily laden, through both secondary and primary jungle, often a matter of pushing blindly and bodily through impenetrable vegetation, beset by leeches and every sort of rodent and serpent. We moved in single file and navigated by compass, with well-established drills for protection.

Singapore was something of a clearing house for military movement – people turned up there unexpectedly, sometimes faces from earlier and distant phases of life. I remember an Eton friend, Humphrey Fitzroy, in the Coldstream, appearing en route from Japan and describing the American occupation of that country – and General MacArthur

– with great admiration. I then, for several weeks, had to train and indoctrinate my company. We sweated a great deal but we never accomplished a major operational success. Our company area of responsibility was in the jungle area west of (and not very far from) Kuala Lumpur itself. 'Terrorists' caught in the act were dealt with by law and the prison in Kuala Lumpur was crowded – and death sentences, we understood, were handed out liberally. Nobody found this in the least troubling.

In the end – but well after our time – the patient and intelligent enterprise of Templer (and some further reinforcements) achieved success. Military and civil powers had been combined under Templer (a most necessary step). Before that, however, the British High Commissioner, Sir Henry Gurney, had been assassinated and a new Conservative administration led by Churchill had taken over the reins in London.

In January 1949 I returned to England, by air, to attend the Army Staff College at Camberley, a course due to last for a year. The first and most powerful impression of Malaya had been the beauty of the country – lush, green, gloriously mountainous, red dirt roads, steamy but somehow balmy atmosphere. Although I was glad to leave, short though my stay had been, I always looked back at it with pleasure; and my company of Grenadiers – my first company command – had been wholly worthwhile. It had also, I felt, been valuable, and often enjoyable, to see something of the British Empire before its final eclipse. It was already clear that, as Burke observed, 'Great Empires and little minds go ill together.'

The course at the Army Staff College was a superb experience. The Staff College was one of the institutions in life – like school if one likes it, or university – where lasting friendships can be made. It was also – and I have no doubt still is – excellently run, with every lecture, exercise, demonstration, study group or whatever a model of how such things should be done. Furthermore it was mentally challenging. Our minds were stimulated, and in good company.

Our fellow-students were, of course, mainly our near-contemporaries and the recent war, with its wide spread of theatres of campaign, meant that experience differed widely, which was excellent. There was considerable dissension about whither our country (and its army) should now be heading. There was no attempt to stifle discussion or impose uniformity of view of any kind. The Commandant was Major General Dudley Ward, who had commanded the 4th Division in Italy – the Division I would one day command myself. He was a first-class instructor – clear in mind and speech, definite in his views and vividly convincing in expounding them, a strong, gifted and articulate soldier. Beneath the Commandant the Staff College was divided into four Divisions, each consisting of about sixty students. In each Division were a sprinkling of foreign officers, including American and Commonwealth and also a few from friendly foreign countries including (in our case) Turkey and Iraq as well as European countries now signing up to the new European Union – Western Union, which had successively several names and ultimately helped produce the future North Atlantic Treaty Organization. Each Division was headed by a Chief Instructor, a sort of housemaster: a Colonel.

I was lucky. My housemaster was Colonel Willie Pike, Royal Artillery, and he became a lifelong friend. He was an excellent professional soldier, but he was much more, and at the Staff College this mattered. He was patient, understanding, considerate and charming. He was a friend to all. He knew how to teach and he knew how to encourage. Our Division was a very happy one.

One of the customs (I don't know when this had started) was to run a dinner club, and one or two students (preferably friends) were nominated to organize it, and produce ideas for choice of guests – mostly distinguished, sometimes controversial – who would be invited to dine and talk on a given theme after dinner. I was asked to be one of the agents of this, with two cavalrymen who became great friends (I hardly knew them before), Martin Abraham of the 12th Lancers and Harry Walker of the Enniskillen Dragoon Guards. This was in every sense an entertaining duty. Our guests – we dined several times in the year – included Lord Goddard, the controversial Lord Chief Justice; politicians Bob Boothby and Douglas Dodds Parker; Richard Crossman, Kingsley Martin, the very left-wing editor of the *New Statesman*, and several others. We always had fun.

The last months at the Staff College (the course was due to end at Christmas 1949) were inevitably dominated for the students by speculation as to what each of us might be sent to do next. Unlike most Army appointments the appraisal of one's performance at Camberley was a closely guarded secret. In most jobs one was subject to a Confidential Report which one was required to read and initial (and to which one could take exception if one regarded it as unjust, although this was very rare). At the Staff College this was all secret. During the final term, at a particular and well-advertised moment, one received an intimation placed in one's pigeon hole, although sometimes there were whispers in the previous day or two.

I can't remember how I heard my own fate but one of the senior Directing Staff, with wide experience, took my arm near the end of term. Was there irony in his voice?

'Congratulations!'

'Really?'

'Really! You won't have a quiet moment for two years. You're going to MO! The War Office!'

I had never been away from my Regiment, except briefly as an instructor. Of higher staffs I knew nothing whatsoever. Of Whitehall, of course, I knew even less. The War Office was completely unknown to me and if asked I would have been happy to keep it that way.

The General Staff in Whitehall was, in those days, large. It had grown vastly during the Second World War and had not yet been pared down. It still had, therefore, a very large number of Directorates, mostly situated in the old War Office building opposite Horse Guards. Of these Directorates (each headed by a major-general) MO – 'Military Operations' – was (at least in our view) the doyen. It had only periodic involvement with actual military operations, despite its name. It was the policy Directorate and its head, the DMO, Director of Military Operations, was the doyen of General Staff Directors. It was he – generally reinforced by the appropriate colonel of a geographic division of the Directorate, of which there were four or five – who briefed the Chief (or Vice Chief) of the Imperial General Staff before meetings of the Chiefs of Staff Committee or before a meeting of the Cabinet.

Preparing the papers and writing the briefs for these meetings constituted a large part of the work of MO. MO1 – my future home – was a coordinating rather than geographic branch. We collected anything which was going.

'What on earth do we do with this one? The Americans [or French; or the Navy; or the Ministry of Aircraft Production] want to know our views on . . . It's coming up in Cabinet. What do the Chiefs think? Or have they no view?'

'Send it to MO 1.'

'Some sort of answer required by this evening!'

Before the meetings (in those days two a week and sometimes more) the folders would need preparing and flagging. The briefs had to be prepared for the Chief, following a system and style deriving from at least Lord Alanbrooke's day. The briefs themselves – the actual substance, what they said – were, of course, the heart of the matter. Sometimes one worked by what, I suppose, a lawyer would call case law: where were the precedents and rulings? At others, always stimulating, one had to work out for oneself the line to be taken. Inter-Service and inter-branch coordination was largely achieved by the Joint Planning Staff, who prepared first drafts of papers for discussion and approval by interested branches. The system had the benefit (and disadvantage) that disagreements tended to be ironed out at a comparatively junior level. This made for smooth running of the machine – sometimes too smooth. The brief would need, of course, the approval of one's next superior, the branch colonel, and ultimately of the DMO, to say nothing of the CIGS himself, Field Marshal Slim, who had taken over from Montgomery in 1948. But there wasn't usually much time.

We juniors sometimes took the briefs we wrote a little too seriously. We thought we were affecting history. Field Marshal Slim, in particular, sometimes settled himself down with a Chiefs of Staff agenda at their meeting and would say, 'I don't know what to think about most of this. I've got a bundle of bumf here, none of it making much sense to me. I suggest we . . .' – and this was generally a shrewd handling of the item.

It was an unnerving world into which to be plunged. It was, however, helped by personalities. My own branch chief – the MO 1 Colonel – was a brilliant lieutenant-colonel of the Royal Engineers, Dick Lloyd. A quiet, inscrutable and very kind man, he had been a King's Scholar at Eton, a shy, reserved, clever person of great shrewdness. Willie Pike, my recent supervisor at Camberley, then arrived as Deputy DMO, a friend indeed. Probably the most helpful of colleagues, however, was a fellow GSO2 (major, which was the rank of all of us below the hierarchy). This was Tom Acton of the Rifle Brigade, a brilliant officer, taciturn, a dedicated trout fisherman, a man with a voluminous memory, capable (like Lloyd) of remembering exactly where some highly relevant reference was probably to be found. He also had an exceptionally clear head and formidable powers of reasoning. He had been taken prisoner with the Rifle Brigade at Calais in 1940 and spent the war incarcerated. Many of my friends had suffered the same fate and it was always impressive to find how resilient some had been, minds and morale steadfast. None more so than Tom Acton. Ultimately promoted to Major-General, he died quite young, a great loss to the Army and the country.

MO1 certainly taught one to face, even on occasion outface, very senior officers with something like confidence. I had been there about ten days when someone said, 'Are MO1 doing these files for the Vice Chief to take to Washington about reviewing classified information?'

I knew there had been much coming and going about this, and a lot of difficulty, but none of it had actually crossed my desk. I was ignorant and showed it.

'He wants to talk about it, quickly. I suppose you know the journey's been brought forward? He'll need the files in final form tomorrow. He wants to talk now to the G2 responsible. Must be you?'

I walked very quickly along a corridor, clutching papers. Panic. A bell rang. A door opened. I found myself inside. A lean, angular figure was sitting at a desk. He glared.

'Name?'

'Fraser, Sir.'

'Regiment?'

'Grenadiers, Sir.'

A grunt.

'Cigarette?' I smoked a lot in those days. So did Sir Gerald Templer.

'Thank you, Sir.'

'Now tell me about this bloody journey to Washington I've got to do tomorrow.'

And so forth. He was formidable, and we loved him.

Much was happening in the world and the Army during my time in

MO 1. One circumstance was particularly merciful. The behaviour of the Soviet Union had finally removed any attempted pretence by our authorities that it was anything except an enemy and a threat. To match it required, and soon received, the wholehearted energy of the United States. The world, by now not pretending otherwise, was divided into two camps and our camp was definitely the weaker in so-called 'conventional' forces – the Russians still had millions of men under arms and had demobilized not at all. There were, however, some weights to be put into the scales on our side and negotiation about them occupied a lot of discussion and paper.

High on the agenda was the whole question of Germany. Rational thought led to the obvious conclusion that a stable world demanded a Germany able to play a part in resisting Soviet aggression – although Germany was physically and morally shattered, plans for recovery could be made. Such plans met, naturally, a great deal of resistance, notably from the French. In time, however, they fructified. And what had been simply an army of occupation, 'Rhine Army', became, by internationally endorsed treaty, a field army of (nominally) four divisions and a tactical air force.

The other makeweight, of course, was the nuclear armoury of the West – threatened as it was by the possibility of the Soviets developing nuclear weapons themselves. A number of highly publicized spy scandals – Fuchs, Burgess, Maclean, Philby in the 1950s – also enlivened life in MO 1.

I have always found these particular betrayals especially odious, particularly when the traitors claimed (and the claim has quite often been supported) to be acting from high motives – to be idealistic even if mistaken. To argue this suggests total blindness to the evils which had been perpetrated – and were still being perpetrated – by the regimes being assisted by the acts of treachery in question. It suggests indifference (for few could plead ignorance) to the mass murder, the deportations, the enslavement of millions. These were, when argument was advanced, excused on grounds of a higher good being sought, an ideological good.

I have never thought this line of defence remotely credible, and throughout have reckoned those who use it to be morally flawed to a fatal degree. Far better plead straightforward if blinkered patriotism;

or greed and the desire for gain. These are sordid motives yet with a human dimension, while the traitor driven (or allegedly driven) by ideological beliefs is condemned twice, first for his or her betrayal of trust, second for the moral blindness which prevents clear sight of the evil being served.

Apart from these skirmishes in what was, I suppose (although not yet so named), 'The Cold War', much of our work in MO was concerned with the inauguration of the North Atlantic Treaty Organization and negotiations about its staffing. I am glad to have witnessed the beginning and growth of this wholly beneficent institution.

But Britain was still a 'World Power', with wide national responsibilities of our own. The Malayan situation was, for most of the time, worsening. There were a whole cluster of small and not-so-small problems – Kenya, Cyprus, Aden – which made demands for troops. The most intractable of these was the situation in Palestine at the end of the British Mandate, over as far as Britain was directly concerned before I went to the War Office; but during my second year the situation in the Middle East – in Egypt – gave sudden concern.

Egypt – a base for British operations against the Germans and Italians in the Second World War – had been for some time comfortably, if erroneously, thought of by the average British soldier as a quasi-colony. It was also regarded as self-evidently important. The Suez Canal ran through it, a lifeline of the British Empire, and should there ever be serious confrontation with the Soviet Union it was an article of faith in London that one of Britain's essential interests was the preservation of a firm base in the Middle East – centre of Imperial communications and treasure house of oil. The British garrison in Egypt (stationed there under earlier agreements) was small, but if necessary it could be reinforced.

But the Egyptians – or many of them – resented this quasi-colonial dependency, and in autumn 1951 the Egyptian Government revoked the Anglo-Egyptian Treaty (which was anyway due shortly to expire). This was the Treaty under which British troops were still in Egypt, and the action of the Egyptians was regarded in England as something not unlike a declaration of war. The immediate question, generating much action and paper in MO, was whether, and to what extent, we should send more troops into the Canal Zone, where only one infantry brigade was in residence. We had troops in England. We had an army in Germany. We had part of an armoured division in Libya. We had a garrison in Cyprus. The issue was complicated by the fact that in June 1950 the Communist army of North Korea had invaded the south – a movement which soon led to the protracted Korean War and more demands for troops. All this made work for MO.

My own time in the War Office was due to end at Christmas 1951. I had found it rather intoxicating. To read the Cabinet minutes during the afternoon of Cabinet was strong medicine for a young man. I knew well, however, that it was high time I became a soldier again, and amidst all the hubbub of major movements and the excitement generated by the Egyptian situation I learned with happiness that I was due to travel, by train and troopship, to Port Said, to join again the 3rd Battalion Grenadiers and again take command of a company.*

* In all I commanded four companies of my Regiment in succession. In each case a smaller one than its predecessor!

14

Times of Turbulence

The Egyptian situation had led to massive reinforcement of the Canal Zone. Ultimately some 70,000 troops were accommodated in this narrow strip of sand astride the Suez Canal, mostly in conditions of discomfort and great heat. Because British relations with Egypt itself were almost non-existent (and for much of the time we were contemplating actual invasion of 'The Delta', as it was called) I spent nearly three years in that fascinating country and yet have never visited Alexandria or Cairo except as an air passenger breaking a journey. No actual state of war existed, but travel beyond the Canal Zone itself was forbidden, with certain exceptions.

Within the Canal Zone duties largely consisted of guards on the extensive depots wherein were the stockpiles required by the Army in case of hostilities (against the Russians, it was presumed). We were occupying a base, allegedly of great strategic importance. We had, therefore, a multiplicity of operational plans, mostly concerned with the contingency of a Soviet advance through Iran towards the Persian Gulf and the Euphrates. These did not impinge much on the life of a Company commander: the immediate task was to acclimatize the troops and train them in desert movement and in the technique of living in desert conditions. We had to rediscover the skills and re-enact the trials of our predecessors in North Africa in the war. Many books had by now been published (from both sides) about the desert war and the doings of the Afrika Korps and the Eighth Army. These were of particular interest to me then because our own training was taking place in desert conditions – of a different kind from that of Cyrenaica, but with a good many points of similarity. The area bordering the west coast of the Red Sea, where our large-scale exercises took place, is remarkable country – sand, certainly, but extraordinary shaped and coloured rock, large ravines and gullies, and, of course, enormous in extent. As a training ground it was matchless – and very beautiful. The army in the Canal Zone at that time amounted to the equivalent of three divisions, including the Parachute Brigade and a brigade of armour – and one of Marines. I still find it difficult to tell people what we were doing all the time but we were enormously busy. When we were freed from internal security duties to go into the desert for major exercises I never remember better training.

In September 1952 I handed over my company in the 3rd Grenadiers and found myself posted to be Brigade Major of the 1st Guards Brigade, based at Fayid on the west of the Great Bitter Lake. The Brigade Commander was Geordie Gordon Lennox, so we were old friends and the experience was one of the best in my life from a professional point of view. The tactical exercises, all taking place (on a huge scale) against the background of country and terrain not dissimilar from that which had seen some of the Army's greatest battles only about ten years previously, were absorbing.

There were few opportunities for wider travel, but one such I took eagerly. Accompanied by a small squad of Guardsmen and three vehicles I set out with Robert Loder, a young Coldstream liaison officer at Brigade Headquarters, to travel to St Catherine's monastery in Sinai.

In those days this was a journey across desert – there were some tracks but no road. With special passes of permission we crossed the Suez Canal to the east bank near Kantara and set out with a few instructions, with compasses and with some rations and a good deal of fuel and water. The journey from the Canal took about three days, in the course of which we drove into an enormous flight of locusts, battering the vehicles of our little convoy deafeningly. I have never encountered this phenomenon before or since. There was a satisfactory biblical feel to the experience.

On the second day of travel we saw the unmistakable shape of the great monastery itself, overshadowed as it was by the huge bulk of Mount Sinai, which we planned to climb on the following day. We set up a little encampment, marched up to the monastery walls, and found a gate. Soon we were inside.

There were, we learned, about fifteen monks still in residence and we were made welcome by the guestmaster, Father Damian, bearded and ingenuous. We gave him a gift, a bottle of brandy.

He acknowledged it. 'That's good. Thank you. I like much to drink. All my family have drunk much.'

He showed us the famous library, from which a copy of the Codex Sinaiticus, original written text of Holy Scripture, was stolen in the last century by the subterfuge of a Russian-German 'scholar', taken to St Petersburg and presented to the Tsar. Stolen property, it was bought by the British Museum from the Bolsheviks after the Russian Revolution. It was our view that it should be restored to the monks of St Catherine's. The monks were charming. Conversation (interpreted by Father Damian) was marked by many wishes for the good of our Queen 'and Prince Philippos? And the little Prince Carolus? Both children well, God is good etc.' One exceptionally dirty old monk ceaselessly muttered to himself, to the obvious embarrassment of the others. 'He is very old,' remarked Father Damian kindly. 'He is old and dirty man, very student, very holy, and mindless'!

We attended Mass in the cold light of dawn in the monastery chapel, where there was chanting by a monk with an exquisite voice, a Chaliapin. Then we climbed Mount Sinai (2,500 feet). At the summit is a small chapel where we paused gratefully – it is a long climb – and planned to eat our sandwiches. After a few minutes we heard the surprising sound of another climber, puffing understandably, who had followed our ascent; soon a middle-aged man of academic appearance appeared over the rim of the crest. We introduced ourselves. He was a distinguished German surgeon who had, before the war, had a large practice in Berlin. He was now, however, touring the Middle East, researching the holy places of antiquity, with a view to a radio programme on Hamburg Radio. He spoke absorbingly about them, and particularly about Jerusalem, whence he had just come.

'There is only one spot,' he told me, 'where archaeology, tradition and faith seem to come together. Outside Jerusalem is the traditional site of the pool where Jesus directed a lame man to be lowered into the water and healed. Archaeology has now shown us that there was, indeed, water and an artificial retaining wall at this point. There, perhaps only there, one can say "Our Lord stood here."'

We called him 'the professor'; conversation with him was highly enjoyable. His name was Peter Bamm. Before we parted I said, 'You have done many and various things in life. You have practised medicine, studied archaeology and theology [on which we had spent some time before our descent] and now you are a broadcaster!'

He smiled gently. 'There was more. For fourteen years I was a member of the German General Staff. When war came I was mostly in Russia.'

He had commanded what in British terms would be called a field ambulance. Horse-drawn. Long afterwards he sent me an autobiography he had written. Its title was *The Invisible Flag*; in 1956 I was delighted to learn that it had been translated into English and published by Faber and Faber.

There was occasional leave permitted from the Canal Zone and I decided to take some. Since our Battalion and their parent brigade – 1st Guards Brigade – had moved to Egypt (in a great hurry) from their official base in Tripoli it was possible to fly free to Tripoli. I did so – staying there with Charles Frederick, a hospitable friend in the Grenadier 'Rear Party' – and enjoyed that fine Italian colonial city. Indeed the Italian settlement was everywhere impressive. Mussolini's dream of a revived Italian Colonial Empire was, at least outwardly, a successful enterprise with splendid buildings, a noble port and all the appearances of culture.

I intended to fly from Tripoli to Rome, a city I had never visited. At our Brigade Headquarters in Egypt one of the most esteemed members was the Roman Catholic chaplain, Father Dan Kellaher. Dan Kellaher was from Kerry. He had been a chaplain with the Irish Brigade in Italy during the war, had won the Military Cross and had a terrific reputation. A dedicated follower of horse racing, a great bridge (and poker) player, he was a true friend to everyone in our Brigade, whatever their rank or creed. Dan was delighted to hear I planned to visit Rome.

'If you've any problems there, David, with currency or things like that' – such things could indeed produce difficulties in an era of currency control such as we still lived in – 'Just go and see O'Flaherty. At the Vatican. He'll help you.'

This was the famous Monsignor O'Flaherty who had masterminded the escape from German hands of a good many British prisoners-of-war, including several friends of mine. They included Paul Freyberg, a Grenadier who later became my second-in-command. O'Flaherty used to shelter them in the Church of St John Lateran, which is Vatican property and thus not within the authority of the occupying German military. The Germans had set a price on his head.

I was not long in Rome (staying at the lovely Hotel Eden) before I felt the need of help, possibly of the sort Dan Kellaher had envisaged. I made my way rather nervously to the Vatican and found the entrance to the *Sanct' Uffizio*, the Holy Office. I asked for Monsignor O'Flaherty.

After a short wait a perfectly enormous man in a soutane swept into the tiny room. He looked at me severely as I introduced myself and conveyed Dan's good wishes. I explained that if it were possible some lire would be a great help. I found myself short of cash. He frowned ferociously. After another pause, he said, 'I can't give you a good rate of exchange.'

'Of course I understand –'

'But it will be better than the official rate. Have you your cheque book with you?'

Thenceforth that superb man constituted himself my guide to Rome and collected me on several occasions from the hotel for an afternoon's expedition in his tiny car: he was a terrifying driver. He was a fund of anecdotes, some from the war; some from the baroque Rome of the Renaissance Popes; some from antiquity. Everywhere he would stop his car (always at some illegal point), struggle out of it and look at some unusual building or object.

'Look here, Major!'

I was always 'Major'. He was the best company in the world. I think his favourite anecdotes, perhaps naturally, concerned the Second World War, when Allied officers had flooded into Rome on short leaves. He once pointed to the 'Holy Steps'.

'That's the Scala Santa, Major. When your officers were here in the war sometimes they'd want to come to confession, and the Scala Santa – so many times up on their knees – was a good penance. There was one boy in the Irish Guards and I gave him a number of Scala Santas. After a while he found there was a lady on the next step up and he was kneeling on her longish skirt. She turned and said, "Would you lift up my skirt"'

O'Flaherty's story was reaching its climax.

'So he said, "No fear! For doing that I'm doing this!"'

He took me to the golf course (he was a passionate golfer) and described Count Ciano, Mussolini's foreign minister and son-in-law, whom the Duce ultimately had shot. Ciano, apparently, was also a dedicated golfer, although I don't remember O'Flaherty describing his prowess at the game. He'd known him quite well.

Afternoons in O'Flaherty's company were never dull, or ordinary. He showed me not only round St Peter's but all over the Vatican, including the Pauline Chapel, the Pope's private chapel. He described to me, rather movingly, the fate of the German police chief in Rome, one Kappler, who had spent a lot of time and energy trying to trap this rascal priest who was known to be smuggling prisoners away but could never be caught red-handed outside Vatican territory. Kappler had said to him as the German forces ultimately withdrew from Rome northward, 'If I'd had my way, Monsignor, you'd have been before a German firing squad, but I failed –'

Then Kappler had asked, as a favour, that O'Flaherty do something for his mother, who was old and ill, living on the Italian coast. He also told O'Flaherty that he wished to be received into the Church. The Monsignor demurred.

'Don't do that, Kappler. You've lived according to your lights. Now they'll shoot you. Die a Nazi and a brave man.'

But Kappler was determined. His death sentence was at the end commuted and, much later, he died a Catholic.

After my stay in Rome I travelled to Trieste, where my dear friend Robin Fyfe was with the Military Mission, and thence I flew back via Tripoli to Egypt, the Canal Zone and duty.

I gave up my job as Brigade Major in December 1954 and returned to my previous Battalion, now doing ceremonial duties in London after a long stint in Egypt; and soon thereafter I was appointed Regimental Adjutant – Staff Officer for the whole Regiment and in charge of such matters as recruitment and general policy. In 1956 the Regiment celebrated the Tercentenary of its formation, as already recorded.

But most notable was the summer of that year and what became known as the Suez crisis.

In Egypt (now evacuated by British forces altogether since my days in the Canal Zone) Colonel Nasser had come to power, amid a ferment of nationalist feeling. An early expression of this was the 'nationalization' of the Suez Canal, which was accompanied by a blockade of Israeli shipping. To a large number of British people (probably a majority) this was an outrageous act of aggression to which Britain had to react vigorously and teach the Egyptians a lesson. The Suez Canal was, in many eyes, almost coterminous with the British Empire.

Following the withdrawal of the previous year, however, there were no troops to protect the base or much else; and the base itself was a widely scattered jumble of workshops, dumps and barbed wire. It was clear that if there were to be a serious military operation to recover the Canal the available British forces would need reinforcement. They would also, probably, need allies. The late summer months of 1956 passed in an atmosphere of considerable confusion. There was widespread agreement, but by no means unanimity, that 'something must be done', and that meant an act of war. Our only friends, it seemed, were the Israelis and the French. The former reckoned, rightly, that Nasser's policies were aimed at them and were probably backed by most of the Arab world, still irreconcilably hostile to Israel because of the circumstances attending the end of the Palestine Mandate. The French were resentful of Arab policies in Algeria, where terror and counter-terror were spilling much blood – they thought that the British could and should take a stronger line with Arab nationalism, and this led them to the pro-Israel camp. All this was the background to a sharp resentment in Britain at Egyptian actions – at Egyptian pretensions, as they were viewed.

Negotiations of one sort or another dragged on, but both sides were preparing for war, whatever it was called. International sensitivities meant that an act of straightforward aggression by either side would need disguise. In England measures of mobilization were ordered. These included the calling-up of sufficient Grenadier reservists (in many cases only recently discharged) to bring my old 3rd Battalion to mobilized strength. At this strength – about 800 men – the Battalion paraded at Windsor in mid-August and sailed from Southampton to Malta, where they were housed in (as we learned from correspondence) a thoroughly unsatisfactory tented camp. In England the atmosphere was one of frustration. It had been supposed that operations were imminent, but they didn't take place.

The course of the Suez operation has been described often. After a massive bombardment (difficult to justify) troops of the Franco-British force were dropped or landed in the Canal Zone, and an elaborate charade was played out whereby the British and French pretended that their movements were part of a plan to safeguard the Canal against external aggression – including, of course, that by Israel, which had been from the start plotted by the British and French themselves. The Egyptians meanwhile found themselves for a while engaged in a fierce contest against the Israelis in mid-Sinai (near, as it happened, where 1st Guards Brigade had carried out a major mock exercise in 1954). Eventually the whistle was blown on all this humbug. It was some time before the degree of deception practised on our own people became clear.

The Suez saga had, I think, more far-reaching consequences for the British than its temporary and not very important strategic outcome suggests. It marked the end of British assurance that a minor campaign of this sort (particularly against the Egyptians) would automatically be popular and boost national confidence and morale. On the contrary, the episode left the British feeling humbled, and in some directions rather ashamed. The deception with which the affair had been launched, together with the ignominious speed with which it was abandoned, left people puzzled and worried. British morale suffered a good deal and in some ways has never been restored. After Suez it was also, of course, a good deal plainer than it had been before that Britain's position in the world was much enfeebled.

The sort of innate certainties with which we had finished the Second World War had gone for ever, washed down the Suez Canal.

I handed over the Regimental Adjutancy and joined once again the 2nd Battalion of the Regiment, as Second-in-Command to one of the most charming of Commanding Officers, James Bowes-Lyon. We had been together in the old wartime 2nd Battalion and now we were serving in the so-called strategic reserve (two infantry divisions) stationed in England to respond to any crisis call. This did not take long to come: in February 1958 we found ourselves, hot and uncomfortable in European clothing, settling into improvised camps in Cyprus.

Our arrival there was not a reaction to the security situation in Cyprus itself, although it might have been, and many supposed this to be the case. Instead our move was a response to yet another turn in the Middle Eastern situation. The friendly regime of King Hussain in Jordan was threatened by the intrigues of Nasser's United Arab Republic, at the same time as a revolution in Iraq which led to the murder of the young King Faisal and a regime hostile to the West. British positions in the area, considered vital to British interests, appeared under threat and the British Parachute Brigade was deployed to Jordan while most of our division (1st) was sent or readied for some sort of operation somewhere in the Middle East.

As a first and precautionary step our Battalion was hurried to Cyprus (and staged there). Because our ultimate destination was secret – and, indeed, undecided – it was a convenient coverplan for the authorities to represent our arrival in Cyprus as a response to local Cypriot conditions. Since we were there (for whatever reason) and since the Cyprus military situation was such that large numbers of troops were required, or thought to be, we naturally were enlisted to join in. We therefore spent the next few months (until October 1958) undertaking various 'internal security operations' in Cyprus.

In Cyprus the main enemy was the Greek terrorist organization, EOKA, who wanted union with Greece. They had committed a considerable number of murders and other atrocities. They had also, unsurprisingly, antagonized the Turkish Cypriot population so that there was intercommunal strife as well as terrorism aimed at the British authorities – and not only the authorities. The Governor until very recently had been Field Marshal Lord Harding, a strong, admired man. His successor was Sir Hugh Foot, a Colonial Governor (I believe a good one) who was of completely different temperament from Harding and who did not (at least on me) make a very good impression when I met him. He seemed equivocal and indecisive – and prone to exaggeration of the dangers of the situation. There was a considerable number of British civilians living in Cyprus, including a good many service families. Some were victims of the assassination campaign and feelings against the Greek Cypriots ran high. Of course, as ever, the huge majority of people, whether Greek Cypriot, Turkish Cypriot, or whatever, were decent and often endearing. But the ferocious brutality of the minority poisoned the atmosphere and there were occasional 'over-reactions' by the security forces – surprisingly few but, of course, fiercely publicized by all who wished Britain ill.

I remember one occasion in, I think, August 1957. James Bowes-Lyon had been ill and was on leave in England. I was commanding the Battalion in his absence. One afternoon an urgent message was received. All commanding officers were personally to attend a meeting called by the Commander British Forces, at once.

I drove to Nicosia – our temporary camp was nearby. The commander was General Kendrew, a fine man with a splendid fighting reputation from the war. He was obviously very upset. He spoke in a very hot marquee.

He told us all that he had visited an internment camp where prisoners were being temporarily held after a recent 'arrest operation'. There had been an outrage – a British wife had been murdered. Our troops had avenged this with acts of violence on a good many of the internees – I think all were Greek Cypriots. Kendrew described what he had seen, or some of it, and made it clear that behaviour of this kind stained the honour of the Army in a completely unpardonable way. No outrage – and nobody had anything but indignant horror at the crime itself – could excuse these indisciplined and brutal reactions. I don't expect there was anybody in the tent who disagreed with him. We dispersed, saddened and anxious. Soon thereafter there were fresh concerns as rumours spread of the treatment being meted out in one or more of the interrogation centres established to support the various operations being undertaken – one of them by our Battalion.

These things were widely discussed and it would be humbug to pretend that opinion was all one way. EOKA was guilty of some appalling cruelty. Nobody – certainly not I – thought their prisoners should be treated with kid gloves. There were, however, limits (and some pretty respectable guidelines issued by the authorities). Furthermore, our Battalion were comparative newcomers to this situation; others had seen more, and worse. There was a lot of hatred for the perpetrators of the atrocities.

One has to find one's way to certain principles in such matters. The letter of the law is seldom a sufficient guide – and certainly not a sufficient defence if defence be needed. I spoke to our officers before the next operation we did, a day or two later, an operation I was due to command. I knew that many were uneasy. I tried to find expressions which might be helpful and not hypocritical. I said that one day, probably quite soon, we would all be gone. Cyprus would simply be a memory. What mattered most, I said, was that when the Cypriots themselves, or their descendants, asked each other 'What sort of people were the British?' the answer should not be one of which to be ashamed.

I returned to England in September 1958. The Cypriot episode is a singularly unpleasant memory. I have probably written enough to indicate why.

I returned from Cyprus to rejoin the 2nd Battalion, who were moving to Germany, to a life and atmosphere now unfamiliar to me. Germany was, of course, transformed by the years since I had last served there. The once-ravaged Ruhr was in full production. Shops were full – and very good. The German population were prosperous and confident. Our tactical exercises (still permitted over large tracts of German farmland) seemed to be tolerated – we were, ostensibly, a force of protection against the enemy in the East. We were stationed in Westphalia, just outside Düsseldorf. The love of the German landscape and culture, which had never died in me, began its reawakening.

In the summer of 1960 I was appointed to command the 1st Battalion of my Regiment. The Battalion were stationed at Tidworth on Salisbury Plain as part of the Strategic Reserve. It was, therefore, unlikely that we would remain for long in England, and sure enough in May 1961 the Battalion was ordered to embark on a troopship at Southampton en route for the British Cameroons.

The Army was in many ways incomparably better than the one I had first joined. Training was more realistic, standards of individual fitness and efficiency were higher, the education of officers was incomparably better. There were many inadequacies in essential equipment still but this was improving all the time. In most ways – and one can never know, since it was never put to the test – I think the Army would have acquitted itself better against a first-class enemy than it did in 1940. I select 1940 rather than a later date for comparison because at later stages of the Second World War the experience of war itself was teaching people; but in the opening stages the shock of hostilities had overwhelmed too many on the British side. It is a prime function of peacetime training to prepare for this shock and I think that in the post-war Regular Army it had to a large extent been done – or was on the way by 1960.

Or probably so, for there were question marks still. In the pre-war and wartime army there was a certain moral robustness which in later years sometimes appeared at risk. Social and cultural trends – the ubiquity of comfortable leisure, the tendency to look for scapegoats if things went wrong, the 'compensation culture', already showing signs of emerging – these things could, and can, erode the essential standards of the warrior. They can soften; and no army can survive and win if it is soft. This elementary lesson had been painfully absorbed after defeat in 1940. Technical training, in the highest sense of the word, can do much, and I think it was and is well understood and practised: but the human and moral dimension is ultimately the most important. I believe strongly in the study of military history, but it is from our defeats we should chiefly learn, and from historical periods when we possessed few material advantages and when the odds were against us.

Battalion command is one of the great ambitions of a soldier's life and I was very lucky. I knew the 1st Battalion well from wartime days when we of the 2nd Battalion had served together with them in the 'Grenadier Group' of the former Guards Armoured Division, and although, of course, almost all faces had changed since those days of more than fifteen years ago the ethos of the 1st Battalion was very familiar to me. The British Cameroons, however, were not. 'Kamerun' had been a German colony until Germany was defeated and forfeited her colonies in 1918. Kamerun was then allocated as a League of Nations Mandate to the Trusteeship of two of the victorious Allied powers, Britain and France. To the British was allocated the western (and very narrow) strip of the country, bordering Nigeria. To the French was assigned the rest – more northerly, and running up to the sub-Sahara desert as well as including a considerable tropical area in the south on the Gulf of Guinea. The British Cameroons were domi-nated in the south by the great mass of Mount Cameroon, rising to 10,500 feet. Much of the country was rainforest, with an exceptionally high rainfall in the wet season. The wet season was due to start when our Battalion arrived.

The British military presence in the Cameroons was comparatively new. It had been thought wise to 'ensure stability' during and after a United Nations plebiscite which had been held in 1960. This plebiscite had been aimed at finding out what the inhabitants wanted done with them. They had once (we gathered) been not unhappy under German colonial government. 'The Germans were hard,' they told us, 'but they taught us honesty. If a man stole, his hand was cut off.' Islamic, in fact. Then they had experienced both French and British rule in different regions of the country, and these had differed widely. There were things to be said for and against each of these Tutelary Powers but – to simplify greatly – the British had believed in encouraging the slow but humanely conceived growth of simple democratic institutions beneath a quasi-colonial supervisory regime. The French had believed in investment and education. The infrastructure – roads and so forth – in the French Cameroons was markedly superior to anything we could show, and the education – of the African elite – was impressive. They were, I think, corrupt and often ruthless, but the outward effect was striking.

The United Nations plebiscite had not led to a result which its organizer, the Tutelary Powers, wished or had expected. The preferred option (in Whitehall) would have been a convincing African vote to merge with the recently independent Nigeria. 'We imagined,' one colonial servant told me in anguished tones, 'that they'd vote to keep to the British way of life! And currency!' They didn't. There had been two options on offer – to join Nigeria, or to join with the Cameroon Republic, recently the French Cameroons but now (at the same time as the British) independent as a Republic in their own right. The Africans chose the latter.

This result of the plebiscite (no dates had yet been set for vesting days) caused a good deal of concern among the people of the Cameroons. They had voted, but now felt they were getting something unexpected and perhaps unwanted. There were plenty of tales rife about the effect of French influence, which was, of course, still very strong in the Cameroon Republic. There were stories about police brutality, contrasting unfavourably with the allegedly easy-going regime to be bequeathed by the British. There were economic fears – the franc was an unknown quantity. More than all this, however, there was in the Cameroon Republic a small but vicious little rebellion and civil war taking place – largely tribal and largely in the north. Thereafter one British battalion, the Border Regiment, had been deployed and after they had done their stint (and made life administratively possible for their successors) we were to succeed them. The rebellion was being suppressed, with variable success, by the forces of the Cameroon Republic, organized and commanded at the top by French officers. A lot of the rebellion was taking place near the border; and French and Cameroonian methods, according to rumour, were harsh. The word was passed that we, the British, were lukewarm in sympathy during this little fight – that the British Cameroons were, in fact, a safe haven for rebels.

Rumour or not, this had its effect on the population. There was a good deal of fear about, as interminable conferences and negotiations were held. The principals in these were the British Government, the Cameroon Government in its independent guise, and the British-sponsored administration of the British Cameroons. The question, always, was what to do with the last-named. I attended all these sessions and tried to be helpful, not always, I fear, with great success. The British Government – and this was both understandable and predictable – were chiefly anxious to get out of the place and not to inherit any commitment, military or otherwise. There was also in some British official and Governmental circles a distrust of the French – of their systems, their motives – as well as a pretty complete ignorance of their language, traditions and culture. This was not a good background from which to encourage happy African cooperation in the future. The Africans – 'our Africans' – inevitably regarded the Africans of the Cameroon Republic as French-inspired and alien to their own more recent loyalties.

It was first necessary to explore once again my Battalion area – it was about 300 miles from north to south and I had been allowed a brief reconnaissance, flying out from England, in the winter. The crux of the future situation must lie with what sort of relations could be promoted with the French, whose influence, albeit unofficial, was likely to be decisive. I reckoned that direct contact would be a good thing.

I was fortunate in that, when taking over responsibility, I had inherited a flight of three rather ancient light aircraft so that I had a measure of independence. I was also, nominally, 'an independent commander under the War Office' – there was no intermediate military headquarters. After an exchange of signals – itself not simple – I set out in a twin Pioneer for Yaoundé, the capital of the Cameroon Republic, to call on the head of the French Military Mission, General Briand. He was purely head of mission, advisers to an independent government, but the odds were that he was still the man whose writ ran. Cameroon had only been independent of France for a year.

I was in luck. General Briand was a charming man, the finest type of French colonial officer (and few finer types exist). He understood the problems and was both sympathetic and intelligent. He had a splendid sense of humour. Delicacy was needed in broaching the subject of African mistrust of what they thought they'd learned of French methods, but he understood perfectly. Our problem was that word had got round that after we, the British, had left, the security forces of the Republic were determined to cross what was now the border and teach the Africans in the British Cameroons a sharp lesson, to punish them for presumed disloyalty. Fear was feeding fear.

Briand undertook to come personally to Buéa (the capital of the British Cameroons) and to tour the territory with me, visiting certain people (many British as well as Africans were anxious) and spreading sense and confidence. This happened, and I think it helped. There were a number of unfortunate incidents which disturbed the internal relationship – cases where the Cameroon authorities seemed to have been heavy-handed, or simply incapable of controlling their more bloodthirsty compatriots. But on the whole the atmosphere lightened and the conduct of our Guardsmen – who we ensured were much in evidence, especially in the last weeks – was all that could be hoped. I was lucky in that my Second-in-Command was my old friend Paul Freyberg, who gave me support and companionship. Command is always lonely.

In conjunction with the Cameroon Republic we agreed to undertake one small operation against a jungle encampment of rebels in a very inaccessible spot high in the mountains; and, sadly, one Guardsman was killed. One immediate consequence was a telegram of sympathy to me from the President of the Cameroon Republic, and, painful though such losses inevitably are, I know that our action had at least persuaded the French Cameroon side that we were serious in our commitment. When we finally sailed away to Southampton we left a small armed police element recruited and trained by our people, in order to give the population some sense of having a force of their own. For at least a while Cameroon was tranquil, although there were – and are – difficult undercurrents. Peace does not last long in Africa.

After Battalion command I was sent to the Staff of London District, an uninteresting appointment lightened by the company of many friends and by the personality of the Major-General commanding, John Nelson, a Grenadier with a great reputation for energy and courage. And while at London District, at the end of 1963 I was, to my considerable surprise, told that my next appointment would be to command a brigade (19 Brigade) in the 3rd Division, again part of the Strategic Reserve. The 3rd Division was commanded by Michael Carver, an officer who had won a considerable name (and very early promotion) in the Desert war; he was an old Desert hand.

He was an exceptionally impressive soldier. A highly intelligent Wykehamist, he suffered fools neither gladly nor agreeably. He believed in expertise and was himself a master of whatever he took up. He was clever, decisive, a commander to his fingertips and the most outstanding soldier of his generation. During the time he was my superior Britain was at peace (save for the sort of minor turbulences I have described); but had we, which the Lord forbid, gone again to war I have never met an officer I would prefer to serve.

Britain's Strategic Reserve was, at that time, being pulled in many different directions. A new situation in Cyprus had led to massive reinforcement there once more (this, mercifully, did not directly affect me). Now a different area was making demands.

Malaysia was the product of Malaya and the former territories of Sabah (formerly North Borneo) and Sarawak, now a colony, previously an independent Rajahdom under the Brooke 'White Rajahs'. Between Sabah and Sarawak was the oil-rich Sultanate of Brunei; these three constituted East Malaysia. The British had a number of agreements, understandings, commitments and near-commitments. The British-controlled Brigade of Gurkhas were all deployed in that part of the world and were greatly respected. The troubled situation in Malaysia was now promoted by the ambitions of President Soekarno of Indonesia; but it was never a matter of direct aggression by Indonesia against Malaysia. More subtly it had its origins in a revolt in Brunei, which had been suppressed by prompt British action in December 1962. Thereafter Soekarno had managed to fan the embers of the original revolt and try to give it the appearance of a popular revolt against the Sultan and his friends and against the concept of Malaysia itself, which was anathema to him. He hoped that ultimately the Borneo Territories might be merged with Indonesia. The subsequent operations were always termed 'Confrontation' – never war; but Indonesian troops nevertheless tried to carry out a raiding policy across the borders into Sarawak and Sabah. There was also a (Chinese) Communist movement in Malaysia which it was hoped (by Soekarno) would assist in the general destabilization of the area: to Indonesian advantage.

By the time my brigade was directly affected the situation in Malaysia had become to an extent routine. A considerable number of troops – British, Gurkha, New Zealand, Malay et al. – were spending a variable number of months in jungle camps near the border with Indonesia, patrolling, gathering information, very occasionally confronting an actual raiding party of the enemy. After a stipulated number of weeks of this a Battalion would be relieved and another take over. The conditions under which the troops were living when not patrolling in the jungle were primitive in the extreme and very, very wet. After a short while of this routine it was decided that another Brigade Headquarters was required and that it would be mine, sent out from England. The frontage (the Sarawak border) was very long and although the number of troops actually deployed must largely depend on the number of 'incidents' – in other words on intensity of combat if there were any – a certain number of overseeing command posts was thought to be a minimum. My own headquarters (moved from Colchester) was at Sibu on the delta of the Rajang river, where we took over some Chinese buildings. I got the impression that the 'threat' (from Indonesia) was to some extent exaggerated – not least by those who wished, for whatever reason, to depict this as a theatre of war requiring reinforcement. The reality was less exciting.

Deployment of troops was almost entirely by helicopter, as was their relief, reinforcement and resupply. Some longboats had outboard motors fitted and movement in these up the great rivers was beautiful and dramatic. Apart from any posts actually on the river there was no other efficient method of movement except the helicopter. Distances were huge and tactical dismounted movement through the jungle (by patrols) was laborious. Helicopters, therefore, were at a premium and my headquarters had a complex and sophisticated system of tasking them so that maximum lift could be obtained from every machine. Safety was a major factor and we had a few tragic accidents – weather was appalling and flying conditions often atrocious.

The native people in Sarawak were a very diverse mixture. There were some indigenous tribes, leading a completely primitive life, and sometimes victims of avoidable or operable ailments as well, of course, as accidents. Then there were the Ibans, land and sea Dayaks, living in their own rather beautifully constructed longhouses. In the cultivated areas there was a large Chinese population. And in particular places there was a Malay sector, for the dominant people before the Europeans had been the Brunei Malays.

Our helicopters were, of course, much in demand and I thought it important to exercise a more stringent control than had hitherto always happened. Because these fairly primitive people, for the first time in their lives, had access to modern medicine and to sophisticated and rapid means of movement it was soon quite common to find both taken for granted in a way which must be dangerous in the long term. Some of our people allocating helicopter missions – actuated by kindness – were apt to forget that we and our helicopters (and our doctors) would one day depart. It was a false sort of kindness to encourage the native population to expect, as of right, a level of medical attention and, where appropriate, urgent hospitalization which would astonish the inhabitants of the Highlands of Scotland. Such service could not and should not last. Our duty must be to be as merciful as conditions allowed but to promote within ourselves and others a sense of realism. This approach was not always popular.

Sarawak is a beautiful land of great forests and awe-inspiring rivers. Among Europeans who served it much affection was generated for the land and its people. One senior District Officer in our area (2nd and 3rd Divisions of Sarawak) had been there most of his life apart from the years brutally disrupted by the Japanese invasion. He had been recruited long before the war by the Brooke rajahs – one of those known as a 'Rajah man'. By name Alan Griffin, he also happened to have been born and bred very near my present home in Hampshire. He described old Sarawak vividly and affectionately.

'It was a happy country,' he used to say; 'the Brookes ruled autocratically but everyone had access to the Rajah in his residence in Kuching [where he also had his private executioner on the establishment]. Anybody could appear with a petition or a confidence. There was no material development whatsoever – that would have necessitated investment and investment would have meant the Chinese. In this completely unprogressive environment the land belonged to the people. And they were happy.' And when one saw him among them, on some rare occasion when something like the old ways were fleetingly recovered, one believed him.

The Sarawak adventure lasted, for me, about nine months. There were few military challenges but it is a fine country and its peoples were continuously interesting. I was – as usual – also lucky in my comrades. The General, Director of Operations, was George Lea, a huge and hugely cheerful soldier who only had to appear for his smile to brighten even the weather. My fellow brigade commanders were Bill Cheyne, who died sadly young soon afterwards but whom I would have backed to go to the top of the Army, or anything else; and Harry Tuzo, a very old friend, once a commander of a Regiment of Horse Artillery next to us at Tidworth and the best and most civilized of companions.

In November 1965 I was told that I had been selected for the next course at the Imperial Defence College, the IDC, at Seaford House, Belgrave Square, London.

15

Allies and Reflections

The Imperial Defence College had been founded in 1927 'to develop understanding of the conduct of war' among selected officers of the fighting services, some civil servants and a number of officers from the Dominion armed services. From the time of the Second World War officers from the United States attended as well, as did some from the Commonwealth. There had been many transformations of composition, charter and syllabus but something of the original ethos always persisted. The course ran in my time for one calendar year and there was an admirable tradition that this should deliberately be made enjoyable. The IDC was not designed as a 'forcing house'. There were no examinations – when I was there, in fact, there was no written work of any kind. The implicit assumption was that if the selection process had worked as it should, the students (all were of mature age and quite senior rank) would have held responsibility in the past, and would again. The IDC year was a time with leisure to read, discuss, think – and make friends. There was an excellent library and within the syllabus were programmes of visits to many installations – military, scientific, industrial, commercial – some in Britain, some abroad. There was always a long overseas tour for which the course (capacity about 75) divided, according mainly to individual choice, into about five or six parties for more far-flung expeditions.

Fairly dominant among the British, of course, was the current thrust of British Defence policy and discussion about its rights and wrongs. This was an era when argument largely raged about the British military presence 'east of Suez', as it was generally, although not quite exactly, called. The background to this was the Vietnam War, which was having its material and moral effect on American policy and which would continue for some time, with escalating consequences. In the Middle East there was to be a brief and pretty decisive war, ending in Israeli victory, in the following year. There was, additionally, a troubled situation in Aden which was to produce violence in 1967, but by the following year this was over.

There was, now, little of the feeling in Britain – very strong until recently – that the British, and British forces, must have a major role to play in the Arab lands or the Far East. British Governmental pronouncements now made it clear that British troops would no longer feature in that area after 1968. We were getting out: and in South East Asia, once the 'confrontation' between Malaysia and Indonesia was over (which it was by August), there was little inclination towards further military involvement beyond the maintenance of our garrison in Hong Kong.

During this whole period of 'disengagement', which was regarded by some as betrayal – including some of my fellow-students – there was a good deal of natural introspection about the British role in the world, and I am glad to have been a student at the IDC at that time. I think there was general agreement that where we had acquired or inherited specific responsibilities these must be discharged; but there was also a wide measure of feeling that in the modern world such responsibilities should be shed as early and as decently as possible. There was general recognition of the fact that not only was the financial penalty of over-extension a pity (or worse) but that – probably more importantly – there was no longer general support in Britain for the sort of tasks we had previously discharged. They had once been not only a duty but in ultimate terms profitable. This was no longer so.

There was, therefore, a general (but not universal) feeling that Britain should primarily 'look to her moat' – defend herself, and those additional (and very few) responsibilities which were unsheddable. Self-defence was, pretty uncontroversially, wrapped up in membership of the NATO Alliance, to which we contributed forces by land, sea and air. These – measured against the notional 'threat' from the forces of the Warsaw Pact – were also clearly inadequate: huge Soviet forces potentially menaced Europe from the east; huge Soviet fleets, recently increased and modernized by the energies of a new generation of Soviet naval officers, posed, or could pose, an unprecedented threat to the freedom of the seas. There appeared to be plenty for the Alliance to do if its citizens were to enjoy real security. And all of this would be increasingly expensive.

There was, therefore, general agreement that NATO was the instrument whereby the Allied nations, including Britain, should seek security; and argument would chiefly turn on the contribution each Allied nation should make to the Allied whole. There was little disagreement that the overall balance of forces was to the Soviet advantage, although less so on sea than on land. Argument, therefore, was chiefly about who should do more for the common cause – an argument which, inevitably, took place primarily within national rather than Allied parameters, since while the spending of money might be an Allied interest the raising of it from taxpayers was essentially national. Arguments at Belgrave Square, therefore, were less about the 'strategic balance' than about whether the Royal Navy, the Royal Air Force or the Army had a superior case for increased investment – or was a proper candidate for retrenchment. These arguments were, obviously, sometimes greatly affected by developments in the strategic sphere; but on the whole the strategic balance was settled.

Much less settled was the future of each Service; and there were issues which aroused great and understandable emotion. Of these, at this time, the most critical was the matter of building, or not, a new aircraft carrier for the Royal Navy. Without it, allegedly, air cover could not be provided for a whole list of far-flung operations; and the counter-arguments tended to be, first, that such cover could possibly be provided by using a number of island bases in the Indian Ocean; and, second, that such operations were decreasingly probable. Huge sums of money were involved. There were, of course, plenty of other issues which caused major difficulties in what is called, rather blandly, 'resource allocation'. The issues in Defence caused great passions to run – and understandably so.

Within the British student body (there were ten of us, the uniformed members), and among the British more widely, opinion tended to polarize between those one might rather crudely call 'the Europeans' and 'the Imperialists'. In the former camp were those who regarded Britain's role as being essentially European, whole-heartedly so; and that this should guide our contribution to NATO and our attitude towards the structure and future of the Alliance. In the latter camp were those who reckoned that Britain traditionally had wider concerns and should nourish them. In this camp, too, were those who much regretted our withdrawal, or near-withdrawal, from the past responsibilities of Empire. Unsurprisingly, most of the students from the Dominions took this line (but not all). There was a general, and I think creditable, recognition that Britain's future could not be excessively dominated by Britain's past.

I have sketched above the outline of a debate which went on for years, and which in one or other form affected my own future for several of them. The IDC was an excellent apprenticeship in this debate, and it was also highly enjoyable. The syllabus was wide and although I have concentrated above on issues which would chiefly occupy the minds of British officers then and later, we read and studied very widely the situations and problems of most parts of the world – helped in my own case by a tour of the United States and Canada. As to the argument I have described as between Europeans and Imperialists, I was unabashedly and strongly in the former camp and have remained so. I did not and do not believe that there is any future for Britain, except as an unimpressive appendage of the United States, unless it embraces with *whole heart* its destiny as a small but potentially important European nation. History, reason, culture and sentiment all pulled my own heart in that direction.

With the advent to power of the Labour Government of 1964 Denis Healey had become Defence Secretary and he had a very powerful effect on the thinking of all who worked in the defence field, whether in uniform or not. He was a man of outstanding ability and remarkable intellectual dedication – one of the giants of political life in our time. I got to know him better after the IDC course ended and my next job took me again to the Ministry of Defence – first as Director of Plans of the Army, then as Director of Defence policy under a reorganization which Healey had done much to inspire.

Denis Healey was formidable. He had an excellent brain and first-class gifts of analysis. A case – and much work of the Ministry of Defence turned on the making of a case or its demolition – had little chance of surviving his relentless forensic powers unless it was unusually well prepared and excellently presented. In the Chiefs of Staff Committee or among the briefing staffs of the Ministry this made him a unique power in the land. Because he was himself so shrewd, so quick-witted and so articulate he also, in many cases, inspired fear. A strong character, he could be a bully if opposition to him was timorous or intellectually inadequate.

Denis Healey had prepared himself for the world of Defence by considerable study when in Opposition. This made him unusually well-trained when he was called to office. It was natural that he came to be greatly admired by the staffs, military, civilian and scientific, which served the defence establishment; and it was also natural that so strong and often ebullient a personality attracted both liking and loathing. There were, as I have indicated, major issues in the world of defence, issues on which great expenditures turned and which would take many years, in some cases, to resolve. With such a personality as Healey around it was inevitable that vigorous parties formed and were often identified with the view an individual took of Healey (or vice versa). The Ministry of Defence was not a tranquil place at that time (Healey would chortle at the idea it ever should be). The danger, of course, of so brilliant and dominant a character and personality is always that opposing views are disregarded or extinguished because so unimpressively argued. Wisdom does not always prevail. Nevertheless Healey – who always took immense trouble personally to master the issues in debate, however complex or technical – did a great deal of good for the level of thinking and arguing about defence matters in our country. I don't think on major decisions he was always right – nobody is. He rated intellectual arguments highly and was apt to disregard points rooted more pragmatically in common sense and experience. I don't believe he was as decisive as a policy-maker in the military field needs to be. But he was a reasoning human being and by the force of his example and his personality he taught others to be the same. He was also, if one was lucky enough to experience more of his company, a particularly charming and splendidly cultivated person, and a witty one.

After I had served some years in Whitehall on the policy staffs by one name or another I was delighted to learn that I had been selected to command a Division in the British Army of the Rhine in Germany from 1969. My Division (4th) was, although not by name, an Armoured Division with a large number of tanks, a considerable assembly of artillery, and many historic Regiments, which changed over quite frequently. Troubles were beginning in Northern Ireland at the same time that I assumed Divisional command and this meant that parts of the Division were regularly detached to that province for duties on the streets of Belfast or somewhere else, an interruption to their primary task but often quite popular with the troops.

Service in Germany gave me an excellent opportunity again to study German and Germany – a very different Germany from that I had known in 1950 or, even more, in 1937. The war and the impact of war were fading memories. There was a very natural reluctance in Germany to dwell much on military matters. As we gradually made more and more friends among Germans there were increasingly ties of understanding with contemporaries who had served in the *Wehrmacht*; and, of course, professional ties with those in the *Bundeswehr*; but the Second World War and its history were, to put it mildly, not popular themes of conversation.

The beauty of much of the country, especially in Lower Saxony, where we carried out numerous exercises, was always present, and the charm and kindness of German friends and their children made our lives particularly agreeable. I rate my time commanding a Division in Germany one of the happiest experiences of my military life. My headquarters and our home was at the historic town of Herford. When, much later, I worked on a biography of Frederick the Great I discovered that that remarkable man wrote with particular warmth and affection about the inhabitants of Herford. He was perfectly right. I improved my knowledge of the German language, a language I have always appreciated; although linguistically I was never as competent as I would have wished.

I have referred to Denis Healey, who left the Ministry of Defence at this time. He was fond of Germany. 'I expect you know,' he said to me, 'Bismarck's solution to the Irish problem?' – which at that time was causing much turbulence in our lives. I shook my head. 'Bismarck,' chuckled Healey, 'said that the solution was simple. The population of Ireland should be exchanged with that of Holland. The Dutch, with their industry and attention to detail, would turn Ireland into an even more thriving pastoral country – the rainfall guarantees it. While the Irish, in the Low Countries, would fail to maintain the dykes and swiftly drown themselves.'

At the end of my two-year stint of Divisional command I returned to Whitehall, to be Assistant Chief of Defence Policy – head of the Branch in which I had served before going to Germany. The problems were much as they had been – they always are. But a considerable change had overtaken the Defence world, with particular implications for me. In the summer of 1970 my old friend Peter Carrington had become Secretary of State for Defence. I was still a Divisional commander and it was a joy to welcome him on a visit to Germany. Soon thereafter I found myself back in Whitehall and seeing him more often. In 1972 I moved offices, not very far, and became Vice Chief of the General Staff – in effect responsible, under the Chief of the General Staff, for the various directorates dealing with the Army, as opposed to 'defence' as a whole.

The 'Army Department', the 'General Staff', was very enjoyable. My boss was the Chief of the General Staff, Michael Carver, whom I have described, knew well and greatly respected. Apart from the inevitable and somewhat routine visits to Northern Ireland there wasn't much travel, and a huge amount of time was concerned with questions of equipment and costs. As VCGS I was chairman of a number of committees, which gave me an overview of the various and often conflicting issues which needed resolution or harmonization so that a General Staff policy line could be evolved. One of the most critical issues was the question of tanks.

The British had sold a considerable number of tanks to Iran and the Shah of Iran took a great interest in their performance. He took a great interest in everything military, especially technical matters; and he had made the modernization and expansion of his country's armed forces a particular concern, even an obsession. We had gladly cooperated, and there were new plans afoot, new training systems, apprentice training for the young and so forth. The Shah (listening with approval to the head of his army, who had paid a recent visit to Britain) was convinced that it was to England he should turn for guidance in military matters. This suited Her Majesty's Government well. Very large sums of money were involved.

At a certain point in the negotiations – which were concerned with a whole host of issues – it was decided that Peter Carrington should visit the Shah; and to my great pleasure I was among several he decided should accompany him. On the first morning after reaching Tehran we approached the Imperial Palace – on foot. Security was such that only a senior minister could drive up to the front door. Soon I was in the huge and splendidly carpeted ante-room. I don't think there was a very long wait – Peter and the Permanent Under Secretary, accompanied by the British Ambassador, Peter Ramsbotham, were already closeted with His Imperial Majesty, the Shah-in-Shah.

Eventually the audience began and lasted nearly an hour. I have seldom been more impressed by an interview. The Shah was complete master of his subject whatever it was (in fact we talked little about tanks: he knew it all). His conversation ranged widely. He was entertaining, very clever, very charming, immensely courteous, and exceptionally well-informed. He was incisive to a remarkable degree. We knew, of course, that there was much intrigue against him and his throne. We knew that there was a great deal of corruption and that he had been weakened by it. None of this alters the fact that he was one of the most impressive human beings I've ever met. When he fell from power not very long afterwards, I felt deeply and personally grieved.

I was also grieved by the fall of the Conservative Government in February 1974; the Government was at first beaten narrowly, but when Harold Wilson asked for a dissolution again in the following October the Labour Party won the ensuing election handsomely. The departure of Peter Carrington was depressing news. Few military men are greatly concerned about Party politics. There is a strong and, I think, healthy tradition in our country that the Government in power deserves loyal support. One has a duty to represent one's views without fear or favour, but that done one gets on with the job. Furthermore anybody of my generation and experience had, by then, served so many different administrations and Party leaders that it was hard to feel too dogmatic or too hostile; or too partisan. Nevertheless the departure from office of such a friend, so calm, so objective a man, hit hard.

When I was VCGS I persuaded the CGS (by that time the particularly charming General, Peter Hunt) that it might be a good thing to involve the support of a wide range of retired officers of seniority in the problems and doings of the Army. He agreed and we launched an enjoyable session – I think in Admiralty House – where a number of Field Marshals and retired generals were given presentations on the current state of the Army. No institution – and certainly no Army – can expect general support unless trouble is taken with its natural constituency – furthermore such information is owed to those whose service is behind them, but whose views and wisdom still belong to the nation. This session went well and became a recognized occasional feature of Army Department life. It makes some work for the busy staff who organize it and clearly the menu can be varied year by year but I am sure the idea is and has remained worthwhile.

The Labour administration of 1974 (Roy Mason was Defence Secretary) was, or seemed to be, largely dominated by recurrent economic problems, as well as by the intractable issues of Northern Ireland, where, in my view, Mason was outstandingly sensible and robust. I, however, was about to begin a new job.

Since the beginning of the North Atlantic Treaty Organization the top stratum of the Alliance has consisted of a committee of senior political – generally diplomatic – permanent representatives at Ambassadorial level. This is, or was, variously called the Defence Policy Committee or the Atlantic Council, somewhat depending on the agenda to be discussed; and the committee or council in planning session consisted of the appropriate ministers – for foreign affairs or defence – while in normal sessions the 'Permanent Representatives', the PERMREPs, spoke with their masters' voices. This was the political hierarchy of NATO, and it was complemented on the military side by a military committee of senior military persons, Chiefs of Defence Staff or in their absence Military Representatives, the MILREPs, who met regularly under the chairmanship of a Chairman of the Military Committee (CMC) appointed by the NATO council.

So far so comparatively simple. There were, however, some variations on the theme which could have considerable effect on the conduct of business. Obviously the first such was the relationship of civilians – ambassadors, ministers or whatever – to the military authorities within each nation. This might be mistrustful, or so warm as to make their views near-identical, or actually sycophantic. Another variation might be the stability or otherwise of a nation's regime at home. Then some nations, or their representatives, took what I regarded as an unrealistically 'pure' attitude to military advice. They thought that the view taken corporately by the Military Committee should be solely based on military factors, objectively considered, and uninfluenced by the political considerations which were bound to differ nation by nation. To those taking that view congress between MILREPs and PERMREPs, whether individually or corporately, was to be regretted.

The British attitude to such matters tends towards informality and relaxation, aided by the traditions of an impartial and professional Civil Service. These traditions make it natural for views to evolve harmoniously in discussion, while all recognized the particular pressures civilians or military men might be under from Government at home. I think the greatest British virtue in such matters is a dislike of striking attitudes; and it is closely followed by another virtue – that of realism. 'Where is all this leading to,' men would ask, 'and what does it really add up to?' The committees of NATO, however, were instructive about the thinking and feelings of others. It was always unwise to leave out of consideration the strong emotions generated by the Second World War and its aftermath, or the passions aroused by developments in the eastern Mediterranean.

Relations between the nations, however, were always interesting. There is a common misapprehension that the French have 'left NATO'. Not so! General De Gaulle withdrew French representation from the integrated command structure of the Alliance. He believed – understandably – that American predominance made this command structure an essentially and excessively American structure. The point of view is tenable. France, however, did not leave the Alliance, and there was always a French MILREP during my time in Brussels (a very engaging General De Favitsky filled the post, just as the equally engaging and distinguished Count François de Rosa was French PERMREP). France is an essential member of the Atlantic Alliance but has sometimes, I think defensibly, reckoned that Alliance objectives will sometimes be best attained by nations acting and thinking with a certain independence. Self-respect, too, comes into this. The United

States is very large and very rich; and, as De Gaulle himself once said, there are times when one is too proud to bow.

For my part I always found, in inter-Allied relations, that the French were particularly congenial – and professionally gifted. There is also a frequent misapprehension that because of the turbulent history of our times, the French and Germans are likely to make uneasy partners. I found the reverse to be true. Finally, it is sometimes supposed that the British find the United States difficult – to some extent through jealousy, through similarity (two nations divided by a single language, and all that). I can only record that to me the friendship and support of Americans was among the most rewarding experiences which Brussels afforded.

Personalities, as always, mattered more than the formal position a man or woman might hold. In my time our country was fortunate. Our Permanent Representative, with the voice of either the British Foreign Office or the Ministry of Defence behind him, was Sir John Killick. John Killick was a charming and unusual diplomat. A brilliant linguist, he had been our Ambassador in Russia, was also an excellent German speaker and graduate of a German university. He was a soldier in the war (and taken prisoner at Arnhem with the 1st Airborne Division). He was witty, articulate and extremely funny, accompanying himself on the guitar through a wide range of songs in many different languages at a Christmas party. Above all, he had a forceful personality, and the Atlantic Council listened when he spoke.

But in any committee the way matters go depends greatly on the chairman. Most people have at some time suffered from an inadequate chairman – ill-prepared, indecisive, personally verbose or indulging to excess a personal view. The Military Committee of NATO for much of my time was led by the British Lord Hill-Norton. Admiral of the Fleet, Chief of the Defence Staff in London when I was heading the Policy Staff, he was a superb leader of an international committee and was greatly respected. Peter Hill-Norton took great trouble to prepare himself for debate – he always had. He knew that a discussion can only be sensibly guided (let alone steered to a rational conclusion) if the person in the chair understands the issues at least as well as any participant. He also knew that there is a great art in allowing free rein to even the most awkward of participants while still keeping control of a discussion: nobody must feel unfairly curtailed in putting a point of view (especially since in NATO this was the point of view of a nation and a representative was probably speaking with explicit national instructions), but the patience of the Committee must not be strained beyond endurance and there are moments when a chairman must, as it were, call 'time'. In all this Peter Hill-Norton was admirable. His French was competent (NATO officially worked in two languages, French and English, but predominantly in English, although knowledge of French was highly desirable). Above all, the Military Committee respected him. So did the Council.

The other main figure in the NATO military hierarchy was, of course, the Supreme Allied Commander, Europe: SACEUR. This had from the beginning been an American officer and while NATO lasts is likely to continue so, if only because of the nuclear dimension to strategy. SACEUR was nominally the subordinate of the Military Committee, embodying, as the latter theoretically did, the corporate wisdom of the Alliance; but in fact SACEUR, as the most senior American military man in Europe and one with the President's ear, was a power in his own right and committees were largely irrelevant. SACEUR, while I was in Brussels, was General Alexander Haig. Al Haig did excellent things for NATO, largely because he understood very clearly how the Allied nations would or would not react to exhortation; to entreaties; to pressures. Faced, as NATO was, with very large forces of the Warsaw Pact which in theory might overrun the forces of the Alliance in an aggressive war, the normal NATO reaction was to describe the dimensions of this threat in uncompromising terms, demonstrating the extent to which the Allies were outnumbered, how great their danger, and to leave the Allied governments to draw the appropriate conclusion; in other words to spend more money on defence or face the possibility of defeat in war and the obloquy of history. A regular cycle of documents and planning targets was used to signpost all this. The result, of course, was absolutely nil. The Allied nations, or their governments, preferred not to look at disagreeable facts; but – more defensibly – were unconvinced that all this talk of threat had much reality behind it. More importantly still, they reckoned that the small amounts they could contribute to improvement would not make the difference between defeat and victory in war – the only difference which matters.

Haig's achievement – one of them – was to see this clearly. He changed the emphasis of presentations. He realized – and the realization was reflected in the way things were shown to the political committees – that if a nation was simply told that huge danger loomed, beyond much hope of remedy, little would be done. But he also realized that if it were shown that a *small* increase of effort (and thus of financing) might make a significant improvement in the ability of the nations to defer an adverse decision in war, even for ever – then this could be regarded as practicable and worthwhile. He therefore concentrated on going for modest but attainable increases in NATO's strength, in all areas; and he achieved not inconsiderable success.

The political committees of NATO met under the chairmanship of the Secretary General of the Alliance. This was Dr Joseph Luns, who had served as Holland's Foreign Minister. He had once been in the Dutch Navy, of which he was extremely proud. An ebullient and social figure, he was a great raconteur who liked the agreeable side of the life in Brussels – and it was very agreeable. I don't think the more intractable problems facing the Alliance kept him awake at night; but probably they shouldn't have done.

Living again in Brussels had, for me, a certain dreamlike quality. Our house was in Boitsfort, near the racecourse where as a child I had been taken by kindly M. Wiener to see Sire d'Halouwin finish first. Much in Brussels was greatly changed, but the trams still clanked into the centre, the Fôret de Soignes was still beautiful, and Waterloo (with its to me always haunting battlefield) was still within reach. And the Belgian families we met had, in most cases, the same names as those I remembered from childhood's friendships in the gardens of the Rue Ducale and the Bois de la Cambre.

I also sometimes returned to the country marked by the First World War, the country which had impressed my childhood and was now again only a few hours' drive or less from our home. I returned again to my father's diaries in that earlier war, to his own letters describing visits in 1918 to scenes of earlier fighting, to the burial place of my mother's first husband, Billy Congreve, at Corbie – 'A tremendous atmosphere of quiet and peace', my father wrote; 'I'm sure he likes the place where he is lying, he always liked high-up places and distant glorious views over flood and field to the faraway hills.' No British soldier can be unmoved by Picardy and Flanders – certainly not I, although of a later generation.

In December 1977 I left Brussels for the last time. I took over the Commandantship of the Royal College of Defence Studies, as the Imperial Defence College had now been named. It was a different establishment from that I had known as the IDC. Great changes had been wrought, mostly in the Healey era. The student body had been widened to include not only NATO European nations but many others deemed friendly – a process which, as I write, has been much extended again. There were equivalent changes made to the syllabus and scope of the College's curriculum and yet another review was under way when I took over. But the essential character of Seaford House had persisted and I hope will continue. It was an interesting, friendly and relaxed place, without such pressure on time that there was inadequate chance to make friends and discuss things at leisure. All relationships need time to develop, and the friendly relationships at that great establishment in Belgrave Square needed time and room to mature. This aspect of the life there was something the Commandant could try to nurture.

It goes without saying that there were always extremely able people in the student body, and to sit with them throughout the two years of my tour of duty – two complete RCDS courses – was a very great pleasure. In February 1980, at the age of 59 and some months, I retired from the Army, time-expired and grateful.

The atmosphere at the Royal College of Defence Studies was a bookish one. I have described the library as excellent and it was – and served by a distinguished succession of librarians, skilled at advising students where, perhaps in other establishments, they could find publications helpful to their particular concerns. It was while I was there that I resolved to take further – indeed, to complete – a project already in my mind and to which I have referred. This was the biography of Lord Alanbrooke, undoubtedly the most distinguished Chairman of the British Chiefs of Staff Committee – and at the most critical time in our history. It was then that the Chiefs of Staff, the service heads of Britain's armed forces, found themselves confronting simultaneously the problems of total war against the Axis Powers and the erratic genius of Winston Churchill as Prime Minister, Minister of Defence and their nominal Chairman.

The writing of *Alanbrooke* thus became a major interest and after I retired it was followed by a large number of other books. Retirement, as often happens, I think, has been a time of considerable activity.

I looked back, as one does. The phases of life and the speed at which they passed were inevitably at first somewhat governed by the outer conventions of life – rank, uniform, appearance. When I became a lieutenant-colonel and a Battalion commander in 1960 I was not only dressed somewhat differently from before but I felt different. Command is a different experience. Until then, whatever the particular duties and responsibilities, I had, somehow, been the same person who had, with a cluster of careless youths, joined the Royal Berkshires after an intoxicating lunch at Oxford twenty years before. The laughter, challenges, risks, and to an extent the fun of life had persisted year on year without too much change. The tempo changed. The people changed. But I did not feel that I changed.

After that I did – no doubt inevitably and rightly. Perhaps in a Service life boyhood is unusually prolonged. The duties successively undertaken resemble each other to an extent and because one has seen them performed by others they are in a way familiar by the time one assumes them. This tends to make military life a continuum, a story without defining breakpoints except those inserted by promotion or posting or operational factors. A significant breakpoint, however, comes with command. It is a unique experience: professional life thereafter resembles less a continuum than a rather jerky sequence of chapters with perhaps one underlying theme but moving inexorably towards an end.

But man is prone to illusion. One especially persistent illusion is that one's predecessors were unbelievably ancient, and different in kind from oneself and one's contemporaries (and stupider, of course!). 'Do you remember' – one would say of some senior of other days – 'He appeared a hundred years old!' Then a moment's calculation and the rejoinder. 'He was about ten years younger than you are now!' And it would be true.

In these years after putting off uniform for the last time my mind has often gone back to those early days of the war when I had made what seemed the momentous decision to leave school and become a soldier as soon as possible. I have never regretted it. My life was varied, sometimes challenging, and almost always interesting. I would choose no other.

Above all my years were packed with the memories of friendship. The friendships of youth are the most memorable, because every day brings a new sensation, a new discovery. For that reason the loss of the beloved friends of youth was the most painful of life's blows. They were not all young themselves; but many were, and I see them and hear them still. The laughter of the young – often irrepressible and irreverent – is something which is not experienced later. For it, and for much else, I can only whisper *Deo Gratias*.

Index

Books written by Sir David Fraser are indexed under their title.